THE ROUTLEDGE ATLAS OF RUSSIAN HISTORY

THE COMPREHENSIVE AND ESSENTIAL GUIDE TO THE GREAT MOSAIC OF RUSSIAN HISTORY

'In this concise atlas, Gilbert uses the geography of the past to elucidate the present'.

Los Angeles Times

'The seventh in an excellent series of historical atlases, this volume by the indefatigable Martin Gilbert . . . takes us from the ancient Slavs to the Soviet-Chinese borderlands in 1970 and covers social unrest, the Jews in Russia, changing place-names etc. Far more detailed than its nearest competitor . . . a valuable adjunct to every course in Russian History.'

Library Journal

The complex and often turbulent history of Russia over the course of 2000 years is brought to life in a series of 176 maps. It covers not only the wars and expansion of Russia, but also a wealth of social and economic details of its history from famine and anarchism to the growth of naval strength and the strengths of the river systems. From 800BC to the fall of the Soviet Union and beyond, this indispensable guide to Russian history covers:

- War and conflict – from the triumph of the Goths between 200 and 400BC to the defeat of Germany at the end of the Second World War, and the end of the Cold War
- Politics – from the rise of Moscow in the Middle Ages to revolution, the fall of the monarch and the collapse of communism
- Industry, economics and transport – from the Trans-Siberian Railway between 1891–1917 to the Virgin Lands Campaign and the growth of heavy industry
- Society, trade and culture – from the growth of monasticism to peasant discontent, Labour Camps and the geographical distribution of ethnic Russians, and Russia's growing arms trading, and gas and oil exports.

Sir Martin Gilbert is one of the leading historians of his generation. An Honorary Fellow of Merton College, Oxford, he is the official biographer of Churchill as well as the author of *Churchill – A Life* and *The First World War* and *Second World War*. For more information please visit www.martingilbert.com.

BOOKS BY MARTIN GILBERT

The Routledge Atlas of American History
The Routledge Atlas of the Arab-Israeli Conflict
The Routledge Atlas of British History
The Routledge Atlas of the First World War
The Routledge Atlas of the Holocaust
The Routledge Atlas of Jewish History
The Routledge Atlas of Russian History

The Appeasers (with Richard Gott)
The European Powers, 1900–1945
The Roots of Appeasement
Children's Illustrated Bible Atlas
Atlas of British Charities
The Holocaust: Maps and Photographs
The Jews of Arab Lands: Their History in Maps
The Jews of Russia: Their History in Maps
Jerusalem Illustrated History Atlas
Sir Horace Rumbold: Portrait of a Diplomat
Jerusalem: Rebirth of a City
Jerusalem in the Twentieth Century
Exile and Return: The Struggle for Jewish
  Statehood
Israel: A History
Auschwitz and the Allies
The Jews of Hope: The Plight of Soviet Jewry
  Today
Shcharansky: Hero of Our Time
The Holocaust: The Jewish Tragedy
The Boys: Triumph over Adversity
The First World War

The Second World War
D-Day
The Day the War Ended
In Search of Churchill
Empires in Conflict: A History of the Twentieth
  Century, 1900–1933
Descent into Barbarism: A History of the
  Twentieth Century, 1934–1951
Challenge to Civilization: A History of the
  Twentieth Century, 1952–1999
From the Ends of the Earth: The Jews in the
  Twentieth Century
Never Again: A History of the Holocaust
The Jews in the Twentieth Century: An
  Illustrated History
Letters to Auntie Fori: The 5,000-Year History
  of the Jewish People and Their Faith
The Righteous: The Unsung Heroes of the
  Holocaust
Churchill and America
Kristallnacht: Prelude to Destruction
Somme: The Heroism and Horror of War

THE CHURCHILL BIOGRAPHY

Volume III: The Challenge of War, 1914–1916
  Document Volume III (in two parts)
Volume IV: World in Torment, 1917–1922
  Document Volume IV (in three parts)
Volume V: The Coming of War, 1922–1939
  Document Volume V: The Exchequer Years,
    1922–1929
  Document Volume V: The Wilderness Years,
    1929–1935
  Document Volume V: The Coming of War,
    1936–1939
Volume VI: Finest Hour, 1939–1941
  Churchill War Papers I: At the Admiralty,
    September 1939–May 1940
  Churchill War Papers II: Never Surrender,
    May–December 1940

Churchill War Papers III: The Ever-Widening
  War, 1941
Volume VII: Road to Victory, 1941–1945
Volume VIII: Never Despair, 1945–1965
Churchill: A Photographic Portrait
Churchill: A Life

EDITIONS OF DOCUMENTS

Britain and Germany between the Wars
Plough My Own Furrow: The Life of Lord
  Allen of Hurtwood
Servant of India: Diaries of the Viceroy's Private
  Secretary, 1905–1910
Surviving the Holocaust: The Kovno Ghetto
  Diary of Avraham Tory
Winston Churchill and Emery Reves:
  Correspondence 1937–1964

THE ROUTLEDGE ATLAS OF
RUSSIAN HISTORY

4th Edition

Martin Gilbert

Routledge
Taylor & Francis Group

LONDON AND NEW YORK

First published 1972 as *The Atlas of Russian History* by Weinfeld & Nicholson

Second edition published 1993 as *The Dent Atlas of Russian History*
by J. M. Dent Ltd.

Third edition published 2002 by Routledge

Fourth edition published 2007 by Routledge
2 Park Square, Milton Park, Abingdon, Oxon OX14 4RN

Simultaneously published in the USA and Canada
by Routledge
270 Madison Ave, New York, NY10016

Routledge is an imprint of the Taylor & Francis Group, an informa business

Typeset in Sabon by
Keystroke, 28 High Street, Tettenhall, Wolverhampton
Printed and bound in Great Britain by
Bell & Bain Ltd, Glasgow

British Library Cataloguing in Publication Data
A catalogue record for this book is available from the British Library
Library of Congress Cataloging in Publication Data
A catalogue record for this book has been requested

ISBN10: 0–415-39483-X (hbk)
ISBN10: 0-415-39484-8 (pbk)

ISBN13: 978-0-415-39483-3 (hbk)
ISBN13: 978-0-415-39484-0 (pbk)

Preface

I have designed this Atlas in the hope that it is possible to present—within the span of 161 maps— a survey of Russian history from the earliest times to the present day. In drafting each map, I drew upon material from a wide range of published works—books, articles, atlases and single sheet maps—each of which I have listed in the bibliography.

On the maps themselves I have included much factual material not normally associated with historical geography, such as the text of one of Stalin's few surviving personal communications—the postcard to his sister-in-law (printed on map 54), and Lenin's telegram to the Bolsheviks in Sweden (printed on map 87). I have drafted each map individually, in such a way as to enable the maximum factual information to be included without making use of a separate page of text; and I have compiled the index in order that it may serve as a means of using the Atlas as if it were a volume of narrative.

I wish to acknowledge the help of many colleagues and friends. In 1962 I began research into Russian history under the supervision of Dr George Katkov, whose insatiable curiosity about elusive historical facts, and whose enthusiasm in tracking them down, have influenced all my subsequent work. I also benefitted from the teaching and encouragement of Mr David Footman, Mr Max Hayward, Dr Harry Willetts and the late Mr Guy Wint. When I was preparing the first sketches for this Atlas, the maps I had drawn and the facts I had incorporated on them were scrutinized by three friends—Mr Michael Glenny, Mr Dennis O'Flaherty and Dr Harry Shukman—to each of whom I am most grateful for many detailed suggestions, and for giving up much time to help me. At the outset of my research I received valuable bibliographical advice from Dr J. G. S. Simmons, and suggestions for specific maps from Mr Norman Davies, Dr Ronald Hingley, Mr John B. Kingston and Mr Ewald Uustalu. Jane Cousins helped me with bibliographical and historical research; Mr Arthur Banks transcribed my sketches into clear, printable maps, and Kate Fleming kept a vigilant eye on the cartography. Susie Sacher helped me to compile the index: Sarah Graham, as well as undertaking all the secretarial work, made many important suggestions, factual and cartographic.

The first 166 maps in this atlas were drawn by Arthur Banks and his team of expert cartographers, including the late Terry Bicknell, who subsequently drew more than six hundred historical maps for me. The last fifteen maps were drawn by Tim Aspden, who also drew the extra maps for several of my other books and historical atlases.

I am particularly grateful to Abe Eisenstat and Kay Thomson for their help over several months in enabling me to bring this atlas up to date for this new edition. The collapse of Soviet Commission and the disintegration of the Soviet Union before the end of its eighth decade, an event which was not conceivable (certainly not to this author) when the atlas was first published in 1972, has led me to prepare fifteen new maps. In designing them, I have tried to show in detail the sequence of events that shook both the

Soviet Union and Eastern Europe within the space of a decade, creating new States and new perspectives as the territorial and ideological monolith dissolved.

3 March 1993

MARTIN GILBERT
Merton College, Oxford

Note to the Fourth Edition

The new maps in this fourth edition bring the history of Russia into the twenty-first century. Despite the disintegration of the Soviet Union in 1991, the Russian Republic retained control of a vast land mass from the Baltic Sea to the Pacific Ocean. With the loss of super-power status, which it had earlier shared with the United States, it sought new means of asserting its power in the world. Enormous resources of crude oil and natural gas provided a considerable source of income and influence.

In 1994 Russia was invited to the G7 table of the world's seven leading industrial nations (Britain, Canada, France, Germany, Italy, Japan, the United States), thus creating the G8, of which Russia became the chairman in 2006, hosting the annual summit in St Petersburg.

In defence policy, the Cold War predominance of the nuclear threat receded. In 2000, the Russian President, Vladimir Putin announced that Russia was interested in reducing its strategic warheads from more than 9,000 to 1,500 or fewer. December 2001 was the START I Treaty deadline for Russia to meet a warhead level of 6,000. It surpassed that goal, reducing its operational warheads to 5,520.

In May 2002, Putin and President George W. Bush agreed to reduce the number of 'operationally deployed' warheads to between 1,700 and 2,200 by the end of 2012. Russia is expected to reach this target even earlier, as Russia continues to transfer its resources from nuclear to conventional forces.

Domestically, Russia struggled at the start of the twentieth-first century with ultra-nationalism, widespread alcoholism, and a falling life expectancy. Russian men have one of the lowest life expectancy rates in the world. A sixteen-year-old Russian boy has a 50 per cent chance of living to sixty, compared with an 85 to 90 per cent chance for a sixteen-year-old in the United States.

Russia has also suffered from a declining place in the global economy, sustaining its economic strength only by having become the world's largest exporter of natural gas (see maps 171 and 173), and, after Saudi Arabia, the second largest exporter of oil (see maps, 169, 170 and 172). Moscow has repeatedly made it clear that neither Gazprom nor Rosneft, the government-owned energy producers, are not open to foreign or domestic bidding; instead, they actively seeks to buy private energy companies in Western Europe.

Some important successes have been noted in Russia's internal life. The number of Russians living below the government-assessed poverty line dropped from 42 million in 2000 to 26 million in 2004. The property-owning middle class reached an estimated 25 per cent of the population in 2006.

In Western Europe and the United States there were concerns that Russia under Putin was drawing closer to the autocratic methods of the Communist era. Thus, even with a much reduced land mass since 1991, and with its tremendous nuclear armament of two decades earlier being decommissioned, Russia remained a source of concern and friction in the wider world.

The Russian national holiday, 12 June, was originally called Independence Day; it marked the Russian Parliament's 1990 declaration of sovereignty from the Soviet Union.

That declaration was a precursor to the breakup of the Soviet Union, which Putin called the 'greatest catastrophe of the 20th century.' In 2002 the holiday was renamed the Day of Russia.

Since he became president in 2000, Putin has permitted the reintroduction of Soviet-era symbols, such as the music to the Soviet anthem and the use of the Red Star by the country's armed forces.

Between 2000 and 2006 Russia came under increasing criticism from the West, which accused it of measures hostile to democracy, media freedoms and human rights. The cutting off of Russian oil to Ukraine on 1 January 2006 was seen as using national wealth as a political weapon, to punish Ukraine for electing Viktor Yushchenko as President over Russia's preferred candidate, the former President Viktor Yanukovich.

Six months later, in June 2006, distress was caused in Moscow when it was announced that Ukraine and the United States of America would hold joint military manoeuvres. This raised fears that Ukraine might follow several former Soviet satellites (including Poland and Hungary) in joining the European Union. The Soviet Foreign Minister, Sergei Lavrov, indicated that this would not be acceptable to Moscow. To the north of Ukraine, Belarus remained the closest of the former Soviet Republics to Russia, though here, as earlier in Ukraine, there were popular demonstrations against the pro-Russian Government.

In the battle for oil exports, Russia was confronted in 2006 by the opening of an alternate route from the Caucasus and Central Asia, that gave both Azerbaijan and Kazakhstan—two former Soviet republics—an ability to be independent of oil pipeline transit routes through Russia (maps 175 and 176).

President Putin emerged as an opponent of the widespread corruption—including the blatant purchase of parliamentary seats—telling the Russian people in a national address in May 2006: 'I believe social responsibility should be the foundation of the work of both officials and business people, and they should bear in mind that the source of the prosperity and well-being of Russia is its people.' The chairman of the National Anti-Corruption Committee commented on this issue: 'Corruption is part and parcel of the system of running the State. It is heavily present in making State decisions.'

This new edition reflects the conflicts and priorities in Russia during the first years of the first decade of the twenty-first century: a history that now—like this atlas—spans more than two thousand years.

26 June 2006   MARTIN GILBERT

Maps

THE SLAVS BY 800 BC

Probable areas of Slavic settlement by 800 BC

Other tribal groups and peoples by 800 BC

Baltic Sea

BALTS

Dvina

GERMANS

SLAVS

Pripet Marshes

SLAVS

Vistula

Carpathians

SLAVS

Dnieper

Don

Volga

Dniester

Danube

Caspian Sea

Caucasus

Black Sea

Byzantium

LAZ

GEORGIANS

GREEKS

ARMENIANS

Mediterranean Sea

ASSYRIANS

MEDES

Euphrates

Tigris

ARABS

Babylon

JEWS

Jerusalem

0   300
Miles

The origin of the Slavs is unknown. Possibly they came from the Caucasus. By 800 BC they were probably settled between the Vistula and the Don, in several separate groups

1

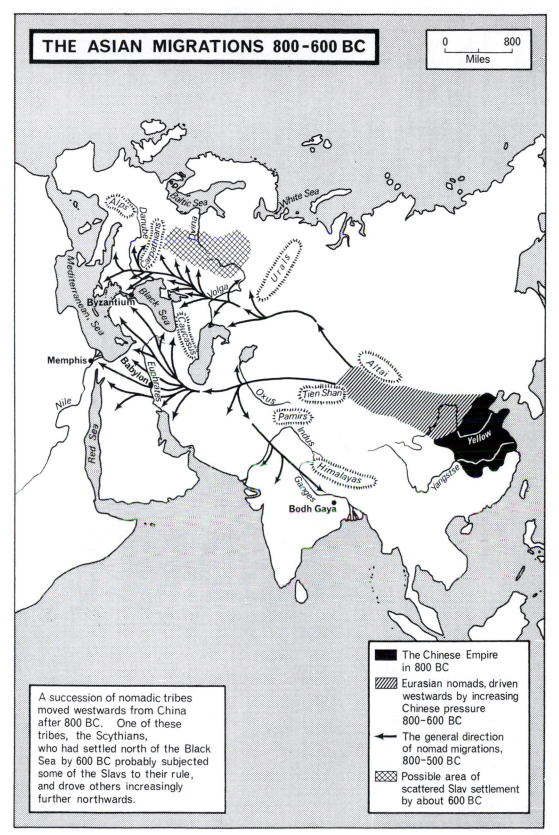

THE ASIAN MIGRATIONS 800-600 BC

0   800
Miles

Alps

Baltic Sea
White Sea
Danube
Vistula
Dvina
Urals

Volga

Mediterranean Sea

Byzantium

Black Sea

Caucasus

Altai

Memphis

Babylon

Euphrates

Oxus

Tien Shan

Pamirs

Indus

Yellow

Nile

Red Sea

Himalayas

Ganges

Yangtse

Bodh Gaya

A succession of nomadic tribes
moved westwards from China
after 800 BC.   One of these
tribes, the Scythians,
who had settled north of the Black
Sea by 600 BC probably subjected
some of the Slavs to their rule,
and drove others increasingly
further northwards.

▇ The Chinese Empire
  in 800 BC

▨ Eurasian nomads, driven
  westwards by increasing
  Chinese pressure
  800-600 BC

← The general direction
  of nomad migrations,
  800-500 BC

▨ Possible area of
  scattered Slav settlement
  by about 600 BC

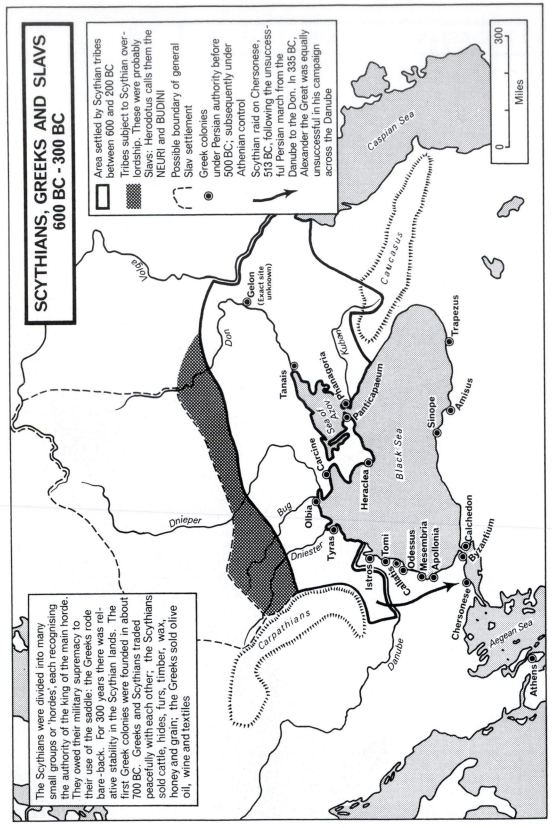

SCYTHIANS, GREEKS AND SLAVS
600 BC - 300 BC

Area settled by Scythian tribes between 600 and 200 BC

Tribes subject to Scythian over-lordship. These were probably Slavs: Herodotus calls them the NEURI and BUDINI

Possible boundary of general Slav settlement

Greek colonies

Greek colonies under Persian authority before 500 BC; subsequently under Athenian control

Scythian raid on Chersonese, 513 BC, following the unsuccess-ful Persian march from the Danube to the Don. In 335 BC, Alexander the Great was equally unsuccessful in his campaign across the Danube

The Scythians were divided into many small groups or 'hordes', each recognising the authority of the king of the main horde. They owed their military supremacy to their use of the saddle: the Greeks rode bare-back. For 300 years there was rel-ative stability in the Scythian lands. The first Greek colonies were founded in about 700 BC. Greeks and Scythians traded peacefully with each other; the Scythians sold cattle, hides, furs, timber, wax, honey and grain; the Greeks sold olive oil, wine and textiles

Caspian Sea

Volga

Caucasus

Don

Gelon (Exact site unknown)

Kuben

Tanais

Phanagoria

Trapezus

Sea of Azov

Panticapaeum

Amisus

Carcine

Sinope

Black Sea

Heraclea

Dnieper

Bug

Olbia

Dniester

Tyras

Calchedon

Istros

Tomi

Callatis

Odessus

Byzantium

Mesembria

Apollonia

Carpathians

Chersonese

Aegean Sea

Danube

Athens

0   300

Miles

3

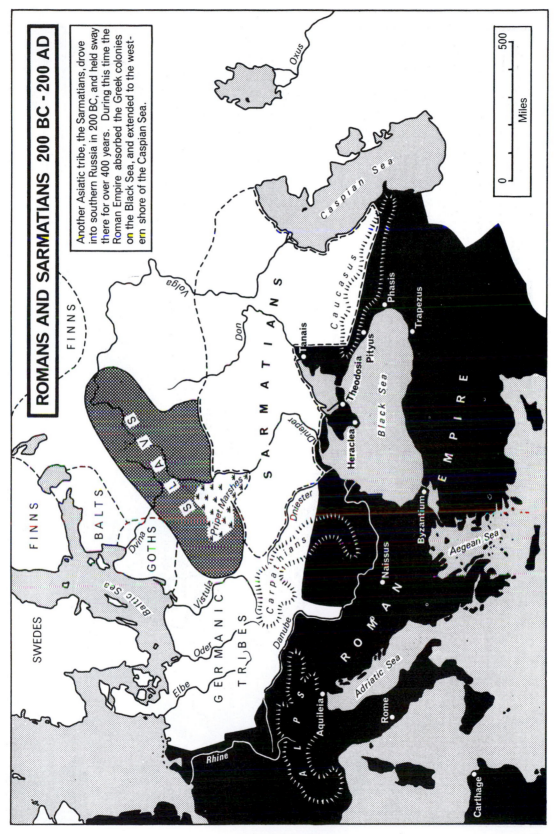

ROMANS AND SARMATIANS 200 BC - 200 AD

Another Asiatic tribe, the Sarmatians, drove into southern Russia in 200 BC, and held sway there for over 400 years. During this time the Roman Empire absorbed the Greek colonies on the Black Sea, and extended to the western shore of the Caspian Sea.

Oxus

Caspian Sea

FINNS

Volga

Don

S A R M A T I A N S

Caucasus

Tanais

Theodosia

Pityus

Phasis

Trapezus

FINNS

Dnieper

S L A V S

Pripet Marshes

Dniester

Heraclea

Black Sea

BALTS

Dvina

GOTHS

Carpathians

Naissus

Byzantium

Aegean Sea

R O M A N

SWEDES

Baltic Sea

Vistula

Oder

GERMANIC TRIBES

Danube

Elbe

A L P S

Aquileia

Adriatic Sea

Rome

E M P I R E

Rhine

Carthage

500

Miles

0

4

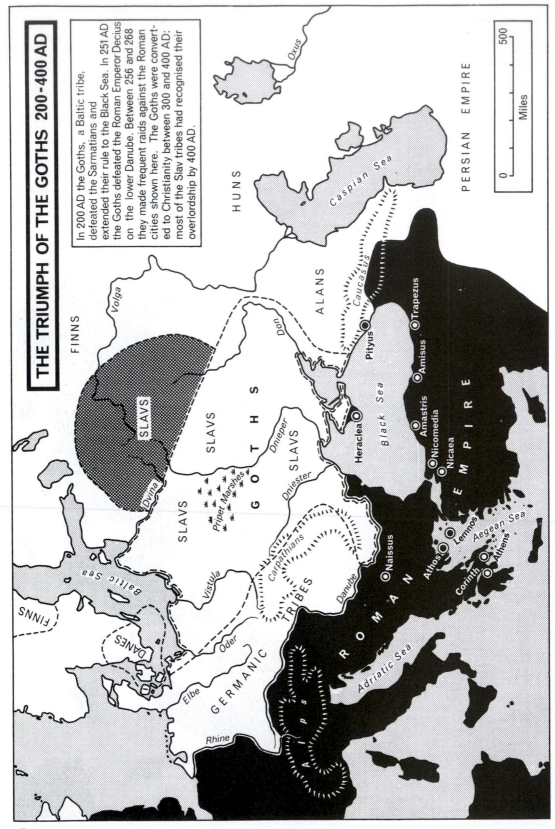

THE TRIUMPH OF THE GOTHS 200-400 AD

In 200 AD the Goths, a Baltic tribe, defeated the Sarmatians and extended their rule to the Black Sea. In 251 AD the Goths defeated the Roman Emperor Decius on the lower Danube. Between 256 and 268 they made frequent raids against the Roman cities shown here. The Goths were converted to Christianity between 300 and 400 AD: most of the Slav tribes had recognised their overlordship by 400 AD.

500

0

Miles

PERSIAN EMPIRE

Oxus

HUNS

Caspian Sea

FINNS

Volga

ALANS

Caucasus

Trapezus

Amisus

Pityus

SLAVS

Don

Black Sea

Amastris

Nicomedia

GOTHS

Dnieper

SLAVS

Heraclea

Nicaea

SLAVS

Dniester

EMPIRE

Pripet Marshes

SLAVS

ROMAN

Lemnos

Aegean Sea

Carpathians

Athos

Athens

Vistula

TRIBES

Naissus

Corinth

Baltic Sea

Danube

FINNS

Oder

GERMANIC

Adriatic Sea

DANES

Elbe

A

l

p

s

Rhine

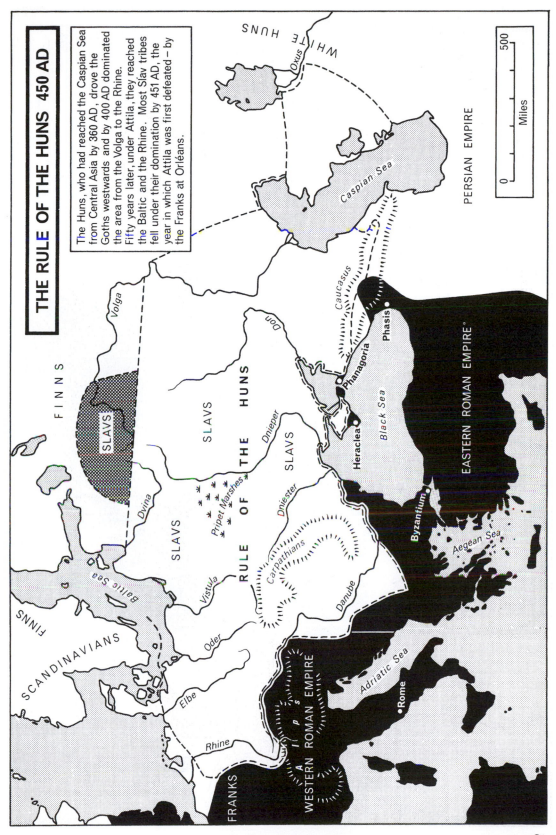

THE RULE OF THE HUNS 450 AD

The Huns, who had reached the Caspian Sea from Central Asia by 360 AD, drove the Goths westwards and by 400 AD dominated the area from the Volga to the Rhine. Fifty years later, under Attila, they reached the Baltic and the Rhine. Most Slav tribes fell under their domination by 451 AD, the year in which Attila was first defeated – by the Franks at Orléans.

WHITE HUNS

Oxus

PERSIAN EMPIRE

Caspian Sea

0   500
Miles

Volga

FINNS

SLAVS

Dvina

SLAVS

Don

Caucasus

Phasis

Phanagoria

Black Sea

EASTERN ROMAN EMPIRE

SLAVS

Dnieper

Heraclea

SLAVS

R U L E   O F   T H E   H U N S

Pripet Marshes

Dniester

Byzantium

Aegean Sea

SLAVS

Carpathians

Baltic Sea

Vistula

Danube

SCANDINAVIANS

FINNS

Oder

A   l   p   s

WESTERN ROMAN EMPIRE

Adriatic Sea

Rome

Elbe

Rhine

FRANKS

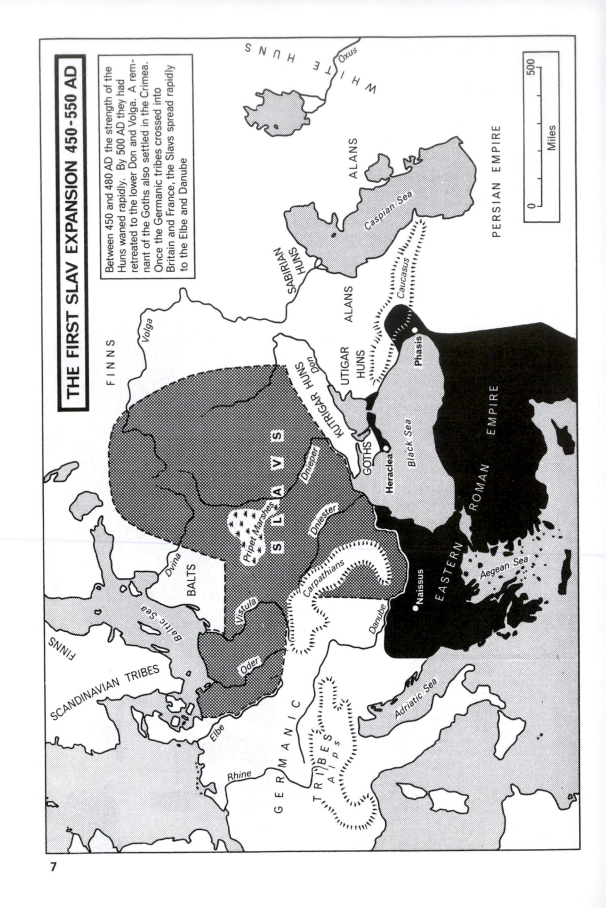

THE FIRST SLAV EXPANSION 450-550 AD

Between 450 and 480 AD the strength of the Huns waned rapidly. By 500 AD they had retreated to the lower Don and Volga. A remnant of the Goths also settled in the Crimea. Once the Germanic tribes crossed into Britain and France, the Slavs spread rapidly to the Elbe and Danube

WHITE HUNS

Oxus

ALANS

Caspian Sea

PERSIAN EMPIRE

SABIRIAN HUNS

Volga

ALANS

UTIGAR HUNS

Caucasus

Phasis

FINNS

KUTRIGAR HUNS

Don

GOTHS

Heraclea

Black Sea

EASTERN ROMAN EMPIRE

Dnieper

S L A V S

Pripet Marshes

Dniester

Aegean Sea

BALTS

Dvina

Carpathians

Naissus

FINNS

Baltic Sea

Vistula

Danube

Adriatic Sea

SCANDINAVIAN TRIBES

Oder

G E R M A N I C   T R I B E S

Elbe

Alps

Rhine

500

0

Miles

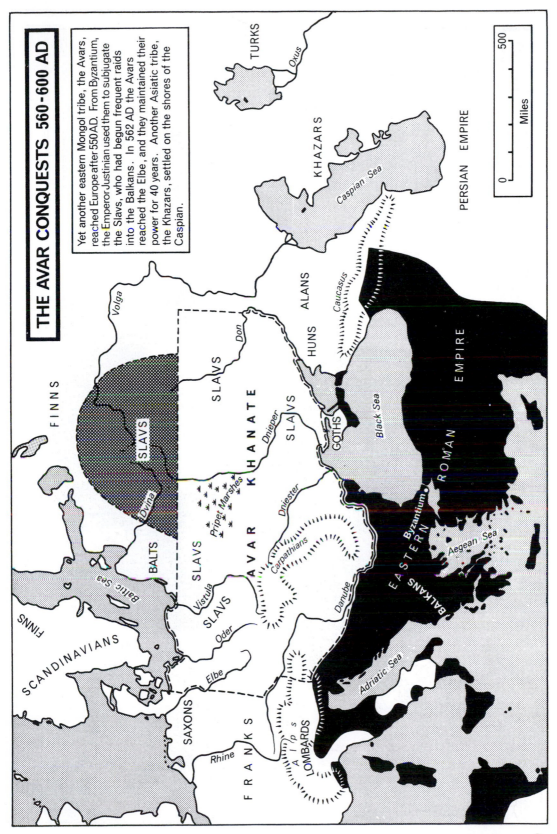

THE AVAR CONQUESTS 560-600 AD

Yet another eastern Mongol tribe, the Avars, reached Europe after 550AD. From Byzantium, the Emperor Justinian used them to subjugate the Slavs, who had begun frequent raids into the Balkans. In 562 AD the Avars reached the Elbe, and they maintained their power for 40 years. Another Asiatic tribe, the Khazars, settled on the shores of the Caspian.

TURKS

Oxus

KHAZARS

Caspian Sea

PERSIAN EMPIRE

500

0

Miles

ALANS

HUNS

Caucasus

Volga

FINNS

Don

SLAVS

SLAVS

A V A R   K H A N A T E

SLAVS

Dnieper

GOTHS

Black Sea

ROMAN EMPIRE

Dvina

Pripet Marshes

SLAVS

Dniester

Carpathians

BALTS

Byzantium

Baltic Sea

SLAVS

Vistula

Oder

Danube

E A S T E R N

BALKANS

Aegean Sea

FINNS

SCANDINAVIANS

Elbe

A l p s

LOMBARDS

Adriatic Sea

SAXONS

F R A N K S

Rhine

8

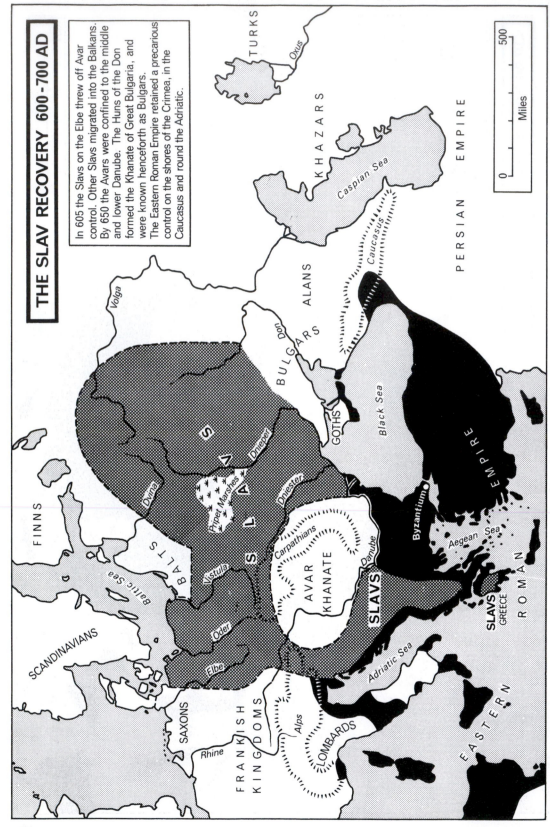

THE SLAV RECOVERY 600-700 AD

In 605 the Slavs on the Elbe threw off Avar control. Other Slavs migrated into the Balkans. By 650 the Avars were confined to the middle and lower Danube. The Huns of the Don formed the Khanate of Great Bulgaria, and were known henceforth as Bulgars. The Eastern Roman Empire retained a precarious control on the shores of the Crimea, in the Caucasus and round the Adriatic.

500

0

Miles

TURKS

Oxus

KHAZARS

Caspian Sea

PERSIAN EMPIRE

Volga

ALANS

Caucasus

BULGARS

Don

GOTHS

Black Sea

EMPIRE

S

Dnieper

Dvina

Pripet Marshes

L

A

V

S

Dniester

Byzantium

Aegean Sea

FINNS

BALTS

Vistula

Carpathians

AVAR KHANATE

Danube

SLAVS

ROMAN

SLAVS

GREECE

SCANDINAVIANS

Baltic Sea

Oder

Elbe

Adriatic Sea

EASTERN

SAXONS

FRANKISH KINGDOMS

Alps

LOMBARDS

Rhine

9

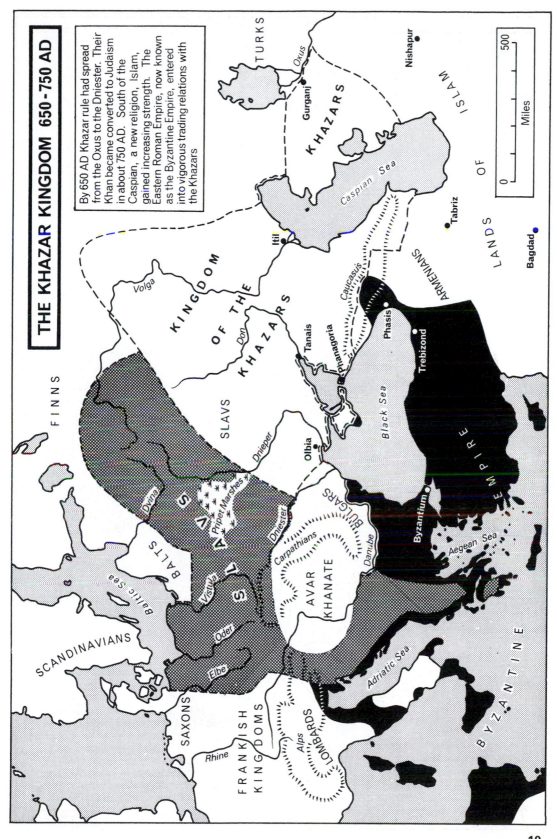

THE KHAZAR KINGDOM 650 - 750 AD

By 650 AD Khazar rule had spread from the Oxus to the Dniester. Their Khan became converted to Judaism in about 750 AD. South of the Caspian, Islam, a new religion, gained increasing strength. The Eastern Roman Empire, now known as the Byzantine Empire, entered into vigorous trading relations with the Khazars

500

0   Miles

TURKS

Nishapur

Oxus

Gurganj

K H A Z A R S

Caspian Sea

Tabriz

Bagdad

L A N D S   O F   I S L A M

Volga

K I N G D O M   O F   T H E

Itil

Don

K H A Z A R S

Caucasus

Tanais

Phanagoria

ARMENIANS

Phasis

Trebizond

SLAVS

Dnieper

Black Sea

FINNS

S L A V S

Dvina

Pripet Marshes

Olbia

BALTS

Dniester

BULGARS

Byzantium

E M P I R E

Vistula

Carpathians

Danube

Aegean Sea

SCANDINAVIANS

Baltic Sea

Oder

AVAR KHANATE

Adriatic Sea

Elbe

B Y Z A N T I N E

SAXONS

FRANKISH KINGDOMS

Rhine

Alps

LOMBARDS

THE SCANDINAVIAN MIGRATIONS 800–1000 AD

VINLAND
(Site unknown)

St. Lawrence

0   400
Miles

GREENLAND

NORTH
ATLANTIC
OCEAN

ICELAND

North
Pole

FAROE
ISLANDS

Iona

Lindisfarne
Jarrow
ENGLAND

Lisbon

SPAIN
Seville

FRANCE   Paris
Pamplona

Valence

Rome

Mediterranean Sea

Novgorod   Ladoga

Kiev   Dnieper

Olbia

KHAZARIA

Constantinople   Black Sea   Tanais   Volga

BYZANTIUM

Itil

Semender

ARMENIA
Antioch   Edessa
SYRIA   Baku   Caspian Sea

Red Sea

PERSIA   Gümüsh Tepe

Persian Gulf

The Scandinavian homelands in 800 AD

← **Principal Scandinavian migrations 800–1000 AD**

The Vikings, or Norsemen, sailed in successive waves from Scandinavia from 793 AD, when they landed at Lindisfarne, to 1098 when they reached Armenia. One line of Norse penetration and settlement was through the Slav lands, from Novgorod to Kiev, along the river trade routes which linked Scandinavia with Constantinople

THE SLAVS AND THE NORSEMEN BY 880 AD

Slav settlement by 880 AD
SERB Principal Slav tribes
BALTS Other tribes
'Kievan Rus', ruled by the Norsemen (Varangarians), who took tribute from the neighbouring Slavs, and protected them against Khazar and Pecheneg attacks

NORSE
SWEDES
DANES
FINNS
Visby
Baltic Sea
OBODRICHI
BALTS
GERMANS
Elbe
POLES
MAZOVIANS
SILESIANS
Pripet Marshes
CZECHS
MORAVIANS
DEREVLIANS
SLOVAKS
Danube
SLOVENES
MAGYARS
Venice
CROATS
Adriatic Sea
SERBS
Preslav
BULGARS
Ægean Sea
Athens
GREEKS

SLOVIANIANS
Novgorod
CHEREMESIANS
Volga
VIATCHIANS
MORDVINS
POLOCHANE
Smolensk
KRIVICHIANS
RADIMICHIANS
SEVERIANS
Kiev
POLIANIANS
VOLHYNIANS
Don
KHAZARS
PECHENEGS
Tmutorokan
Black Sea
Caucasus
Constantinople
ARMENIANS

The Norse settlers between Novgorod and Kiev quickly dominated the local Slavs, over whom they established political control. Known as "Varangarians", these Norse overlords moulded the Slavs into a coherent federation, "Kievan Rus". Originally Norse speaking, Kievan Rus, or Russia, saw a close mingling of Scandinavian and Slav culture; and the emergence of a strong Kievan, or Russian national consciousness. The first Varangarian ruler, Rurik, led an expedition against Constantinople in 860 AD. His successor Oleg established his capital at Kiev in about 880 AD.

0   300
Miles

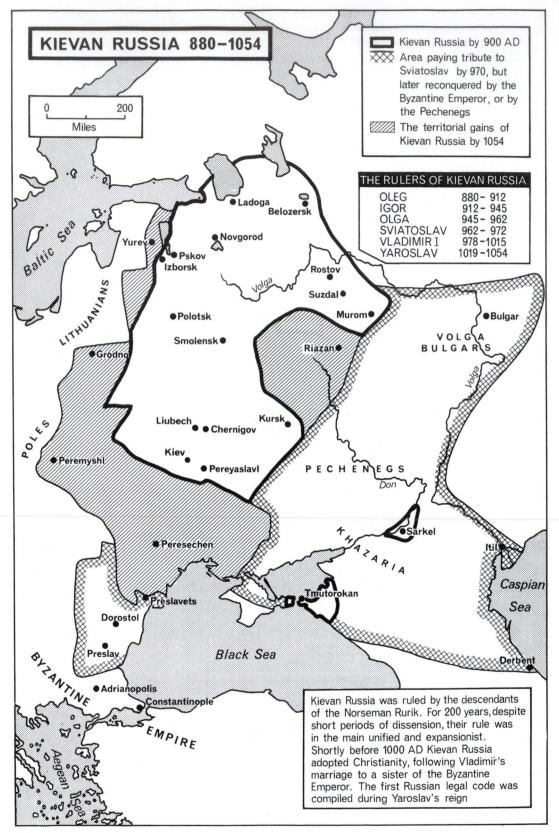

KIEVAN RUSSIA 880–1054

0 — 200
Miles

Legend:
- Kievan Russia by 900 AD
- Area paying tribute to Sviatoslav by 970, but later reconquered by the Byzantine Emperor, or by the Pechenegs
- The territorial gains of Kievan Russia by 1054

THE RULERS OF KIEVAN RUSSIA

OLEG	880– 912
IGOR	912– 945
OLGA	945– 962
SVIATOSLAV	962– 972
VLADIMIR I	978–1015
YAROSLAV	1019–1054

Baltic Sea

Ladoga
Belozersk
Yurev
Novgorod
Pskov
Izborsk
Rostov
Volga
Suzdal
Murom
Bulgar
LITHUANIANS
Polotsk
VOLGA BULGARS
Smolensk
Riazan
Volga
Grodno
POLES
Liubech
Kursk
Chernigov
Kiev
Pereyaslavl
PECHENEGS
Peremyshl
Don
Peresechen
Sarkel
KHAZARIA
Itil
Caspian Sea
Preslavets
Tmutorokan
Dorostol
Preslav
Black Sea
Derbent
BYZANTINE
Adrianopolis
Constantinople
EMPIRE
Aegean Sea

Kievan Russia was ruled by the descendants of the Norseman Rurik. For 200 years, despite short periods of dissension, their rule was in the main unified and expansionist. Shortly before 1000 AD Kievan Russia adopted Christianity, following Vladimir's marriage to a sister of the Byzantine Emperor. The first Russian legal code was compiled during Yaroslav's reign

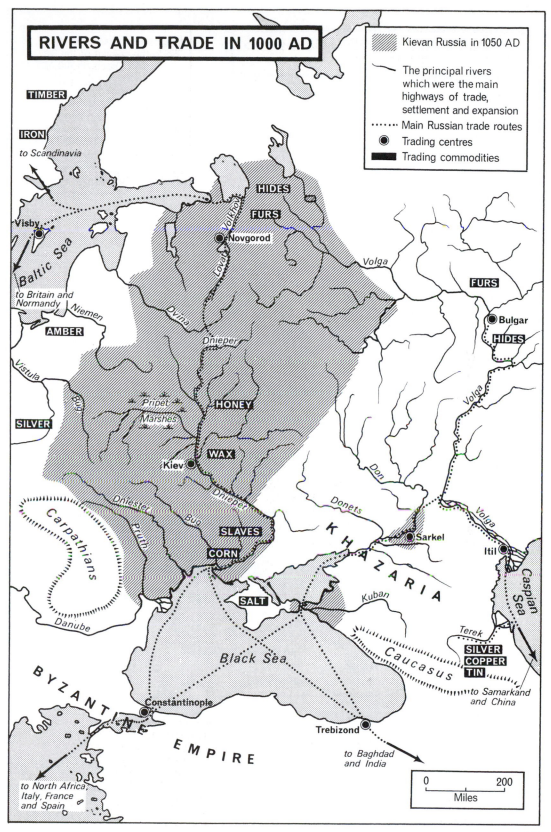

RIVERS AND TRADE IN 1000 AD

Kievan Russia in 1050 AD

The principal rivers which were the main highways of trade, settlement and expansion

Main Russian trade routes

Trading centres

Trading commodities

TIMBER

IRON

to Scandinavia

HIDES

FURS

Visby

Baltic Sea

Novgorod

Volkhov

Volga

FURS

to Britain and Normandy

Niemen

Bulgar

AMBER

HIDES

Dvina

Vistula

Bug

Dnieper

HONEY

Pripet Marshes

SILVER

WAX

Kiev

Dniester

Dnieper

Don

Donets

Prut

Bug

K H A Z A R I A

Sarkel

SLAVES

Volga

CORN

Itil

Carpathians

Caspian Sea

SALT

Kuban

Danube

Black Sea

Caucasus

Terek

SILVER
COPPER
TIN

to Samarkand and China

B Y Z A N T I N E

Constantinople

E M P I R E

Trebizond

to Baghdad and India

to North Africa, Italy, France and Spain

0   200
Miles

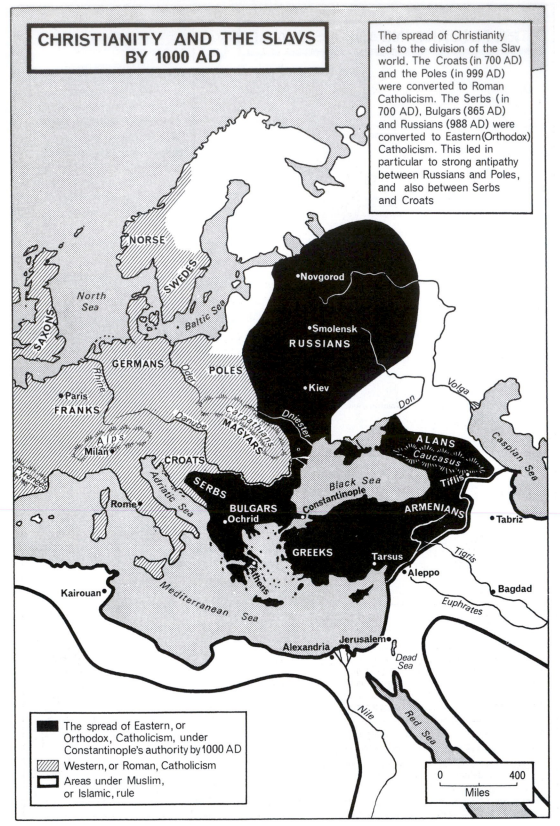

CHRISTIANITY AND THE SLAVS BY 1000 AD

The spread of Christianity led to the division of the Slav world. The Croats (in 700 AD) and the Poles (in 999 AD) were converted to Roman Catholicism. The Serbs (in 700 AD), Bulgars (865 AD) and Russians (988 AD) were converted to Eastern (Orthodox) Catholicism. This led in particular to strong antipathy between Russians and Poles, and also between Serbs and Croats

NORSE

SWEDES

North Sea

Baltic Sea

SAXONS

GERMANS

POLES

•Novgorod

•Smolensk

RUSSIANS

Oder

Rhine

•Paris

FRANKS

•Kiev

Volga

Don

Danube

Carpathians

MAGYARS

Dniester

Alps

Milan•

CROATS

ALANS

Caucasus

Caspian Sea

SERBS

Adriatic Sea

Black Sea

Constantinople

Tiflis•

Rome•

BULGARS

•Ochrid

ARMENIANS

•Tabriz

GREEKS

Tarsus•

Tigris

Athens

•Aleppo

Kairouan•

Mediterranean

Sea

•Bagdad

Euphrates

Alexandria•

Jerusalem•

Dead Sea

Nile

Red Sea

The spread of Eastern, or Orthodox, Catholicism, under Constantinople's authority by 1000 AD

Western, or Roman, Catholicism

Areas under Muslim, or Islamic, rule

0   400
Miles

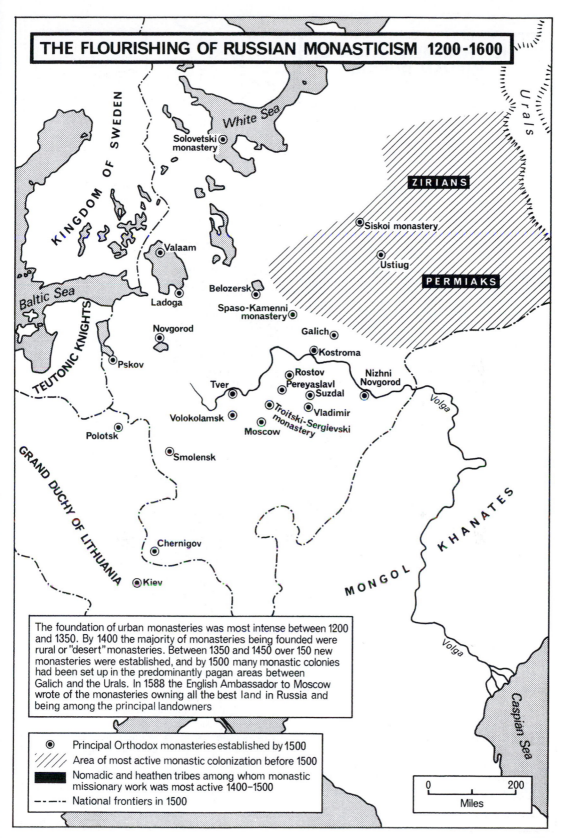

THE FLOURISHING OF RUSSIAN MONASTICISM 1200-1600

White Sea

Urals

KINGDOM OF SWEDEN

Solovetski monastery

ZIRIANS

Siskoi monastery

Valaam

Ustiug

Belozersk

PERMIAKS

Baltic Sea

Ladoga

Spaso-Kamenni monastery

Novgorod

Galich

TEUTONIC KNIGHTS

Pskov

Kostroma

Nizhni Novgorod

Tver

Rostov

Pereyaslavl

Suzdal

Volokolamsk

Troitski-Serglevski monastery

Vladimir

Volga

Moscow

Polotsk

Smolensk

GRAND DUCHY OF LITHUANIA

MONGOL KHANATES

Chernigov

Kiev

Volga

Caspian Sea

The foundation of urban monasteries was most intense between 1200 and 1350. By 1400 the majority of monasteries being founded were rural or "desert" monasteries. Between 1350 and 1450 over 150 new monasteries were established, and by 1500 many monastic colonies had been set up in the predominantly pagan areas between Galich and the Urals. In 1588 the English Ambassador to Moscow wrote of the monasteries owning all the best land in Russia and being among the principal landowners

⊚   Principal Orthodox monasteries established by 1500

/////   Area of most active monastic colonization before 1500

▬   Nomadic and heathen tribes among whom monastic missionary work was most active 1400–1500

–·–·–   National frontiers in 1500

0   200

Miles

THE FRAGMENTATION OF KIEVAN RUSSIA 1054–1238

0   200
Miles

DEPENDENCIES OF NOVGOROD

FINNS

Ustiug

Ladoga

Belozersk

REPUBLIC OF NOVGOROD
• Novgorod

VLADIMIR–SUZDAL

Reval

Kostroma •
• Yaroslavl
• Rostov

VOLGA BULGARS

• Pskov

Torzhok •

Tver •

Suzdal •

Izborsk

Moscow •

Vladimir •

Riga

SMOLENSK

Murom •

LITHUANIA

Polotsk •

Viazma •

Riazan •

Kovno •

Vitebsk •

Smolensk •

MUROM–RIAZAN

POLOTSK
• Minsk

CHERNIGOV

Bialystok •

TUROV
• Pinsk

NOVGOROD–SEVERSK

POLAND

Turov •

Chernigov •

VOLHYNIA

KIEV
Kiev •

PEREYASLAVL
• Pereyaslavl

Cracow •

Zhitomir •

GALICIA
• Galich

Don

Vistula

Dvina

Dniester   CUMANS or POLOVTSI

Carpathians

HUNGARY

Black Sea

Constantinople •

On the death of Yaroslav in 1054, Kievan Russia was divided among his sons. Their constant feuds led to the fragmentation of the once powerful kingdom. United briefly from 1113 to 1125 by Vladimir Monomakh, the Russian lands were again divided and in conflict during the hundred years before the Mongol invasion of 1238. In 1199 Galicia and Volhynia were united, and in 1254 recognised by the Pope as an independent kingdom. In 1307 Polotsk came under Lithuanian suzerainty

☐ The twelve Principalities of Russia in 1100

Baltic Sea

17

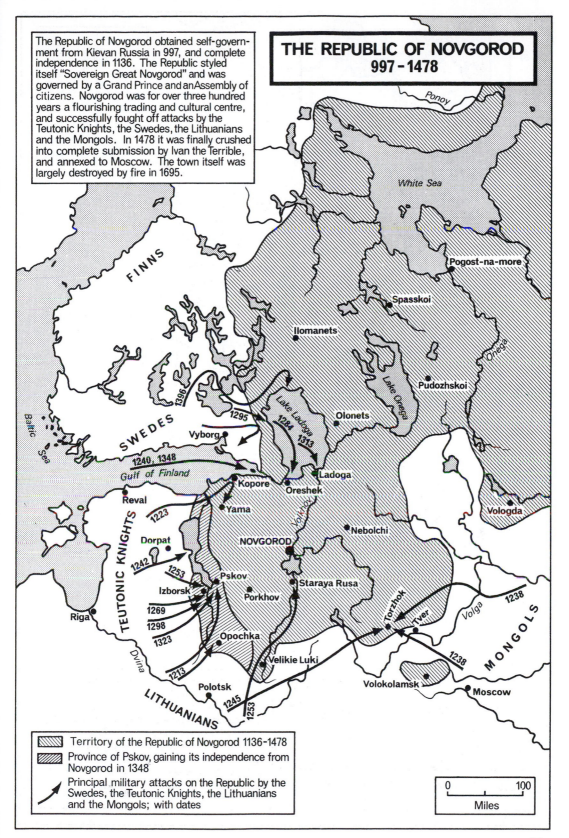

THE REPUBLIC OF NOVGOROD
997-1478

The Republic of Novgorod obtained self-government from Kievan Russia in 997, and complete independence in 1136. The Republic styled itself "Sovereign Great Novgorod" and was governed by a Grand Prince and an Assembly of citizens. Novgorod was for over three hundred years a flourishing trading and cultural centre, and successfully fought off attacks by the Teutonic Knights, the Swedes, the Lithuanians and the Mongols. In 1478 it was finally crushed into complete submission by Ivan the Terrible, and annexed to Moscow. The town itself was largely destroyed by fire in 1695.

Ponoy

White Sea

Pogost-na-more

FINNS

Spasskoi

Ilomanets

Pudozhskoi

Lake Onega

Onega

Olonets

Lake Ladoga

SWEDES

1386

1295

1284

1313

Vyborg

Baltic Sea

1240, 1348

Gulf of Finland

Kopore

Ladoga

Oreshek

Reval

Yama

Vologda

1223

Volkhov

Nebolchi

Dorpat

NOVGOROD

1242

TEUTONIC KNIGHTS

1253

Pskov

Staraya Rusa

Izborsk

Porkhov

1238

1269

Riga

1298

Volga

Torzhok

Tver

1323

Opochka

MONGOLS

Dvina

Velikie Luki

1238

1213

Volokolamsk

Moscow

LITHUANIANS

Polotsk

1245

1253

Territory of the Republic of Novgorod 1136-1478

Province of Pskov, gaining its independence from Novgorod in 1348

Principal military attacks on the Republic by the Swedes, the Teutonic Knights, the Lithuanians and the Mongols; with dates

0   100
Miles

18

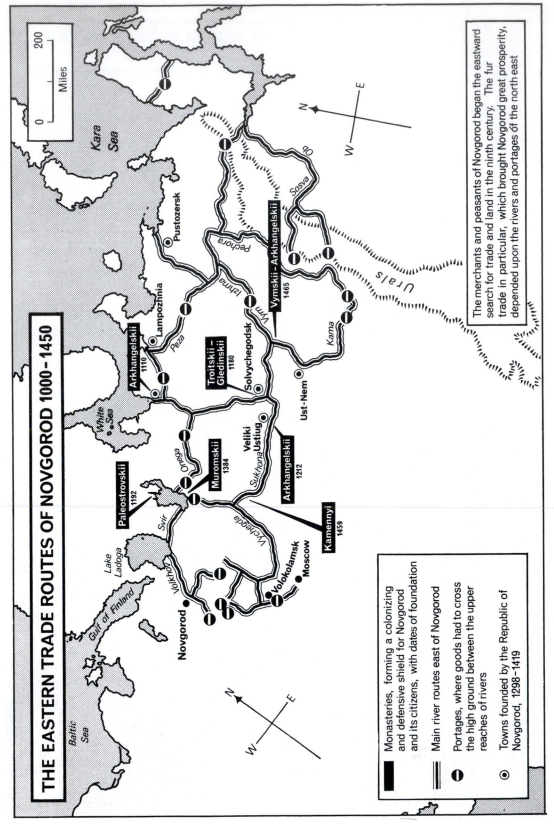

THE EASTERN TRADE ROUTES OF NOVGOROD 1000–1450

Kara Sea

Baltic Sea

Gulf of Finland

White Sea

Lake Ladoga

Volkhov

Svir

Onega

Peza

Pechora

Izhma

Sosva

Ob

Urals

Kama

Vym

Sukhona

Vychegda

Novgorod

Pustozersk

Lampozhnia

Arkhangelskii
1110

Troitskii –
Gledinskii
1180

Solvychegodsk

Ust-Nem

Veliki Ustiug

Vymskii – Arkhangelskii
1465

Paleostrovskii
1192

Muromskii
1384

Arkhangelskii
1212

Kamennyi
1459

Volokolamsk

Moscow

200 Miles
0

The merchants and peasants of Novgorod began the eastward search for trade and land in the ninth century. The fur trade in particular, which brought Novgorod great prosperity, depended upon the rivers and portages of the north east

Monasteries, forming a colonizing and defensive shield for Novgorod and its citizens, with dates of foundation

Main river routes east of Novgorod

Portages, where goods had to cross the high ground between the upper reaches of rivers

Towns founded by the Republic of Novgorod, 1298–1419

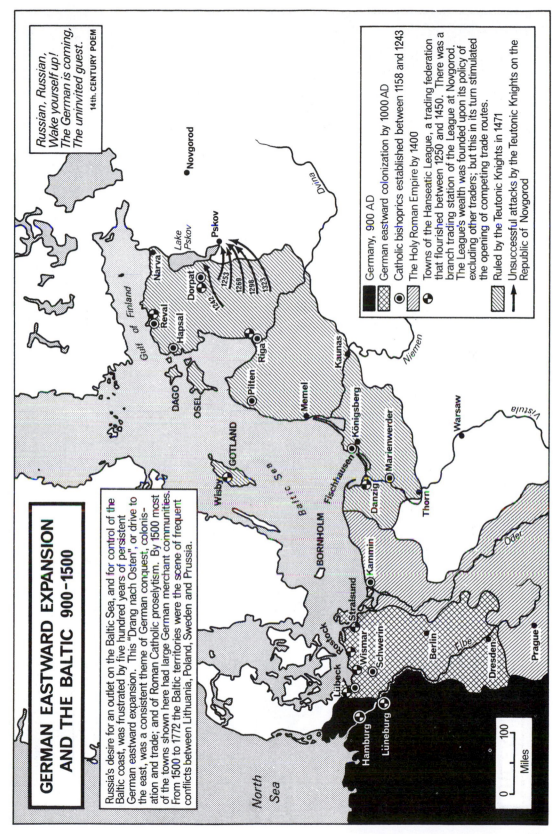

GERMAN EASTWARD EXPANSION AND THE BALTIC 900–1500

Russia's desire for an outlet on the Baltic Sea, and for control of the Baltic coast, was frustrated by five hundred years of persistent German eastward expansion. This "Drang nach Osten", or drive to the east, was a consistent theme of German conquest, colonisation and trade; and of Roman Catholic proselytism. By 1500 most of the towns shown here had large German merchant communities. From 1500 to 1772 the Baltic territories were the scene of frequent conflicts between Lithuania, Poland, Sweden and Prussia.

Russian, Russian,
Wake yourself up!
The German is coming.
The uninvited guest.

14th. CENTURY POEM

Germany, 900 AD

German eastward colonization by 1000 AD

Catholic bishoprics established between 1158 and 1243

The Holy Roman Empire by 1400

Towns of the Hanseatic League, a trading federation that flourished between 1250 and 1450. There was a branch trading station of the League at Novgorod. The League's wealth was founded upon its policy of excluding other traders; but this in its turn stimulated the opening of competing trade routes.

Ruled by the Teutonic Knights in 1471

Unsuccessful attacks by the Teutonic Knights on the Republic of Novgorod

Novgorod

Lake Pskov

Pskov

Narva

Dorpat

Reval

Hapsal

Riga

Pilten

DAGO

OSEL

Memel

Kaunas

Königsberg

Marienwerder

Warsaw

Gulf of Finland

Dvina

Niemen

Vistula

GOTLAND

Wisby

Baltic Sea

BORNHOLM

Fischhausen

Danzig

Thorn

Kammin

Stralsund

Rostock

Wismar

Schwerin

Lübeck

Hamburg

Lüneburg

Berlin

Dresden

Prague

Oder

Elbe

North Sea

1253
1269
1298
1323
1242

0   100

Miles

20

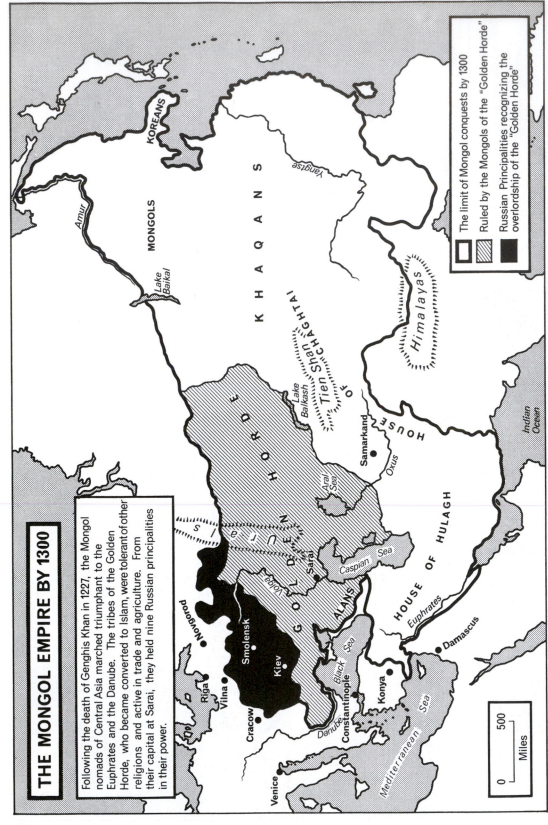

THE MONGOL EMPIRE BY 1300

Following the death of Genghis Khan in 1227, the Mongol nomads of Central Asia marched triumphant to the Euphrates and the Danube. The tribes of the Golden Horde, who became converted to Islam, were tolerant of other religions and active in trade and agriculture. From their capital at Sarai, they held nine Russian principalities in their power.

The limit of Mongol conquests by 1300

Ruled by the Mongols of the "Golden Horde"

Russian Principalities recognizing the overlordship of the "Golden Horde"

KOREANS

MONGOLS

KHAQANS

Amur

Yangtse

Lake Baikal

Tien Shan

CHAGHTAI

HOUSE OF

Himalayas

Indian Ocean

Lake Balkash

Samarkand

Oxus

Aral Sea

GOLDEN HORDE

URALS

Novgorod

Smolensk

Kiev

Volga

Sarai

Caspian Sea

ALANS

HOUSE OF HULAGH

Euphrates

Damascus

Riga

Vilna

Cracow

Black Sea

Constantinople

Konya

Venice

Danube

Mediterranean Sea

0   500
Miles

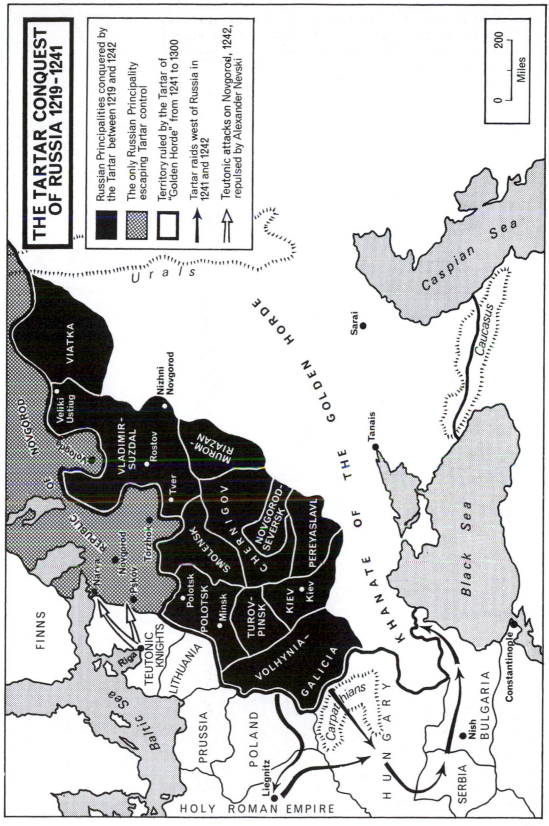

THE TARTAR CONQUEST OF RUSSIA 1219-1241

Russian Principalities conquered by the Tartar between 1219 and 1242

The only Russian Principality escaping Tartar control

Territory ruled by the Tartar of "Golden Horde" from 1241 to 1300

Tartar raids west of Russia in 1241 and 1242

Teutonic attacks on Novgorod, 1242, repulsed by Alexander Nevski

Caspian Sea

Urals

GOLDEN HORDE

Sarai

Caucasus

VIATKA

Nizhni Novgorod

NOVGOROD

Veliki Ustiug

Vologda

VLADIMIR-SUZDAL

Rostov

MUROM-RIAZAN

Tanais

Black Sea

REPUBLIC

Tver

CHERNIGOV

NOVGOROD-SEVERSK

PEREYASLAVL

SMOLENSK

KHANATE OF THE

FINNS

Novgorod

Pskov

Torzhok

Polotsk

Minsk

POLOTSK

TUROV-PINSK

KIEV

Kiev

Constantinople

Narva

Riga

TEUTONIC KNIGHTS

LITHUANIA

VOLHYNIA-GALICIA

Carpathians

HUNGARY

BULGARIA

Nish

SERBIA

Baltic Sea

PRUSSIA

POLAND

Liegnitz

HOLY ROMAN EMPIRE

Constantinople

200

0

Miles

22

THE LITHUANIAN CONQUESTS 1240 - 1462

Baltic Sea

ROSTOV

NOVGOROD

Riga

TEUTONIC KNIGHTS

PSKOV

TVER

MOSCOW

Polotsk

Viazma

Vitebsk

Kovno

Smolensk

TEUTONIC KNIGHTS

Vilna

RIAZAN

Grodno

Minsk

Brest-Litovsk

Slonim

Briansk

Warsaw

Pinsk

Turov

KINGDOM

Vladimir

Chernigov

OF

Zhitomir

Kiev

POLAND

Lvov

Poltava

CRIMEAN KHANATE Mongols

CRIMEAN KHANATE Mongols

Haji-bey

Sea of Azov

Black Sea

0   150
Miles

■ Grand Principality of Lithuania, 1240

▨ Lithuanian conquests by 1340, including the Russian Principalities of Polotsk and Pinsk-Turov

▨ Ruled by Lithuania in 1462

□ Russian Principalities unconquered by Lithuania

Shattered by Mongol invasions, and divided among themselves, the Russian Principalities fell easy victims to Lithuanian expansion after 1240.
In 1386, Lithuania and the Kingdom of Poland united under a single king. The Catholicism of this powerful kingdom was an extra cause of conflict with Russia.

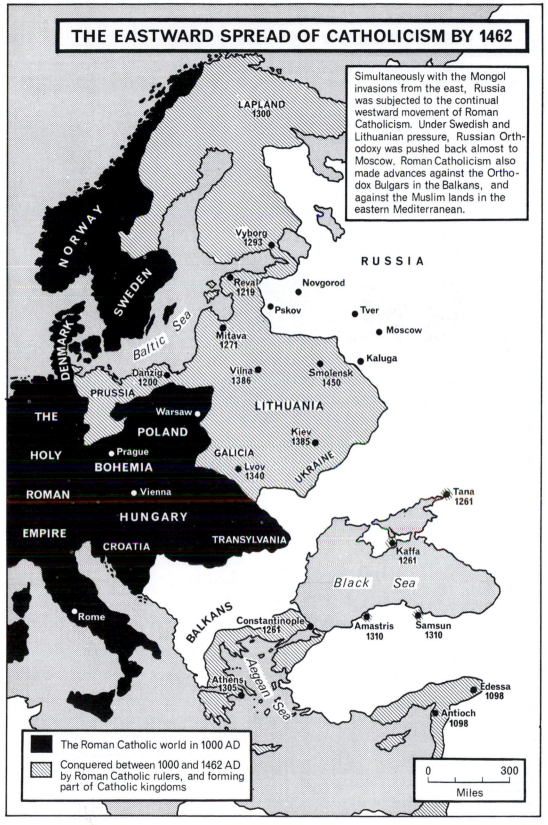

THE EASTWARD SPREAD OF CATHOLICISM BY 1462

Simultaneously with the Mongol invasions from the east, Russia was subjected to the continual westward movement of Roman Catholicism. Under Swedish and Lithuanian pressure, Russian Orthodoxy was pushed back almost to Moscow. Roman Catholicism also made advances against the Orthodox Bulgars in the Balkans, and against the Muslim lands in the eastern Mediterranean.

LAPLAND
1300

NORWAY

SWEDEN

DENMARK

Baltic Sea

RUSSIA

Vyborg
1293

Reval
1219

Novgorod

Pskov

Tver

Moscow

Mitava
1271

Kaluga

Danzig
1200

Vilna
1386

Smolensk
1450

PRUSSIA

LITHUANIA

THE

Warsaw

POLAND

HOLY

Prague

GALICIA

Kiev
1385

BOHEMIA

ROMAN

Vienna

Lvov
1340

UKRAINE

EMPIRE

HUNGARY

Tana
1261

CROATIA

TRANSYLVANIA

Kaffa
1261

BALKANS

Black Sea

Rome

Constantinople
1261

Amastris
1310

Samsun
1310

Athens
1305

Aegean Sea

Edessa
1098

Antioch
1098

The Roman Catholic world in 1000 AD

Conquered between 1000 and 1462 AD by Roman Catholic rulers, and forming part of Catholic kingdoms

0   300
Miles

24

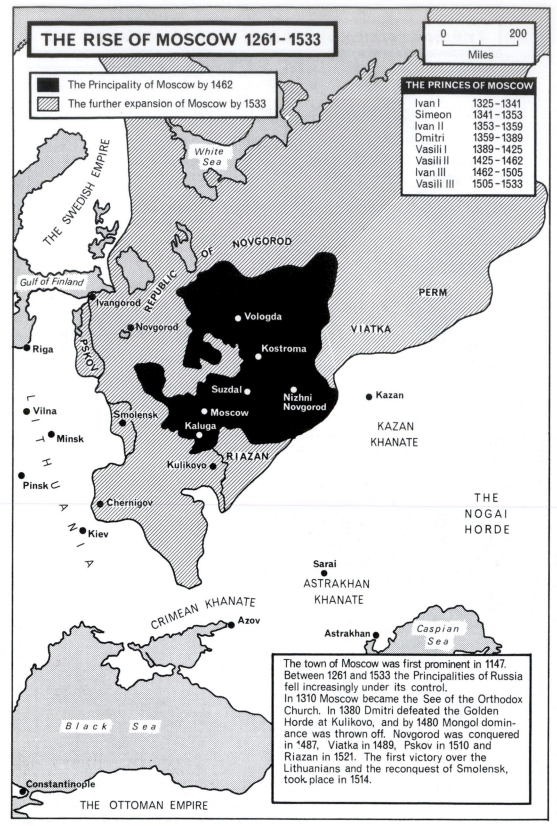

THE RISE OF MOSCOW 1261-1533

0   200
Miles

■ The Principality of Moscow by 1462
▨ The further expansion of Moscow by 1533

THE PRINCES OF MOSCOW

Ivan I	1325-1341
Simeon	1341-1353
Ivan II	1353-1359
Dmitri	1359-1389
Vasili I	1389-1425
Vasili II	1425-1462
Ivan III	1462-1505
Vasili III	1505-1533

THE SWEDISH EMPIRE

White Sea

Gulf of Finland

REPUBLIC OF NOVGOROD

PERM

Ivangorod

Novgorod

Vologda

VIATKA

Riga

PSKOV

Kostroma

Suzdal

Kazan

Vilna

Smolensk

Moscow

Nizhni Novgorod

KAZAN KHANATE

L I T H U A N I A

Minsk

Kaluga

Pinsk

RIAZAN

Kulikovo

THE NOGAI HORDE

Chernigov

Kiev

Sarai

ASTRAKHAN KHANATE

CRIMEAN KHANATE

Azov

Astrakhan

Caspian Sea

Black   Sea

The town of Moscow was first prominent in 1147. Between 1261 and 1533 the Principalities of Russia fell increasingly under its control.
In 1310 Moscow became the See of the Orthodox Church. In 1380 Dmitri defeated the Golden Horde at Kulikovo, and by 1480 Mongol dominance was thrown off. Novgorod was conquered in 1487, Viatka in 1489, Pskov in 1510 and Riazan in 1521. The first victory over the Lithuanians and the reconquest of Smolensk, took place in 1514.

Constantinople

THE OTTOMAN EMPIRE

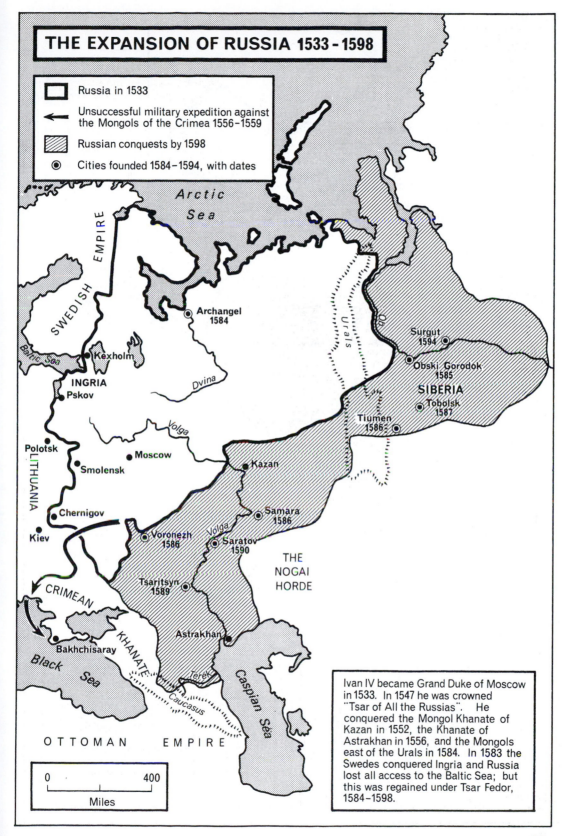

THE EXPANSION OF RUSSIA 1533-1598

Russia in 1533

Unsuccessful military expedition against the Mongols of the Crimea 1556-1559

Russian conquests by 1598

◉ Cities founded 1584-1594, with dates

Arctic Sea

SWEDISH EMPIRE

◉ **Archangel** 1584

Kexholm

INGRIA

Pskov

Baltic Sea

Dvina

Urals

Ob

Surgut 1594 ◉

◉ **Obski Gorodok** 1585

SIBERIA

◉ **Tobolsk** 1587

Tiumen 1586 ◉

Volga

Polotsk

LITHUANIA

Smolensk

• **Moscow**

• **Kazan**

Chernigov

• **Kiev**

◉ **Samara** 1586

◉ **Voronezh** 1586

◉ **Saratov** 1590

Volga

THE NOGAI HORDE

Tsaritsyn 1589 ◉

CRIMEAN

Bakhchisaray

Black Sea

KHANATE

Astrakhan

Terek

Caucasus

Caspian Sea

OTTOMAN EMPIRE

Ivan IV became Grand Duke of Moscow in 1533. In 1547 he was crowned "Tsar of All the Russias". He conquered the Mongol Khanate of Kazan in 1552, the Khanate of Astrakhan in 1556, and the Mongols east of the Urals in 1584. In 1583 the Swedes conquered Ingria and Russia lost all access to the Baltic Sea; but this was regained under Tsar Fedor, 1584-1598.

0 ___ 400
Miles

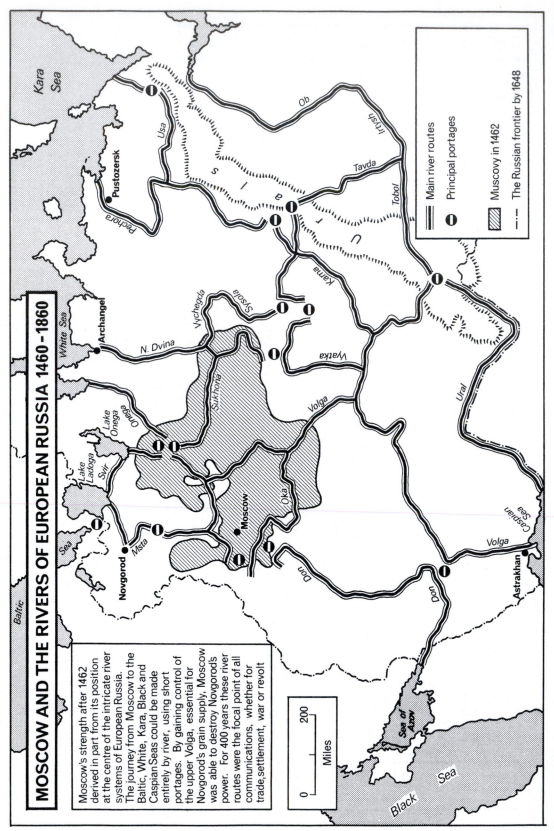

MOSCOW AND THE RIVERS OF EUROPEAN RUSSIA 1460–1860

Moscow's strength after 1462 derived in part from its position at the centre of the intricate river systems of European Russia. The journey from Moscow to the Baltic, White, Kara, Black and Caspian Seas could be made entirely by river, using short portages. By gaining control of the upper Volga, essential for Novgorod's grain supply, Moscow was able to destroy Novgorod's power. For 400 years these river routes were the focal point of all communications, whether for trade, settlement, war or revolt

Legend:

‖	Main river routes
0	Principal portages
(hatched)	Muscovy in 1462
–·–·–	The Russian frontier by 1648

Miles: 0 — 200

Kara Sea

Ob

Irtysh

Tavda

Usa

Tobol

Pechora

Pustozersk

S i b e r i a

U r a l

Kama

Vychegda

Sysola

Archangel

White Sea

N. Dvina

Sukhona

Vyatka

Volga

Ural

Onega

Lake Onega

Lake Ladoga

Svir

Baltic Sea

Novgorod

Msta

Moscow

Oka

Don

Volga

Caspian Sea

Astrakhan

Sea of Azov

Black Sea

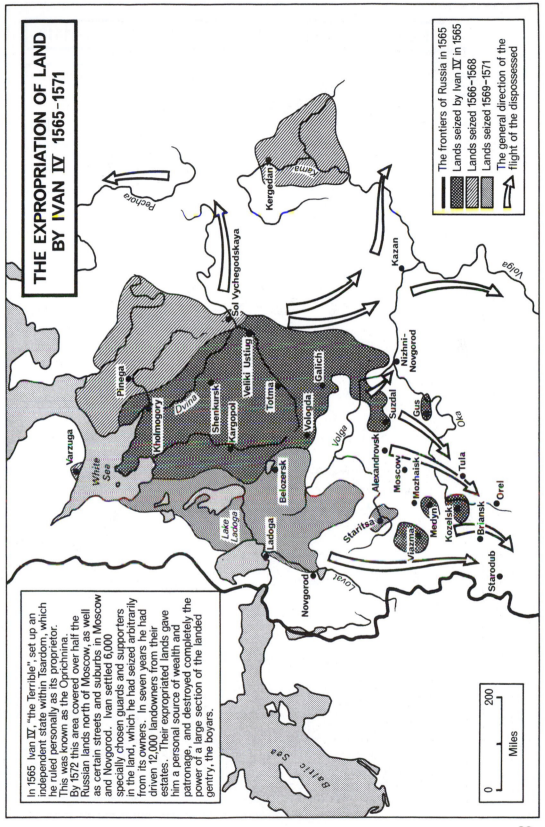

THE EXPROPRIATION OF LAND BY IVAN IV 1565-1571

In 1565 Ivan IV, "the Terrible", set up an independent state within Tsardom, which he ruled personally as its proprietor. This was known as the Oprichnina.
By 1572 this area covered over half the Russian lands north of Moscow, as well as certain streets and suburbs in Moscow and Novgorod. Ivan settled 6,000 specially chosen guards and supporters in the land, which he had seized arbitrarily from its owners. In seven years he had driven 12,000 landowners from their estates. Their expropriated lands gave him a personal source of wealth and patronage, and destroyed completely the power of a large section of the landed gentry, the boyars.

The frontiers of Russia in 1565
Lands seized by Ivan IV in 1565
Lands seized 1566-1568
Lands seized 1569-1571
The general direction of the flight of the dispossessed

Baltic Sea

White Sea

Lake Ladoga

Varzuga
Pinega
Kholmogory
Dvina
Shenkursk
Kargopol
Veliki Ustiug
Totma
Vologda
Galich
Belozersk
Ladoga
Novgorod
Lovat
Starodub
Staritsa
Viazma
Medyn
Kozelsk
Briansk
Orel
Moscow
Mozhaisk
Tula
Alexandrovsk
Suzdal
Gus
Oka
Nizhni-Novgorod
Volga
Kazan
Sol Vychegodskaya
Pechora
Kergedan
Kama
Volga

0   200
Miles

28

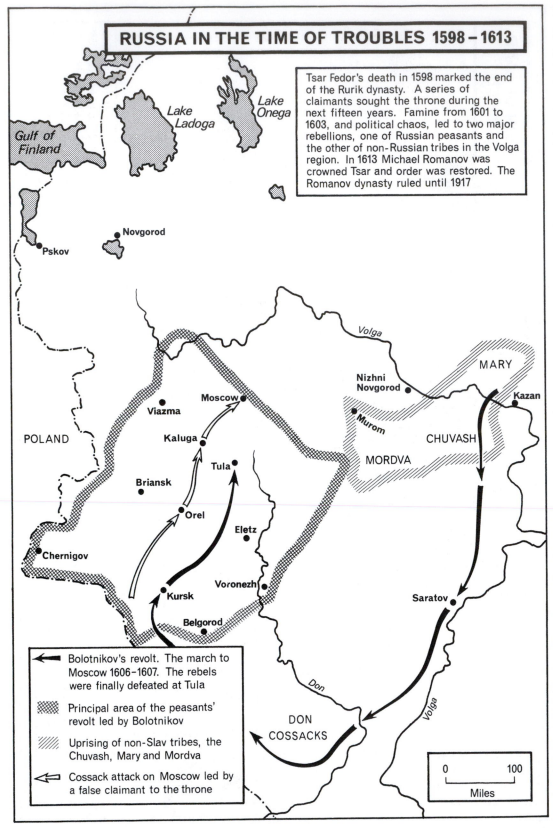

RUSSIA IN THE TIME OF TROUBLES 1598 – 1613

Tsar Fedor's death in 1598 marked the end of the Rurik dynasty. A series of claimants sought the throne during the next fifteen years. Famine from 1601 to 1603, and political chaos, led to two major rebellions, one of Russian peasants and the other of non-Russian tribes in the Volga region. In 1613 Michael Romanov was crowned Tsar and order was restored. The Romanov dynasty ruled until 1917

Gulf of Finland

Lake Ladoga

Lake Onega

Pskov

Novgorod

POLAND

Volga

Viazma

Moscow

Kaluga

Briansk

Tula

Orel

Eletz

Chernigov

Kursk

Belgorod

Voronezh

Nizhni Novgorod

Murom

MORDVA

MARY

Kazan

CHUVASH

Saratov

Don

Volga

DON COSSACKS

Bolotnikov's revolt. The march to Moscow 1606–1607. The rebels were finally defeated at Tula

Principal area of the peasants' revolt led by Bolotnikov

Uprising of non-Slav tribes, the Chuvash, Mary and Mordva

Cossack attack on Moscow led by a false claimant to the throne

0   100
Miles

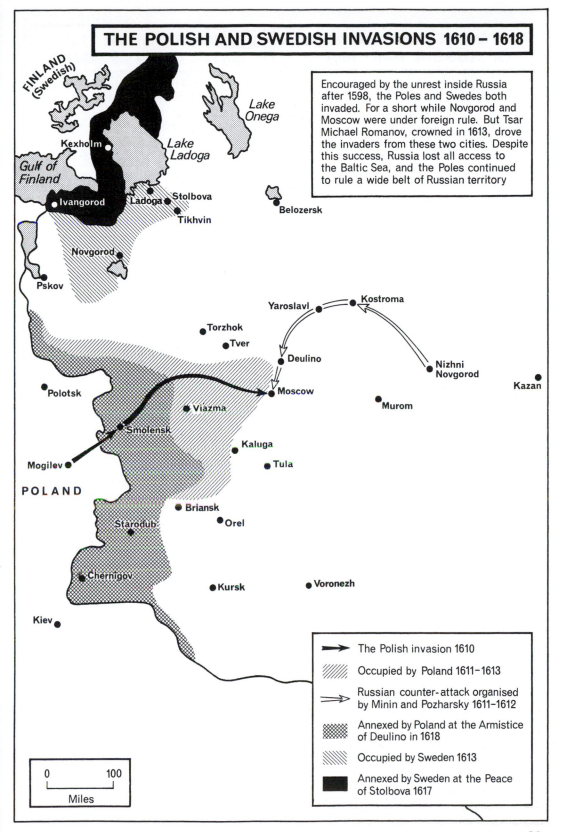

THE POLISH AND SWEDISH INVASIONS 1610 – 1618

Encouraged by the unrest inside Russia after 1598, the Poles and Swedes both invaded. For a short while Novgorod and Moscow were under foreign rule. But Tsar Michael Romanov, crowned in 1613, drove the invaders from these two cities. Despite this success, Russia lost all access to the Baltic Sea, and the Poles continued to rule a wide belt of Russian territory

FINLAND (Swedish)

Lake Onega

Lake Ladoga

Kexholm

Gulf of Finland

Ivangorod

Ladoga

Stolbova

Tikhvin

Belozersk

Novgorod

Pskov

Yaroslavl

Kostroma

Torzhok

Tver

Deulino

Nizhni Novgorod

Kazan

Polotsk

Moscow

Viazma

Murom

Smolensk

Kaluga

Mogilev

Tula

POLAND

Briansk

Starodub

Orel

Chernigov

Kursk

Voronezh

Kiev

The Polish invasion 1610

Occupied by Poland 1611–1613

Russian counter-attack organised by Minin and Pozharsky 1611–1612

Annexed by Poland at the Armistice of Deulino in 1618

Occupied by Sweden 1613

Annexed by Sweden at the Peace of Stolbova 1617

0   100

Miles

30

THE WESTWARD EXPANSION OF RUSSIA 1640-1667

Western Russia in 1640

Cossack revolt of 1648 against Polish landowners and gentry. The revolt was led by Bogdan Khmelnitski. After defeating the Polish army, the Cossacks joined with the Polish peasantry, murdering over 100,000 Jews

Towns in which Jews were murdered by Cossacks and Poles 1648-1652

Advance of Russian and Ukrainian forces against the Poles 1654-1655

Polish territory ceded to Russia at the Armistice of Andrusovo in 1667

Baltic Sea

PRUSSIA

LITHUANIA

Nevel

Moscow

Polotsk

Viazma

Königsberg

Kovno

Vilna

Vitebsk

Smolensk

Andrusovo

Orsha

Borisov

Mogilev

Grodno

Minsk

WHITE RUSSIA

Briansk

Orel

Wa saw

Gomel

Starodub

POLAND

Brest-Litovsk

Pinsk

Mozyr

Kursk

Turov

Lublin

Pripet   Marshes

Kovel

WESTERN UKRAINE

Chernigov

EASTERN UKRAINE

Belgorod

Zamosc

Berestechke

Lutsk

Rovno

Przemysl

Belz

Zhitomir

Kiev

Kharkov

Lvov

Pereyaslavl

Zbarazh

Poltava

Bar

Korsun

Carpathians

Kamenets

Vinnitsa

Kodak

HUNGARY

ZAPOROZHE

OTTOMAN EMPIRE

Sech

0   100

Miles

CRIMEAN KHANATE

Haji-bey

SOCIAL UNREST 1648 and 1670

In 1648 uprisings took place in many of the principal Russian towns. As a result, a new code of laws was drawn up, protecting the rights of traders and town-dwellers. In 1670 a Don Cossack, Stenka Razin, led a widespread revolt of Cossacks, peasants, small traders, minor officials and the dispossessed of the Volga, Don and Donets river valleys. The revolt was crushed in 1671 and Razin broken on the wheel in Moscow.

Kargopol

Solvychegodsk
Veliki Ustiug
Cherdin

Olonets

Solikamsk

Totma

Gdov

Novgorod

Romanov

Pskov

Ostrov

Volga

Vladimir

Ruza
Yadrin

Moscow

Simbirsk

Koslov
Penza

Tambov

Samara

Donets

Kursk
Saratov

Voronezh

Don

Tsaritsyn

DON
COSSACKS

Gurev

Sea of
Azov

Astrakhan

Black Sea

Terski
Gorodok

Caspian Sea

◎   Urban uprisings of 1648–1650

▇   The peasants' revolt led by Stenka Razin 1670–1671

—   The Russian frontier in 1670

0   500

Miles

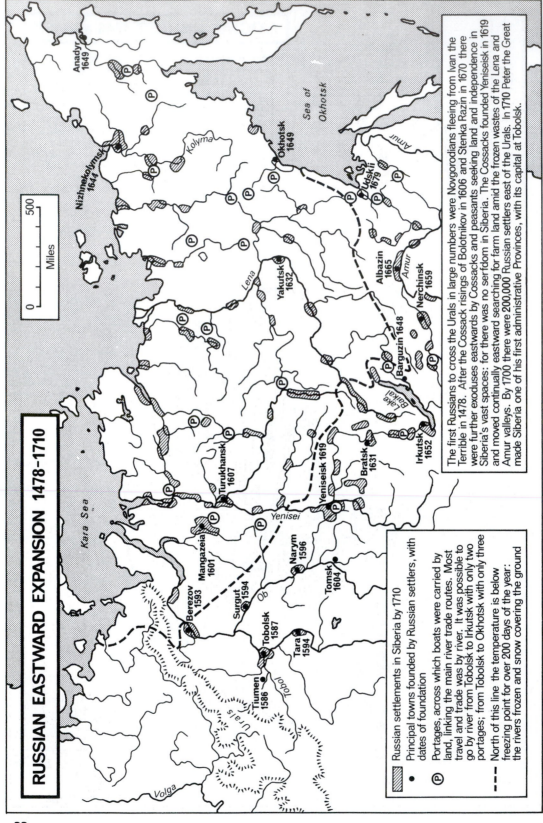

RUSSIAN EASTWARD EXPANSION 1478–1710

Anadyr 1649

Nizhnekolymsk 1644

Kolyma

Okhotsk 1649

Sea of Okhotsk

Amur

Udskii 1679

Lena

Yakutsk 1632

Albazin 1665

Nerchinsk 1659

Barguzin 1648

Lake Baikal

Bratsk 1631

Irkutsk 1652

Amur

Turukhansk 1607

Yeniseisk 1619

Yenisei

Mangazeia 1601

Narym 1596

Tomsk 1604

Berezov 1593

Surgut 1594

Tobolsk 1587

Tara 1594

Ob

Tiumen 1586

Tobol

Urals

Kara Sea

Volga

500

Miles

0

The first Russians to cross the Urals in large numbers were Novgorodians fleeing from Ivan the Terrible in 1478. After the Cossack risings of Bolotnikov in 1606 and Stenka Razin in 1670 there were further exoduses eastwards by Cossacks and peasants seeking land and independence in Siberia's vast spaces: for there was no serfdom in Siberia. The Cossacks founded Yeniseisk in 1619 and moved continually eastward searching for farm land amid the frozen wastes of the Lena and Amur valleys. By 1700 there were 200,000 Russian settlers east of the Urals. In 1710 Peter the Great made Siberia one of his first administrative Provinces, with its capital at Tobolsk.

Russian settlements in Siberia by 1710

• Principal towns founded by Russian settlers, with dates of foundation

Ⓟ Portages, across which boats were carried by land, linking the main river trade routes. Most travel and trade was by river. It was possible to go by river from Tobolsk to Irkutsk with only two portages; from Tobolsk to Okhotsk with only three portages

--- North of this line the temperature is below freezing point for over 200 days of the year: the rivers frozen and snow covering the ground

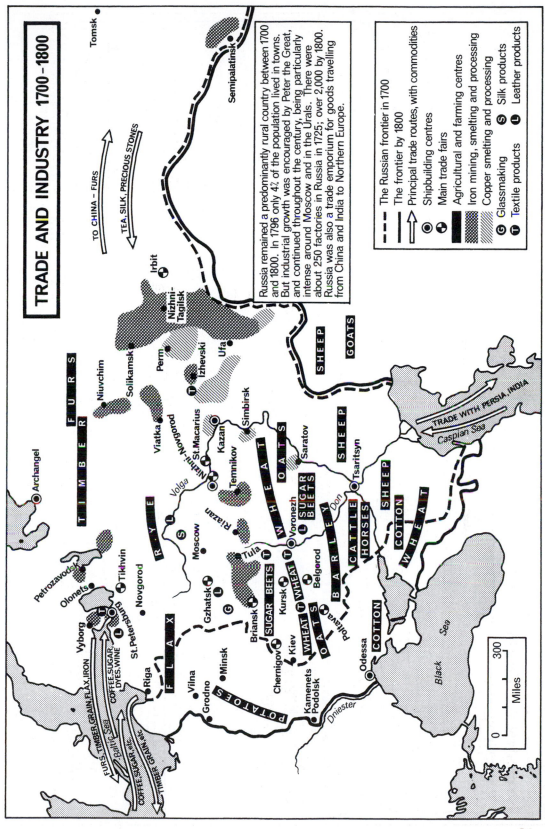

TRADE AND INDUSTRY 1700 – 1800

Russia remained a predominantly rural country between 1700 and 1800. In 1796 only 4% of the population lived in towns. But industrial growth was encouraged by Peter the Great, and continued throughout the century, being particularly intense around Moscow and in the Urals. There were about 250 factories in Russia in 1725; over 2,000 by 1800. Russia was also a trade emporium for goods travelling from China and India to Northern Europe.

- – – – The Russian frontier in 1700
- ───── The frontier by 1800
- ⬆ Principal trade routes, with commodities
- ◉ Shipbuilding centres
- ◐ Main trade fairs
- ━━ Agricultural and farming centres
- ▨ Iron mining, smelting and processing
- ▧ Copper smelting and processing
- **G** Glassmaking **S** Silk products
- **T** Textile products **L** Leather products

TO CHINA – FURS

TEA, SILK, PRECIOUS STONES

Tomsk

Semipalatinsk

Irbit

Nizhni-Tagilsk

SHEEP

GOATS

Perm

Solikamsk
Niuvchim

Izhevski

Ufa

F U R S

T I M B E R

Archangel

Viatka

Nizhni-Novgorod
St.Macarius

Kazan

Simbirsk

Temnikov

Saratov

SHEEP

W H E A T

O A T S

R Y E

Volga

Riazan

Moscow

Petrozavodsk

Olonets

Tikhvin

Novgorod

Vyborg

St.Petersburg

Riga

F L A X

Vilna

Grodno

Minsk

P O T A T O E S

Gzhatsk

Briansk

SUGAR BEETS

Kursk

Chernigov

Kiev

WHEAT

O A T S

Kamenets
Podolsk

Dniester

Tula

WHEAT

Belgorod

B A R L E Y

Poltava

COTTON

Odessa

COTTON

Voronezh

SUGAR
BEETS

CATTLE

HORSES

SHEEP

W H E A T

Tsaritsyn

Don

TRADE WITH PERSIA, INDIA

Caspian Sea

Black Sea

FURS, TIMBER, GRAIN, FLAX, IRON

Baltic Sea

COFFEE, SUGAR, DYES, WINE

TIMBER, GRAIN, etc.

COFFEE, SUGAR, etc.

0   300
Miles

34

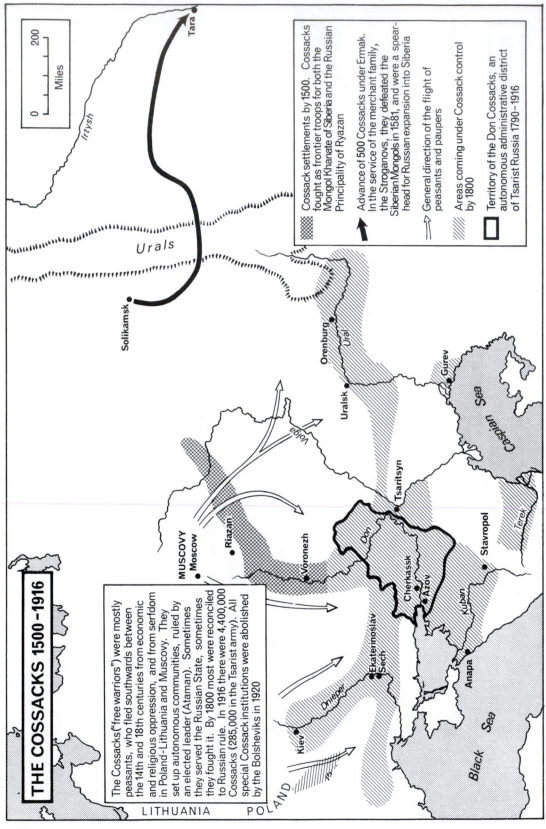

THE COSSACKS 1500–1916

The Cossacks ("free warriors") were mostly peasants, who fled southwards between the 14th and 18th centuries from economic and religious oppression, and from serfdom in Poland-Lithuania and Muscovy. They set up autonomous communities, ruled by an elected leader (Ataman). Sometimes they served the Russian State, sometimes they fought it. By 1800 most were reconciled to Russian rule. In 1916 there were 4,400,000 Cossacks (285,000 in the Tsarist army). All special Cossack institutions were abolished by the Bolsheviks in 1920

Cossack settlements by 1500. Cossacks fought as frontier troops for both the Mongol Khanate of Siberia and the Russian Principality of Ryazan

Advance of 500 Cossacks under Ermak. In the service of the merchant family, the Stroganovs, they defeated the Siberian Mongols in 1581, and were a spearhead for Russian expansion into Siberia

General direction of the flight of peasants and paupers

Areas coming under Cossack control by 1800

Territory of the Don Cossacks, an autonomous administrative district of Tsarist Russia 1790–1916

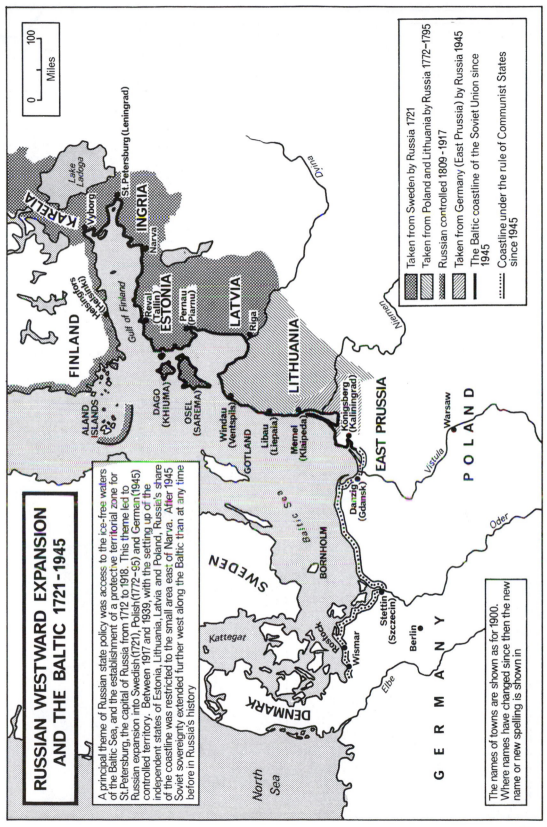

RUSSIAN WESTWARD EXPANSION AND THE BALTIC 1721-1945

A principal theme of Russian state policy was access to the ice-free waters of the Baltic Sea, and the establishment of a protective territorial zone for St.Petersburg, the capital of Russia from 1712 to 1918. This theme led to Russian expansion into Swedish (1721), Polish (1772-95) and German (1945) controlled territory. Between 1917 and 1939, with the setting up of the independent states of Estonia, Lithuania, Latvia and Poland, Russia's share of the coastline was restricted to the small area east of Narva. After 1945 Soviet sovereignty extended further west along the Baltic than at any time before in Russia's history

The names of towns are shown as for 1900. Where names have changed since then the new name or new spelling is shown in

Taken from Sweden by Russia 1721

Taken from Poland and Lithuania by Russia 1772-1795

Russian controlled 1809 -1917

Taken from Germany (East Prussia) by Russia 1945

The Baltic coastline of the Soviet Union since 1945

Coastline under the rule of Communist States since 1945

FINLAND

Helsingfors (Helsinki)

Lake Ladoga

Vyborg

St.Petersburg (Leningrad)

INGRIA

Narva

KARELIA

Dvina

Reval (Tallin)
ESTONIA

Pernau (Piarnu)

LATVIA

Riga

Gulf of Finland

ALAND ISLANDS

DAGO (KHIUMA)

OSEL (SAREMA)

Windau (Ventspils)

GOTLAND

Libau (Liepaia)

Memel (Klaipeda)

LITHUANIA

Königsberg (Kaliningrad)

EAST PRUSSIA

Niemen

Baltic Sea

BORNHOLM

Danzig (Gdansk)

Warsaw

POLAND

Vistula

Oder

SWEDEN

Stettin (Szczecin)

Rostock

Wismar

Berlin

GERMANY

Kattegat

North Sea

DENMARK

Elbe

0 ... 100
Miles

36

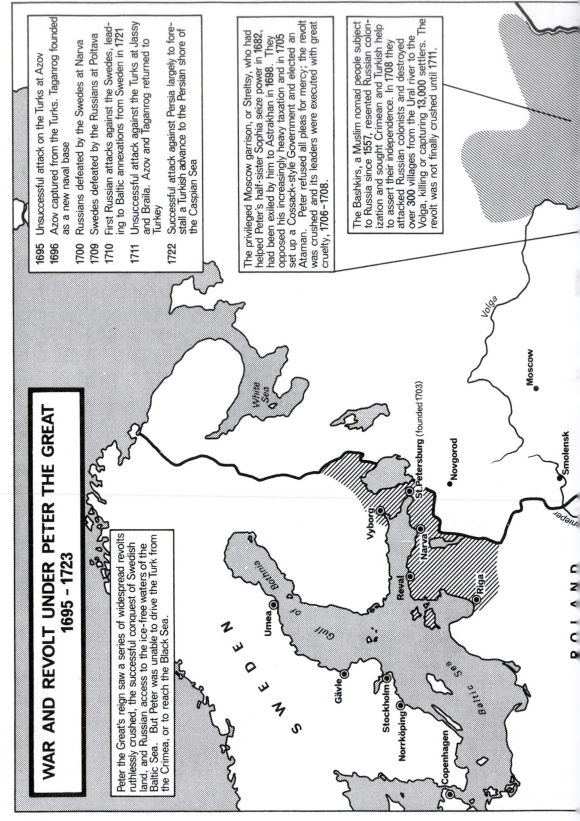

WAR AND REVOLT UNDER PETER THE GREAT
1695 – 1723

Peter the Great's reign saw a series of widespread revolts ruthlessly crushed, the successful conquest of Swedish land, and Russian access to the ice-free waters of the Baltic Sea. But Peter was unable to drive the Turk from the Crimea, or to reach the Black Sea.

1695	Unsuccessful attack on the Turks at Azov
1696	Azov captured from the Turks. Taganrog founded as a new naval base
1700	Russians defeated by the Swedes at Narva
1709	Swedes defeated by the Russians at Poltava
1710	First Russian attacks against the Swedes, leading to Baltic annexations from Sweden in 1721
1711	Unsuccessful attack against the Turks at Jassy and Braila. Azov and Taganrog returned to Turkey
1722	Successful attack against Persia largely to forestall a Turkish advance to the Persian shore of the Caspian Sea

The privileged Moscow garrison, or Streltsy, who had helped Peter's half-sister Sophia seize power in 1682, had been exiled by him to Astrakhan in 1698. They opposed his increasingly heavy taxation and in 1705 set up a Cossack-style Government and elected an Ataman. Peter refused all pleas for mercy; the revolt was crushed and its leaders were executed with great cruelty, 1706–1708.

The Bashkirs, a Muslim nomad people subject to Russia since 1557, resented Russian colonization and sought Crimean and Turkish help to assert their independence. In 1708 they attacked Russian colonists and destroyed over 300 villages from the Ural river to the Volga, killing or capturing 13,000 settlers. The revolt was not finally crushed until 1711.

White Sea

Volga

● Moscow

● Smolensk

● Novgorod

St. Petersburg (founded 1703)

Vyborg

Reval

Narva

Riga

Dnieper

POLAND

SWEDEN

Gulf of Bothnia

● Umeå

● Gävle

Stockholm ●

Norrköping ●

● Copenhagen

Baltic Sea

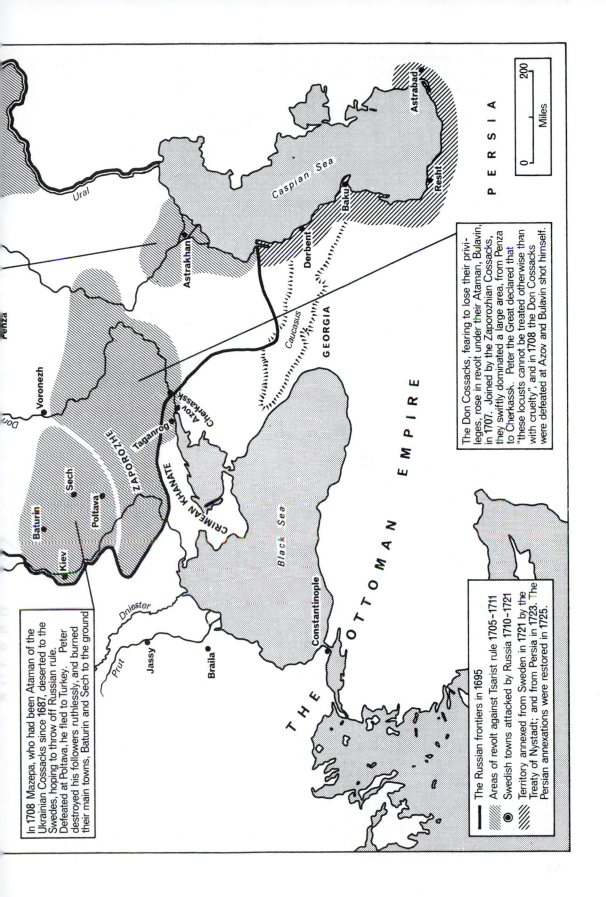

In 1708 Mazepa, who had been Ataman of the Ukrainian Cossacks since 1687, deserted to the Swedes, hoping to throw off Russian rule. Peter defeated at Poltava, he fled to Turkey. Peter destroyed his followers ruthlessly, and burned their main towns, Baturin and Sech to the ground

The Don Cossacks, fearing to lose their privileges, rose in revolt under their Ataman, Bulavin, in 1707. Joined by the Zaporozhian Cossacks, they swiftly dominated a large area, from Penza to Cherkassk. Peter the Great declared that "these locusts cannot be treated otherwise than with cruelty", and in 1708 the Don Cossacks were defeated at Azov and Bulavin shot himself.

The Russian frontiers in 1695
Areas of revolt against Tsarist rule 1705–1711
Swedish towns attacked by Russia 1710–1721
Territory annexed from Sweden in 1721 by the Treaty of Nystadt; and from Persia in 1723. The Persian annexations were restored in 1725.

PERSIA

Caspian Sea

Astrabad
Resht
Baku
Derbent
Astrakhan

Ural
Penza
Voronezh
Don

GEORGIA
Caucasus

ZAPOROZHE
Baturin
Sech
Kiev
Poltava
Taganrog
Azov
Cherkassk

CRIMEAN KHANATE

Black Sea

THE OTTOMAN EMPIRE

Constantinople
Braila
Jassy
Prut
Dniester

0   200
Miles

THE PROVINCES AND POPULATION OF RUSSIA IN 1724

0   300

Miles

St.Petersburg

Selected as the site of a new town by Peter the Great in 1703, and built at great cost in human life by serf labour, St.Petersburg became the seat of the Russian Government in 1712. Courtiers and noble families were compelled by law to live there from 1725. The city had a population of 200,000 by 1788.

White Sea

Archangel

A R C H A N G E L

Dvina

S I B E R I A

Gulf of Finland

St.Petersburg

Novgorod

Viatka

Perm

Pskov

Vologda

S T.   P E T E R S B U R G

Kostroma

Tver

Volga

Kazan

Moscow

Nizhni Novgorod

K A Z A N

Smolensk

M O S C O W

Simbirsk

Mogilev

SMOLENSK

Riazan

Samara

Tula

Orel

Tambov

Penza

Orenburg

Chernigov

A Z O V

Saratov

Ural

C O S S A C K S

Dnieper

K I E V

Voronezh

Kiev

Poltava

Kharkov

Don

Volga

Dniester

C O S S A C K S

Azov

C O S S A C K S

Caspian Sea

Black Sea

COSSACKS

COSSACKS

It was Peter the Great who first divided Russia into Provinces (known as "Gubernii" or "Governments"). These administrative divisions served a military, financial and judicial purpose. They enabled Peter to supervise the whole kingdom by means of Governors responsible directly to himself. Catherine the Great later divided these Provinces into smaller units. The establishment of Provincial administrations led to a rapid growth of bureaucracy, and a complex hierarchy of local seniority. The population of Russia in 1724 was just over 15 million, of whom only ½ million lived in towns.

—·— Russia's frontiers by 1725

▬▬ Provinces established by Peter the Great

Area with over 20 inhabitants in every square verst. (One verst = two-thirds of a mile)

Area with between 10 and 20 inhabitants per square verst

Russian territory with less than 10 inhabitants per square verst is not shaded

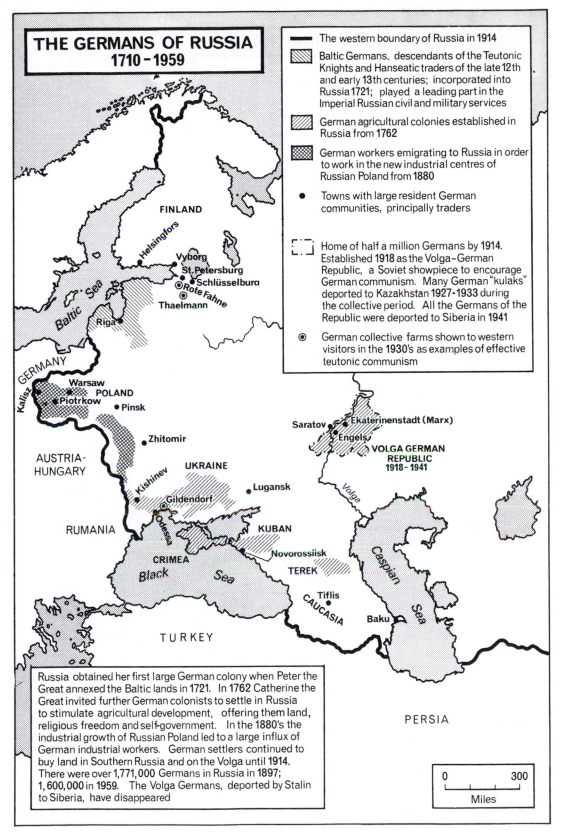

THE GERMANS OF RUSSIA
1710 – 1959

— The western boundary of Russia in 1914

Baltic Germans, descendants of the Teutonic Knights and Hanseatic traders of the late 12th and early 13th centuries; incorporated into Russia 1721; played a leading part in the Imperial Russian civil and military services

German agricultural colonies established in Russia from 1762

German workers emigrating to Russia in order to work in the new industrial centres of Russian Poland from 1880

● Towns with large resident German communities, principally traders

⌐⌐ Home of half a million Germans by 1914. Established 1918 as the Volga–German Republic, a Soviet showpiece to encourage German communism. Many German "kulaks" deported to Kazakhstan 1927-1933 during the collective period. All the Germans of the Republic were deported to Siberia in 1941

◉ German collective farms shown to western visitors in the 1930's as examples of effective teutonic communism

FINLAND

Helsingfors
Vyborg
St. Petersburg
Schlüsselburg
◉Rote Fahne
Thaelmann
Baltic Sea
Riga

GERMANY
Kalisz
Warsaw
POLAND
Piotrkow
Pinsk
Zhitomir
AUSTRIA-HUNGARY
Kishinev
UKRAINE
Gildendorf
Lugansk
RUMANIA
Odessa
KUBAN
CRIMEA
Novorossiisk
Black Sea
TEREK
CAUCASIA
Tiflis
Baku

Saratov
Ekaterinenstadt (Marx)
Engels
VOLGA GERMAN REPUBLIC
1918-1941
Volga
Caspian Sea

TURKEY

PERSIA

Russia obtained her first large German colony when Peter the Great annexed the Baltic lands in 1721. In 1762 Catherine the Great invited further German colonists to settle in Russia to stimulate agricultural development, offering them land, religious freedom and self-government. In the 1880's the industrial growth of Russian Poland led to a large influx of German industrial workers. German settlers continued to buy land in Southern Russia and on the Volga until 1914. There were over 1,771,000 Germans in Russia in 1897; 1,600,000 in 1959. The Volga Germans, deported by Stalin to Siberia, have disappeared

0   300
Miles

THE EXPANSION OF CHINA 1720 – 1760

THE

RUSSIAN

EMPIRE

U r a l s

Okhotsk ⊙

Yakutsk ⊙

Tobolsk ⊙

Yeniseisk ⊙

Tomsk ⊙

Krasnoyarsk ⊙

Omsk ⊙

Nerchinsk ⊙

Albazin ●

Amur

Irkutsk ⊙

Lake Baikal

Harbin ●

Semipalatinsk ⊙

Ustkamenogorsk ⊙

Maimachin ●

M O N G O L S

Lake Balkhash

Kulja ●

Urumchi ●

Hami ●

Peking ●

DOMINIONS OF THE
ZUNGAR KALMUKS

Nanking ○

Yarkand ●

Sian ●

Khotan ●

C H I N A

T I B E T

Chengtu ●

Lhasa ●

H i m a l a y a s

Canton ●

Yunnan ●

⊙ Cities founded by the Russians before 1720

■ The Chinese Empire in 1720, ruled by the Manchu Dynasty

▨ Under Chinese control by 1720, providing the Manchus with a reservoir of military power

▨ Conquered by China between 1724 and 1764

▨ Conquered by China in 1780

0   500
Miles

40

RUSSIAN EXPANSION UNDER
CATHERINE THE GREAT
1762–1796

The Provinces of Russia
in 1750

Territory annexed by
Russia 1762–1796, giving
Russia an outlet on the
Black Sea, and a common
frontier with Prussia
and Austria

White Sea

Archangel
ARCHANGEL

FINLAND

Helsingfors

Perm

ESTONIA
ST. PETERSBURG
Novgorod
NOVGOROD
Vologda
Viatka

Baltic Sea
LIVONIA
Pskov
KAZAN

KURLAND
Tver
Kazan
Ufa

Vilna
Minsk
SMOLENSK
MOSCOW
UFA

PRUSSIA
LITHUANIA
Moscow
NIZHNI
NOVGOROD

WHITE
RUSSIA
Orel
Stavropol
Samara

Warsaw
Pinsk
BELGOROD

AUSTRIA
PODLESIA
KIEV
VORONEZH

Lutsk
Kiev
ASTRAKHAN

Dniester
Belgorod

PODOLIA
Dnieper

Jassy
ZAPOROZHE

Odessa
Taganrog
Astrakhan

CRIMEA
KUBAN

Kutchuk
Kainardji
Sebastopol
KABARDA
Tarki

THE
Black Sea
Caspian Sea

OTTOMAN
Constantinople

EMPIRE
Kars

0   200
Miles

PERSIA

41

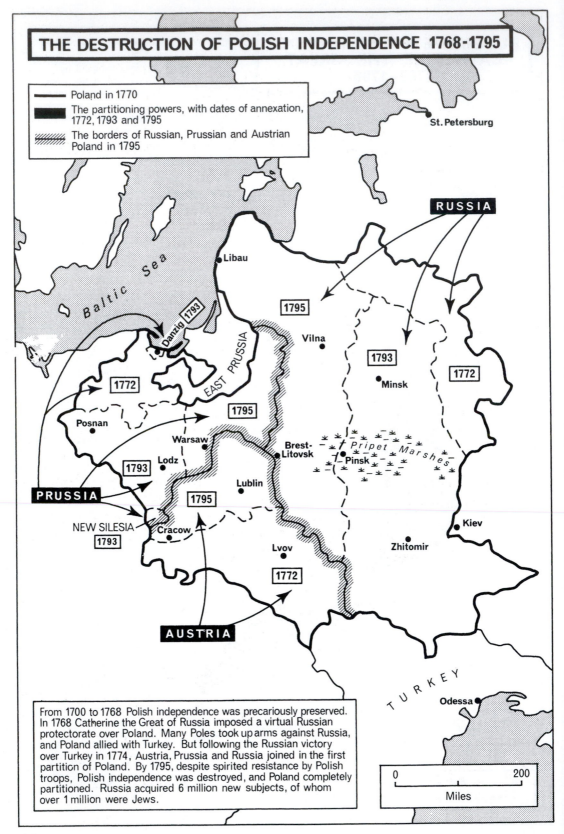

THE DESTRUCTION OF POLISH INDEPENDENCE 1768-1795

Poland in 1770

The partitioning powers, with dates of annexation, 1772, 1793 and 1795

The borders of Russian, Prussian and Austrian Poland in 1795

St. Petersburg

RUSSIA

Baltic Sea

Libau

1795

Danzig 1793

Vilna

EAST PRUSSIA

1772

1793

Minsk

1772

1795

Posnan

Warsaw

1795

Brest-Litovsk

Pripet Marshes

Lodz

Pinsk

1793

Lublin

PRUSSIA

Kiev

NEW SILESIA
1793

Cracow

1795

Lvov

1772

Zhitomir

AUSTRIA

T U R K E Y

Odessa

From 1700 to 1768 Polish independence was precariously preserved. In 1768 Catherine the Great of Russia imposed a virtual Russian protectorate over Poland. Many Poles took up arms against Russia, and Poland allied with Turkey. But following the Russian victory over Turkey in 1774, Austria, Prussia and Russia joined in the first partition of Poland. By 1795, despite spirited resistance by Polish troops, Polish independence was destroyed, and Poland completely partitioned. Russia acquired 6 million new subjects, of whom over 1 million were Jews.

0   200

Miles

THE RUSSIAN ANNEXATIONS OF POLAND 1772-1795

0   150

Miles

Baltic Sea

LATVIA

Pskov

Windau

Riga

Libau

Mitau

Dvinsk

Nevel

Palanga

Memel

Dvina

Polotsk

LITHUANIA

Kovno

1795

Vitebsk

Smolensk

Königsberg

Vilna

1793

1772

Orsha

Troki

Borisov

Mogilev

Mstislav

**EAST
PRUSSIA**

Suvalki

Lida

Minsk

Dnieper

Grodno

**WHITE
RUSSIA**

Novogrudok

Vilkoviski

Mir

Bobruisk

Starodub

Bialystok

Baranovichi

Slutsk

Gomel

Warsaw

Brest-Litovsk

Pinsk

Pripet   **Marshes**

Turov

Mozyr

Pripet

Chernigov

Lublin

Kovel

Olevsk

UKRAINE

VOLHYNIA

**WESTERN
UKRAINE**

**AUSTRIAN - ANNEXED
POLAND**

Lutsk

Rovno

Zhitomir

Kiev

Dubno

Pereyaslavl

Lvov

Przemysl

Staro-
Konstantinov

Berdychev

Boguslav

G A L I C I A

Tarnopol

Vinnitsa

Dnieper

Stanislavov

P O D O L I A

Kamenets-
Podolsk

Bug

B E S S A R A B I A

Dniester

Balta

AUSTRIA

**RUSSIAN-
ANNEXED**

TURKEY

T U R K E Y

1791
Odessa

Kherson

1774

Dnieper

*Black
Sea*

PRUSSIAN-ANNEXED POLAND

The western part of Russia in 1770

Partition lines

Principal Polish military resistance
to the Russians

The western frontier of Russia 1795

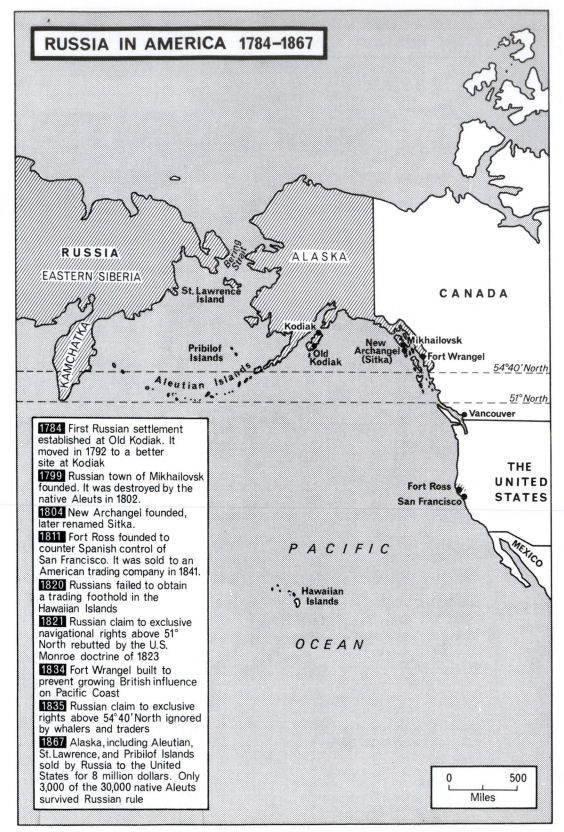

RUSSIA IN AMERICA 1784–1867

RUSSIA
EASTERN SIBERIA

KAMCHATKA

Bering Strait

St. Lawrence Island

Pribilof Islands

Aleutian Islands

ALASKA

CANADA

Kodiak

Old Kodiak

New Archangel (Sitka)

Mikhailovsk

Fort Wrangel

54°40' North

51° North

Vancouver

THE UNITED STATES

Fort Ross
San Francisco

PACIFIC

OCEAN

Hawaiian Islands

MEXICO

1784 First Russian settlement established at Old Kodiak. It moved in 1792 to a better site at Kodiak

1799 Russian town of Mikhailovsk founded. It was destroyed by the native Aleuts in 1802.

1804 New Archangel founded, later renamed Sitka.

1811 Fort Ross founded to counter Spanish control of San Francisco. It was sold to an American trading company in 1841.

1820 Russians failed to obtain a trading foothold in the Hawaiian Islands

1821 Russian claim to exclusive navigational rights above 51° North rebutted by the U.S. Monroe doctrine of 1823

1834 Fort Wrangel built to prevent growing British influence on Pacific Coast

1835 Russian claim to exclusive rights above 54°40' North ignored by whalers and traders

1867 Alaska, including Aleutian, St. Lawrence, and Pribilof Islands sold by Russia to the United States for 8 million dollars. Only 3,000 of the 30,000 native Aleuts survived Russian rule

0   500
Miles

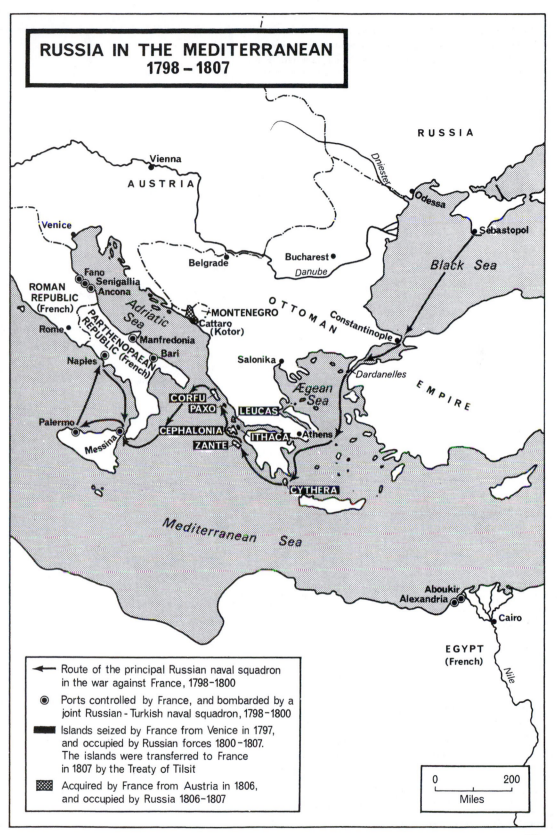

RUSSIA IN THE MEDITERRANEAN
1798 – 1807

RUSSIA

Vienna

AUSTRIA

Dniester

Odessa

Venice

Sébastopol

Belgrade

Bucharest

Black Sea

Danube

Fano
Senigallia
Ancona

ROMAN
REPUBLIC
(French)

Adriatic Sea

MONTENEGRO
Cattaro
(Kotor)

OTTOMAN

Constantinople

Rome

PARTHENOPAEAN
REPUBLIC (French)

Manfredonia
Bari

Salonika

EMPIRE

Naples

Ægean
Sea

Dardanelles

CORFU
PAXO

LEUCAS

Palermo

CEPHALONIA

ITHACA

Athens

Messina

ZANTE

CYTHERA

Mediterranean   Sea

Aboukir
Alexandria

Cairo

EGYPT
(French)

Nile

Route of the principal Russian naval squadron
in the war against France, 1798–1800

Ports controlled by France, and bombarded by a
joint Russian - Turkish naval squadron, 1798–1800

Islands seized by France from Venice in 1797,
and occupied by Russian forces 1800–1807.
The islands were transferred to France
in 1807 by the Treaty of Tilsit

Acquired by France from Austria in 1806,
and occupied by Russia 1806–1807

0   200
Miles

RUSSIA AND TURKEY 1721-1829

Kiev

Dnieper

Khotin
1788

Uman
1738

Dniester

Bug

Kishinev
1739

BESSARABIA

Jassy
1806

Prut

Riabaya
Mogila
1770

Bendery
1770

Ochakov
1788

1771

Perekop
1730

1789
1770, 1806

Fokshani

1790

Kilia
1791

Braila
1806

Ismail
1791, 1806

1788

Belgrade

Craiova
1807, 1828

Bucharest
1770, 1806,
1828

Bakhchisarai
1736

CR

Negotin
1810

Danube

Silistria
1810

1828
Kustenje
1809

Vidin
1811, 1828

Rushchuk
1771
1811

1774, 1828
Kutchuk
Kainardji

Mangalia
1810, 1828

Nikopol
1829

1774
Shumla
1810

1829

Varna
1810

1791

Turnovo
1810

Black

TURKEY IN EUROPE

Adrianople
1829

Midia
1829

Bosphorus

Enos
1829

Corlu
1829

Constantinople

The Straits

Dardanelles

Aegean Sea

TURKEY   IN

THE BLACK SEA AND THE STRAITS

1739 Treaty of Belgrade: Russian ships not allowed
into the Sea of Azov or the Black Sea

1774 Treaty of Kutchuk Kainardji: Russian merchant
ships gained the right to navigate the Black
Sea and pass the Straits; but cargoes could
be requisitioned at will

1829 Treaty of Adrianople: Russia obtained the
right of unhindered passage of unarmed ships

0   100

Miles

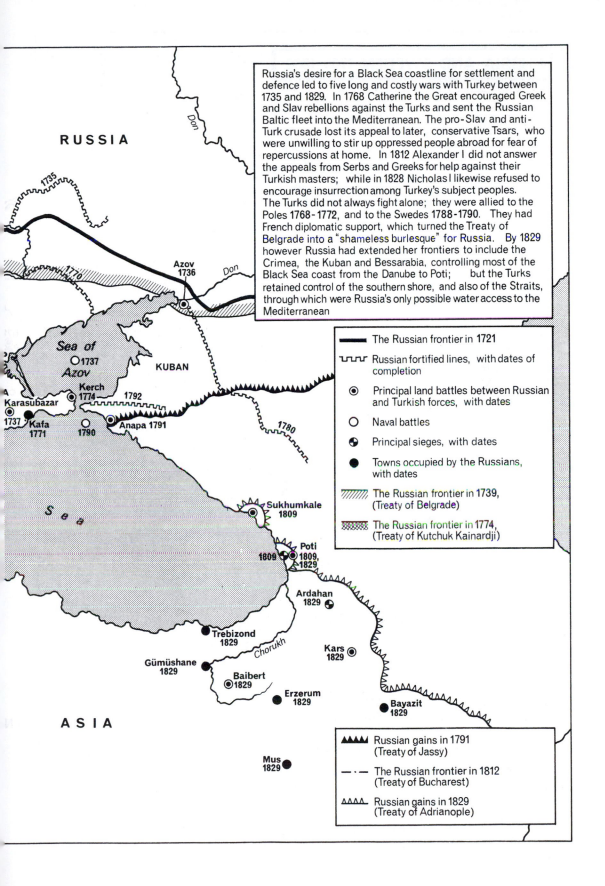

RUSSIA

Don

Don

Azov
1736

Sea of
Azov
○1737

KUBAN

Kerch
1774

Karasubazar

1792

1737

Kafa
1771

○
1790

Anapa 1791

1780

Sea

Sukhumkale
1809

Poti
1809 ●1809,
1829

Ardahan
1829

Trebizond
1829

Chorukh

Kars
1829

Gümüshane
1829

Baibert
1829

Erzerum
1829

Bayazit
1829

ASIA

Mus
1829

Russia's desire for a Black Sea coastline for settlement and
defence led to five long and costly wars with Turkey between
1735 and 1829. In 1768 Catherine the Great encouraged Greek
and Slav rebellions against the Turks and sent the Russian
Baltic fleet into the Mediterranean. The pro-Slav and anti-
Turk crusade lost its appeal to later, conservative Tsars, who
were unwilling to stir up oppressed people abroad for fear of
repercussions at home. In 1812 Alexander I did not answer
the appeals from Serbs and Greeks for help against their
Turkish masters; while in 1828 Nicholas I likewise refused to
encourage insurrection among Turkey's subject peoples.
The Turks did not always fight alone; they were allied to the
Poles 1768-1772, and to the Swedes 1788-1790. They had
French diplomatic support, which turned the Treaty of
Belgrade into a "shameless burlesque" for Russia. By 1829
however Russia had extended her frontiers to include the
Crimea, the Kuban and Bessarabia, controlling most of the
Black Sea coast from the Danube to Poti; but the Turks
retained control of the southern shore, and also of the Straits,
through which were Russia's only possible water access to the
Mediterranean

▬▬▬	The Russian frontier in 1721
⎍⎍⎍	Russian fortified lines, with dates of completion
◉	Principal land battles between Russian and Turkish forces, with dates
○	Naval battles
✛	Principal sieges, with dates
●	Towns occupied by the Russians, with dates
▨▨▨	The Russian frontier in 1739, (Treaty of Belgrade)
▨▨▨	The Russian frontier in 1774, (Treaty of Kutchuk Kainardji)

▲▲▲▲	Russian gains in 1791 (Treaty of Jassy)
— · —	The Russian frontier in 1812 (Treaty of Bucharest)
△△△△	Russian gains in 1829 (Treaty of Adrianople)

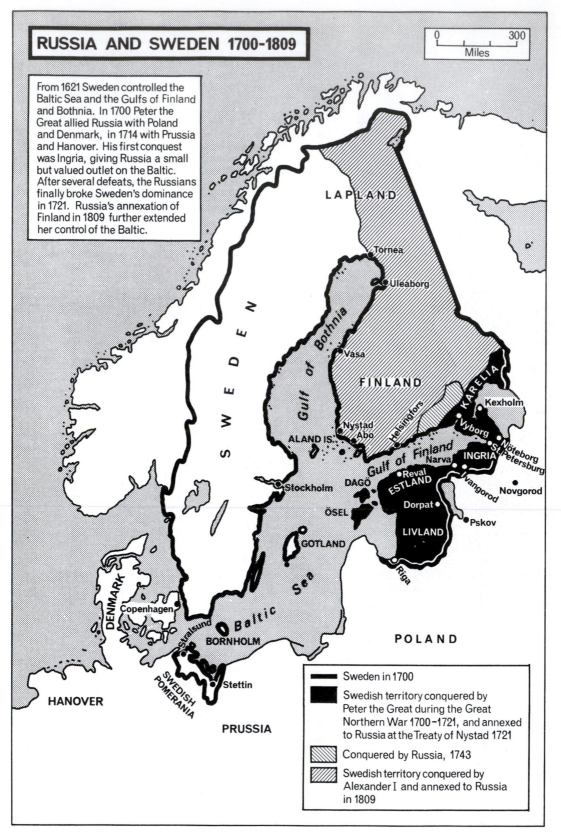

RUSSIA AND SWEDEN 1700-1809

0   300
Miles

From 1621 Sweden controlled the
Baltic Sea and the Gulfs of Finland
and Bothnia. In 1700 Peter the
Great allied Russia with Poland
and Denmark, in 1714 with Prussia
and Hanover. His first conquest
was Ingria, giving Russia a small
but valued outlet on the Baltic.
After several defeats, the Russians
finally broke Sweden's dominance
in 1721. Russia's annexation of
Finland in 1809 further extended
her control of the Baltic.

LAPLAND

Tornea

Uleaborg

Gulf of Bothnia

S W E D E N

Vasa

F I N L A N D

KARELIA

Kexholm

Helsingfors

Nystad
Abo

Vyborg

ALAND IS.

Nöteborg
St. Petersburg

Narva

INGRIA

Gulf of Finland

Reval

Ivangorod

DAGO

ESTLAND

Novgorod

Stockholm

OSEL

Dorpat

Pskov

GOTLAND

LIVLAND

Baltic Sea

Riga

DENMARK

Copenhagen

POLAND

Stralsund

BORNHOLM

SWEDISH
POMERANIA

Stettin

HANOVER

PRUSSIA

Sweden in 1700

Swedish territory conquered by
Peter the Great during the Great
Northern War 1700-1721, and annexed
to Russia at the Treaty of Nystad 1721

Conquered by Russia, 1743

Swedish territory conquered by
Alexander I and annexed to Russia
in 1809

47

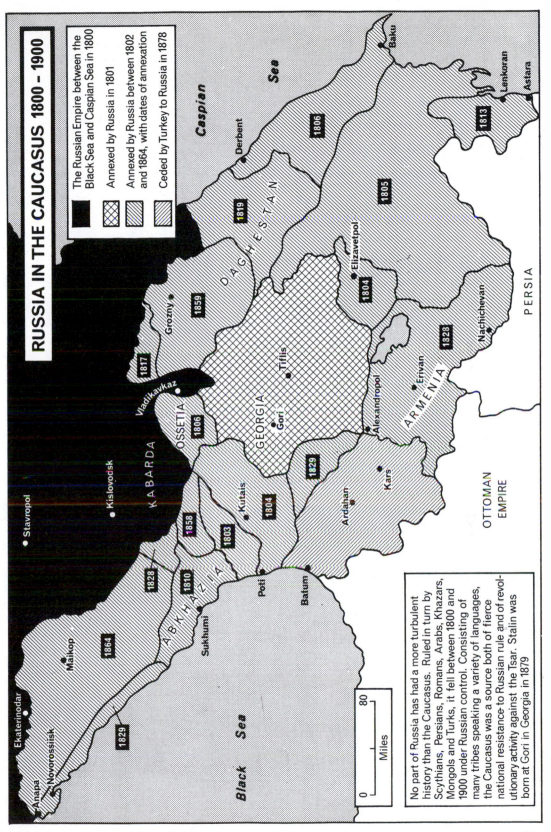

RUSSIA IN THE CAUCASUS 1800 – 1900

The Russian Empire between the Black Sea and Caspian Sea in 1800

Annexed by Russia in 1801

Annexed by Russia between 1802 and 1864, with dates of annexation

Ceded by Turkey to Russia in 1878

Caspian Sea

Baku

Lenkoran

Astara

1813

1806

Derbent

1805

DAGHESTAN

1819

Elizavetpol

1804

Grozny

1859

1817

Vladikavkaz

OSSETIA

1806

KABARDA

Kislovodsk

Tiflis

GEORGIA

Gori

Erivan

ARMENIA

Alexandropol

Nachichevan

1828

PERSIA

Kars

1829

Ardahan

Kutais

1804

1858

1803

ABKHAZIA

1810

1828

Sukhumi

Poti

Batum

OTTOMAN EMPIRE

Stavropol

Malkop

1864

Ekaterinodar

Anapa

Novorossiisk

1829

Black Sea

0

80

Miles

No part of Russia has had a more turbulent history than the Caucasus. Ruled in turn by Scythians, Persians, Romans, Arabs, Khazars, Mongols and Turks, it fell between 1800 and 1900 under Russian control. Consisting of many tribes speaking a variety of languages, the Caucasus was a source both of fierce national resistance to Russian rule and of revolutionary activity against the Tsar. Stalin was born at Gori in Georgia in 1879

48

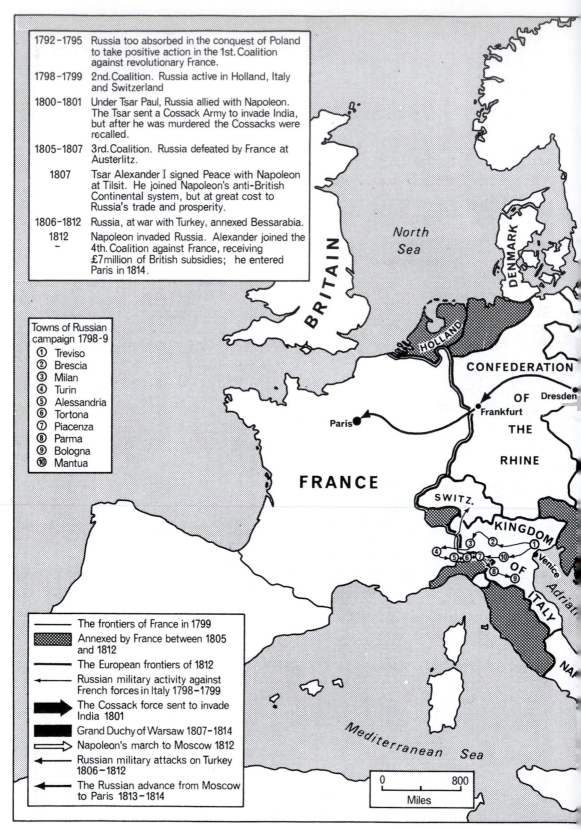

1792–1795   Russia too absorbed in the conquest of Poland to take positive action in the 1st. Coalition against revolutionary France.

1798–1799   2nd. Coalition. Russia active in Holland, Italy and Switzerland

1800–1801   Under Tsar Paul, Russia allied with Napoleon. The Tsar sent a Cossack Army to invade India, but after he was murdered the Cossacks were recalled.

1805–1807   3rd. Coalition. Russia defeated by France at Austerlitz.

1807   Tsar Alexander I signed Peace with Napoleon at Tilsit. He joined Napoleon's anti-British Continental system, but at great cost to Russia's trade and prosperity.

1806–1812   Russia, at war with Turkey, annexed Bessarabia.

1812   Napoleon invaded Russia. Alexander joined the 4th. Coalition against France, receiving £7 million of British subsidies; he entered Paris in 1814.

Towns of Russian campaign 1798-9
① Treviso
② Brescia
③ Milan
④ Turin
⑤ Alessandria
⑥ Tortona
⑦ Piacenza
⑧ Parma
⑨ Bologna
⑩ Mantua

The frontiers of France in 1799
Annexed by France between 1805 and 1812
The European frontiers of 1812
Russian military activity against French forces in Italy 1798–1799
The Cossack force sent to invade India 1801
Grand Duchy of Warsaw 1807–1814
Napoleon's march to Moscow 1812
Russian military attacks on Turkey 1806–1812
The Russian advance from Moscow to Paris 1813–1814

0   800
Miles

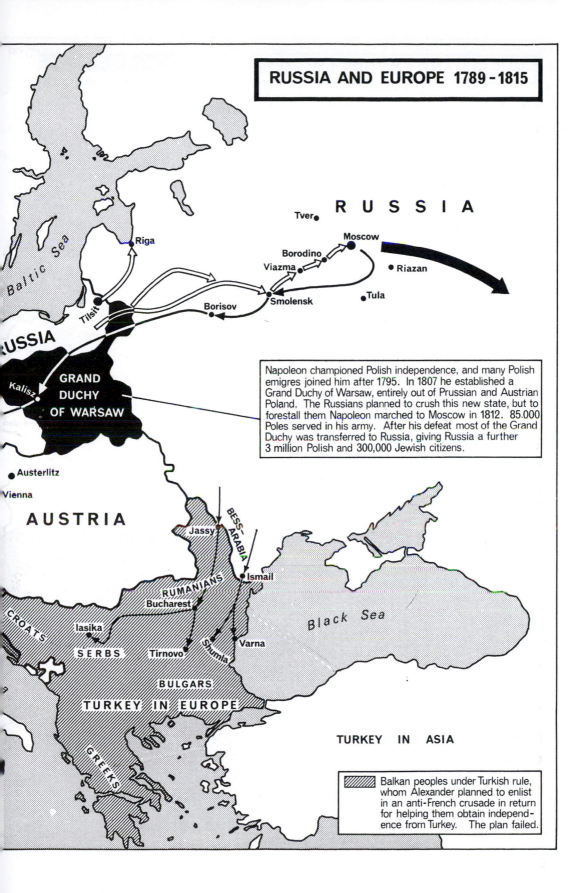

RUSSIA AND EUROPE 1789-1815

R U S S I A

Tver

Moscow

Borodino

Viazma

Riazan

Smolensk

Tula

Riga

Tilsit

Borisov

RUSSIA

Kalisz

GRAND DUCHY OF WARSAW

Baltic Sea

Napoleon championed Polish independence, and many Polish emigres joined him after 1795. In 1807 he established a Grand Duchy of Warsaw, entirely out of Prussian and Austrian Poland. The Russians planned to crush this new state, but to forestall them Napoleon marched to Moscow in 1812. 85,000 Poles served in his army. After his defeat most of the Grand Duchy was transferred to Russia, giving Russia a further 3 million Polish and 300,000 Jewish citizens.

Austerlitz

Vienna

AUSTRIA

Jassy

BESS-ARABIA

Ismail

RUMANIANS

Bucharest

Black Sea

CROATS

Iasika

SERBS

Tirnovo

Shumla

Varna

BULGARS

TURKEY IN EUROPE

GREEKS

TURKEY IN ASIA

Balkan peoples under Turkish rule, whom Alexander planned to enlist in an anti-French crusade in return for helping them obtain independence from Turkey. The plan failed.

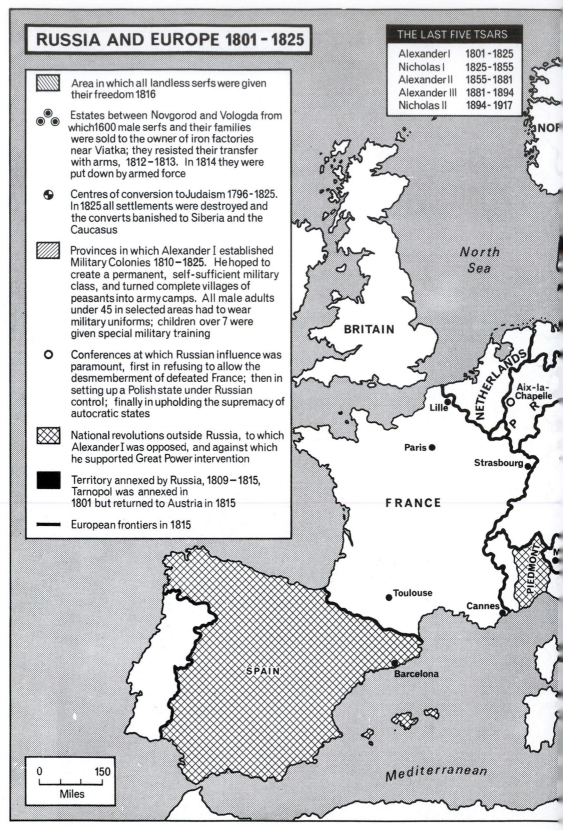

RUSSIA AND EUROPE 1801-1825

Area in which all landless serfs were given their freedom 1816

Estates between Novgorod and Vologda from which 1600 male serfs and their families were sold to the owner of iron factories near Viatka; they resisted their transfer with arms, 1812 – 1813. In 1814 they were put down by armed force

Centres of conversion to Judaism 1796 - 1825. In 1825 all settlements were destroyed and the converts banished to Siberia and the Caucasus

Provinces in which Alexander I established Military Colonies 1810 – 1825. He hoped to create a permanent, self-sufficient military class, and turned complete villages of peasants into army camps. All male adults under 45 in selected areas had to wear military uniforms; children over 7 were given special military training

Conferences at which Russian influence was paramount, first in refusing to allow the desmemberment of defeated France; then in setting up a Polish state under Russian control; finally in upholding the supremacy of autocratic states

National revolutions outside Russia, to which Alexander I was opposed, and against which he supported Great Power intervention

Territory annexed by Russia, 1809 – 1815, Tarnopol was annexed in 1801 but returned to Austria in 1815

European frontiers in 1815

NORTH

North Sea

BRITAIN

NETHERLANDS

Aix-la-Chapelle

Lille

EUROPE

Paris

Strasbourg

FRANCE

PIEDMONT

M

Toulouse

Cannes

SPAIN

Barcelona

0   150

Miles

Mediterranean

FINLAND

ALAND
ISLANDS

SWEDEN

St.
Petersburg

Novgorod

Viatka ●

Vologda

● Moscow

Tula ⊕

Saratov ●

R U S S I A

Mogilev ●

Bobrov ⊕

Pavlovsk ⊕

Baltic Sea

S S I A

POLAND

Ekaterinoslav ●

Carlsbad ○

Lemberg ●
Tarnopol

Nikolaev ●

Prague ●   Troppau ○

BESSARABIA

Vienna ○

AUSTRIA–
HUNGARY

Laibach ○

Bucharest ●

Black Sea

Belgrade ●

T   U

Cattaro

R

Constantinople ●

K   E   Y

NAPLES

Naples ●

GREECE

Athens

Like Catherine the Great on her accession,
Alexander I was looked to on his accession
(in 1801) as a potential source of liberal-
ization. In the war against Napoleon he acted
as the enemy of tyrants and friend of the
oppressed. But by 1820 he had become a
pillar of autocracy both in Russia and
abroad. Under Alexander, Russia's western
frontier reached its furthest western extent,
and from 1820 to 1917 it was unchanged

Sea

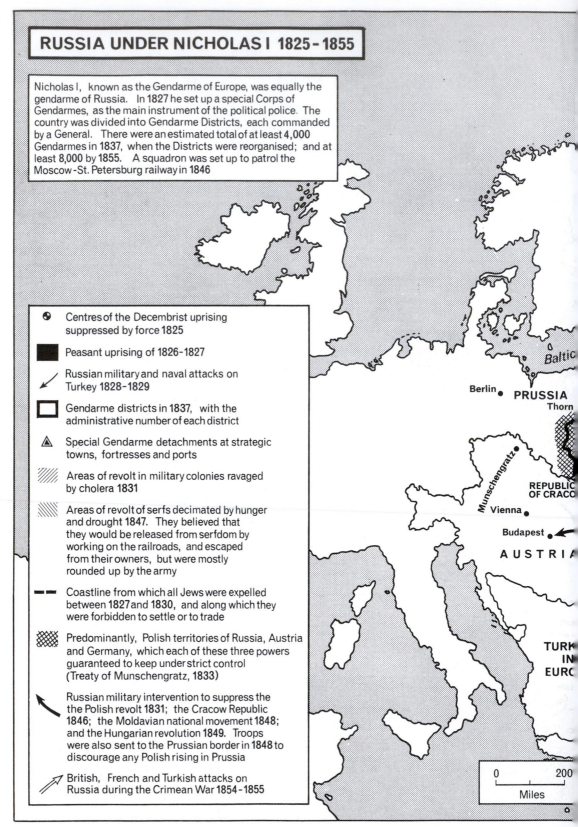

RUSSIA UNDER NICHOLAS I 1825-1855

Nicholas I, known as the Gendarme of Europe, was equally the gendarme of Russia. In 1827 he set up a special Corps of Gendarmes, as the main instrument of the political police. The country was divided into Gendarme Districts, each commanded by a General. There were an estimated total of at least 4,000 Gendarmes in 1837, when the Districts were reorganised; and at least 8,000 by 1855. A squadron was set up to patrol the Moscow-St. Petersburg railway in 1846

⊕ Centres of the Decembrist uprising suppressed by force 1825

■ Peasant uprising of 1826-1827

↙ Russian military and naval attacks on Turkey 1828-1829

▢ Gendarme districts in 1837, with the administrative number of each district

△ Special Gendarme detachments at strategic towns, fortresses and ports

▨ Areas of revolt in military colonies ravaged by cholera 1831

▨ Areas of revolt of serfs decimated by hunger and drought 1847. They believed that they would be released from serfdom by working on the railroads, and escaped from their owners, but were mostly rounded up by the army

– – Coastline from which all Jews were expelled between 1827 and 1830, and along which they were forbidden to settle or to trade

▨ Predominantly, Polish territories of Russia, Austria and Germany, which each of these three powers guaranteed to keep under strict control (Treaty of Munschengratz, 1833)

↖ Russian military intervention to suppress the the Polish revolt 1831; the Cracow Republic 1846; the Moldavian national movement 1848; and the Hungarian revolution 1849. Troops were also sent to the Prussian border in 1848 to discourage any Polish rising in Prussia

↗ British, French and Turkish attacks on Russia during the Crimean War 1854-1855

Baltic

Berlin ● **PRUSSIA**
Thorn

Munschengratz

REPUBLIC OF CRACO

Vienna ●

Budapest ●←

AUSTRIA

TURK IN EURO

0   200
Miles

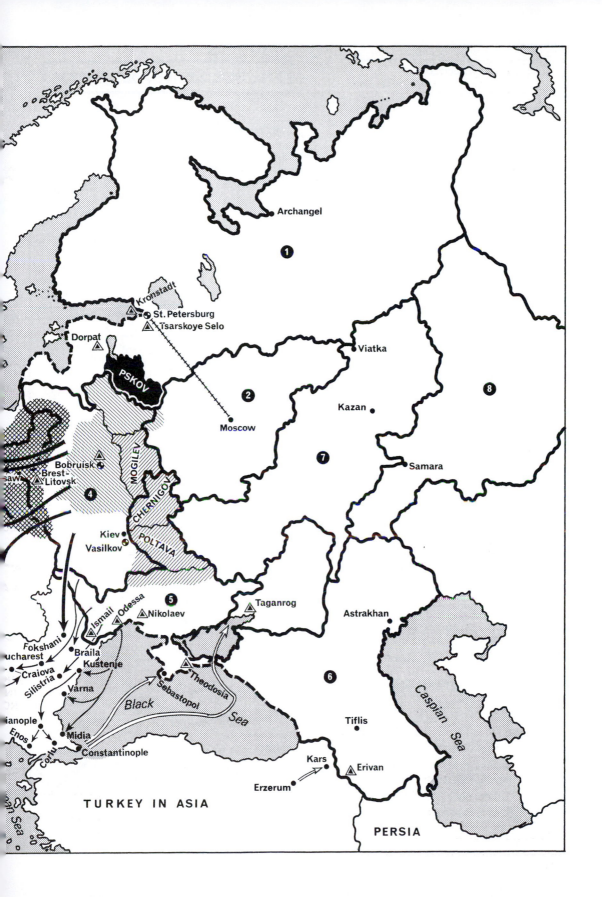

Archangel

❶

Kronstadt
St. Petersburg
Tsarskoye Selo

Dorpat

PSKOV

Viatka

❷

❽

Kazan

Moscow

MOGILEV

Bobruisk
Brest-
Litovsk
saw

❹

CHERNIGOV

❼

Samara

POLTAVA

Kiev
Vasilkov

❺

Odessa

Ismail
Nikolaev

Taganrog

Astrakhan

Fokshani
ucharest
Craiova
Silistria

Braila
Kustenje

Varna

Sebastopol

Theodosia

❻

Tiflis

Caspian
Sea

ianople
Enos

Midia

Black

Sea

Corfu

Constantinople

Kars

Erzerum

Erivan

TURKEY IN ASIA

PERSIA

an Sea

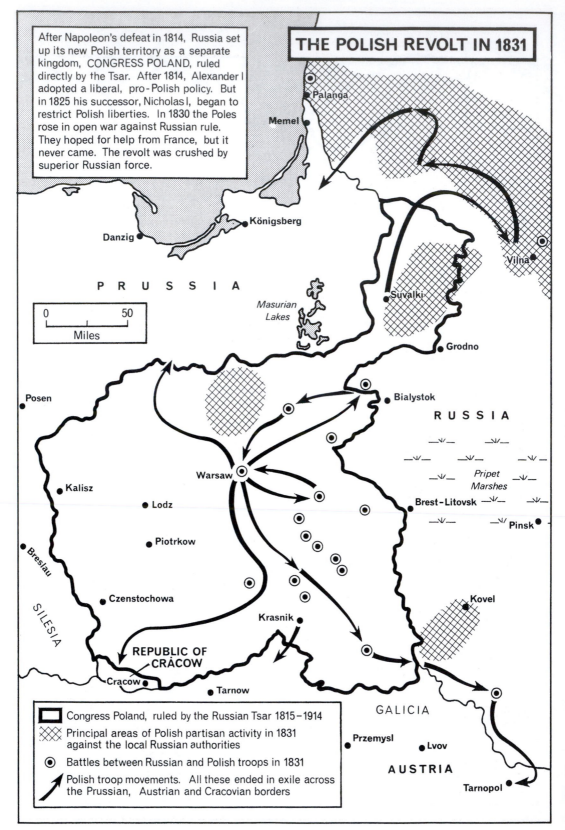

THE POLISH REVOLT IN 1831

After Napoleon's defeat in 1814, Russia set up its new Polish territory as a separate kingdom, CONGRESS POLAND, ruled directly by the Tsar. After 1814, Alexander I adopted a liberal, pro-Polish policy. But in 1825 his successor, Nicholas I, began to restrict Polish liberties. In 1830 the Poles rose in open war against Russian rule. They hoped for help from France, but it never came. The revolt was crushed by superior Russian force.

Palanga

Memel

Vilna

Königsberg

Danzig

P R U S S I A

Masurian Lakes

Suvalki

0   50
Miles

Grodno

Posen

Bialystok

R U S S I A

Warsaw

Kalisz

Lodz

Pripet Marshes

Brest-Litovsk

Piotrkow

Pinsk

Breslau

SILESIA

Czenstochowa

Kovel

Krasnik

REPUBLIC OF CRACOW

Cracow

Tarnow

GALICIA

Przemysl

Lvov

AUSTRIA

Tarnopol

☐ Congress Poland, ruled by the Russian Tsar 1815–1914

▨ Principal areas of Polish partisan activity in 1831 against the local Russian authorities

⊙ Battles between Russian and Polish troops in 1831

↗ Polish troop movements. All these ended in exile across the Prussian, Austrian and Cracovian borders

52

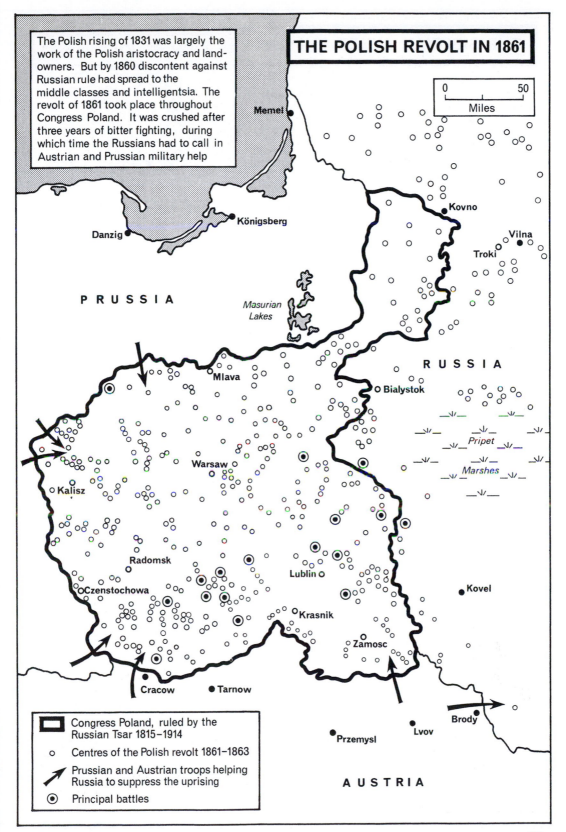

THE POLISH REVOLT IN 1861

The Polish rising of 1831 was largely the work of the Polish aristocracy and landowners. But by 1860 discontent against Russian rule had spread to the middle classes and intelligentsia. The revolt of 1861 took place throughout Congress Poland. It was crushed after three years of bitter fighting, during which time the Russians had to call in Austrian and Prussian military help

0   50
Miles

Memel

Kovno

Vilna

Troki

Danzig   Königsberg

P R U S S I A

Masurian Lakes

Mlava

R U S S I A

O Bialystok

Warsaw

Pripet

Marshes

O Kalisz

Radomsk

Lublin O

Kovel

O Czenstochowa

O Krasnik

Cracow   ● Tarnow   Zamosc

Brody

Przemysl   Lvov

A U S T R I A

Congress Poland, ruled by the Russian Tsar 1815–1914

o   Centres of the Polish revolt 1861–1863

Prussian and Austrian troops helping Russia to suppress the uprising

⊙   Principal battles

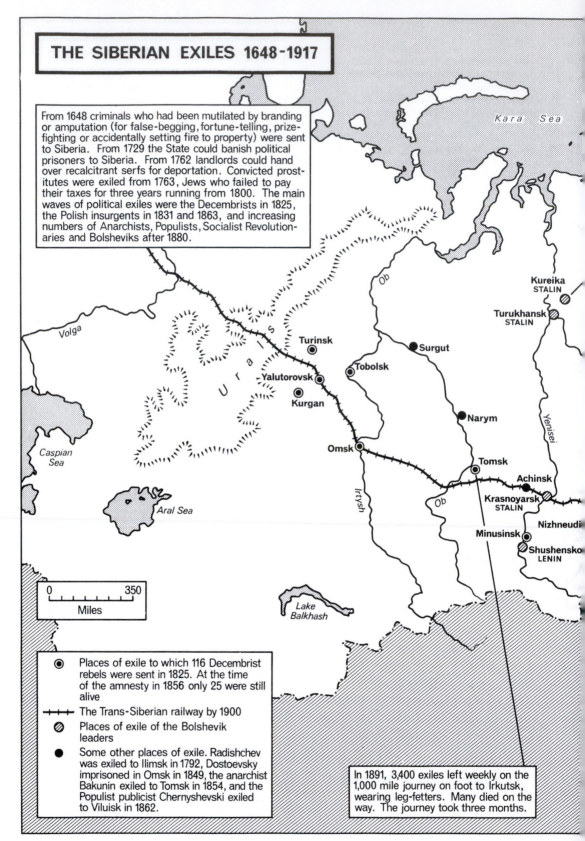

THE SIBERIAN EXILES 1648-1917

From 1648 criminals who had been mutilated by branding or amputation (for false-begging, fortune-telling, prize-fighting or accidentally setting fire to property) were sent to Siberia. From 1729 the State could banish political prisoners to Siberia. From 1762 landlords could hand over recalcitrant serfs for deportation. Convicted prostitutes were exiled from 1763, Jews who failed to pay their taxes for three years running from 1800. The main waves of political exiles were the Decembrists in 1825, the Polish insurgents in 1831 and 1863, and increasing numbers of Anarchists, Populists, Socialist Revolutionaries and Bolsheviks after 1880.

Kara Sea

Ob

Kureika
STALIN

Turukhansk
STALIN

Volga

Turinsk

Surgut

Tobolsk

U r a l s

Yalutorovsk

Kurgan

Narym

Yenisei

Caspian Sea

Omsk

Irtysh

Ob

Tomsk

Achinsk

Krasnoyarsk
STALIN

Aral Sea

Nizhneudi

Minusinsk

Shushensko
LENIN

0	350
Miles	

Lake Balkhash

◉ Places of exile to which 116 Decembrist rebels were sent in 1825. At the time of the amnesty in 1856 only 25 were still alive

+++ The Trans-Siberian railway by 1900

⊘ Places of exile of the Bolshevik leaders

● Some other places of exile. Radishchev was exiled to Ilimsk in 1792, Dostoevsky imprisoned in Omsk in 1849, the anarchist Bakunin exiled to Tomsk in 1854, and the Populist publicist Chernyshevski exiled to Viluisk in 1862.

In 1891, 3,400 exiles left weekly on the 1,000 mile journey on foot to Irkutsk, wearing leg-fetters. Many died on the way. The journey took three months.

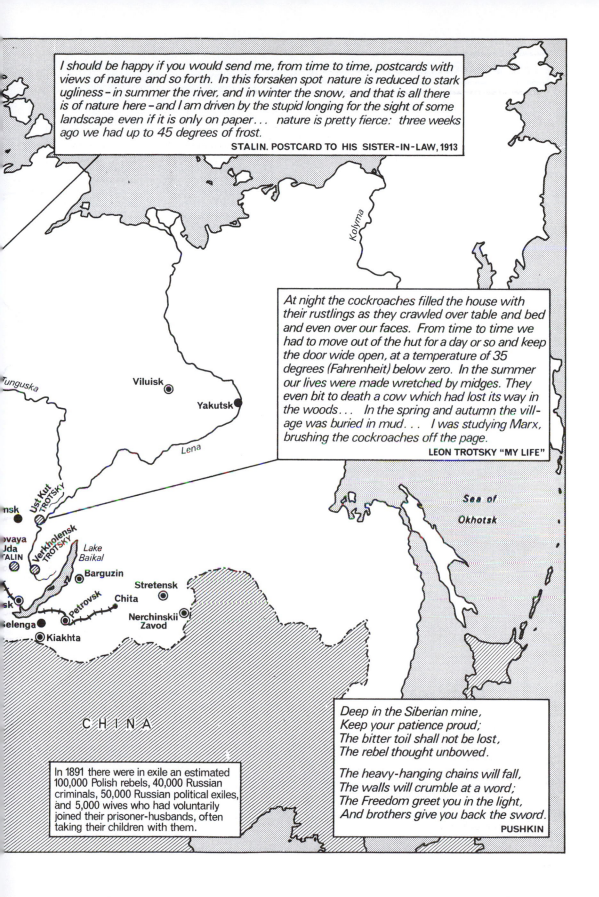

I should be happy if you would send me, from time to time, postcards with views of nature and so forth. In this forsaken spot nature is reduced to stark ugliness – in summer the river, and in winter the snow, and that is all there is of nature here – and I am driven by the stupid longing for the sight of some landscape even if it is only on paper... nature is pretty fierce: three weeks ago we had up to 45 degrees of frost.

STALIN. POSTCARD TO HIS SISTER-IN-LAW, 1913

At night the cockroaches filled the house with their rustlings as they crawled over table and bed and even over our faces. From time to time we had to move out of the hut for a day or so and keep the door wide open, at a temperature of 35 degrees (Fahrenheit) below zero. In the summer our lives were made wretched by midges. They even bit to death a cow which had lost its way in the woods... In the spring and autumn the village was buried in mud... I was studying Marx, brushing the cockroaches off the page.

LEON TROTSKY "MY LIFE"

Kolyma

Tunguska

Viluisk

Yakutsk

Lena

Ust Kut
TROTSKY

nsk

ovaya
Jda
ALIN

Verkholensk
TROTSKY

Lake
Baikal

Barguzin

Stretensk

Petrovsk

Chita

sk

Nerchinskii
Zavod

Selenga

Kiakhta

Sea of

Okhotsk

CHINA

Deep in the Siberian mine,
Keep your patience proud;
The bitter toil shall not be lost,
The rebel thought unbowed.

The heavy-hanging chains will fall,
The walls will crumble at a word;
The Freedom greet you in the light,
And brothers give you back the sword.

PUSHKIN

In 1891 there were in exile an estimated 100,000 Polish rebels, 40,000 Russian criminals, 50,000 Russian political exiles, and 5,000 wives who had voluntarily joined their prisoner-husbands, often taking their children with them.

THE ANARCHISTS 1840-1906

"What is property? Property is theft" wrote the French philosopher Proudhon, the father of anarchism, in 1840. He urged the destruction of officialdom, bureaucracy money and state organisation in order to make all men equal and free. But he shunned violent revolt, fearing that revolution might bring new tyranny. The Russian, Bakunin, bent anarchism to violence. "The passion to destroy is at the same time a passion to create," he wrote in 1842. Bakunin believed that the Russian peasant would be the instrument of anarchic revolt, and encouraged terrorist acts. The murder of Tsar Alexander II at St. Petersburg in 1881 encouraged further assassinations, aimed at provoking revolution. The Russian anarchist, Prince Kropotkin, said after the execution of one of the 5 assassins: "By her death she was dealing an even more terrible blow, from which the autocracy will never recover."

Baltic Sea

St.Petersburg

Viatka

Riga

LITHUANIA

Kovno

Vilna

Grodno Minsk

Bialystok

Warsaw

POLAND

Moscow

Tula

Orel

Nizhni
Novgorod

Volga

Samara

Nezhin

Kiev

Kharkov

UKRAINE

Ekaterinoslav

Kishinev

Odessa

Volga

Sebastopol

Yalta

Black Sea

Caspian Sea

Batum Tiflis

CAUCASIA

Baku

Anarchist groups meeting from the 1840's to 1880's

Revolutionary anarchist groups in existence from 1903 and "revolting" in 1905-1906

The "Forest Brethren" carrying out terrorist activity in 1905-1906

0 300
Miles

55

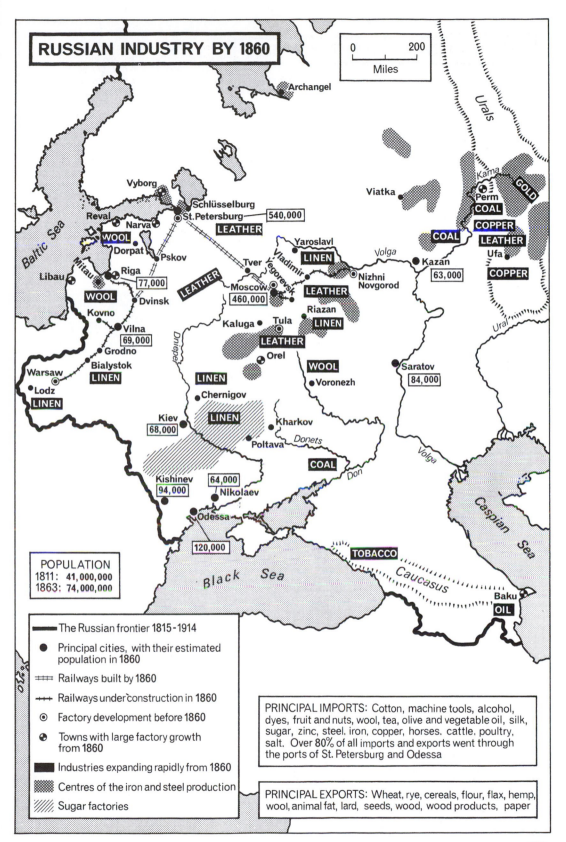

RUSSIAN INDUSTRY BY 1860

0   200
Miles

Archangel

Ural s

Vyborg

Schlüsselburg

Reval   St. Petersburg   540,000   LEATHER

Narva   Dorpat   Pskov

Viatka

Kama

Perm

COAL

COPPER

COAL   LEATHER

Ufa

COPPER

Baltic Sea

WOOL

Libau   Mitau   Riga   77,000

Dvinst   WOOL

Kovno

Vilna   69,000

Grodno

Bialystok

Warsaw   LINEN

Lodz

LINEN

Yaroslavl   LINEN

Tver   Vladimir   Volga

Egorevsk   Nizhni   Kazan   63,000

Moscow   Novgorod

460,000   LEATHER

LEATHER

Riazan   LINEN

Kaluga   Tula

LEATHER

Orel   WOOL

Voronezh

Saratov

84,000

LINEN

Chernigov

Kiev   LINEN

68,000

Kharkov

Poltava   Donets

COAL   Don

Volga

Kishinev   64,000

94,000   Nikolaev

Odessa

120,000

TOBACCO

Caucasus

Caspian Sea

Baku

OIL

Dnieper

Ural

Black Sea

POPULATION
1811: 41,000,000
1863: 74,000,000

The Russian frontier 1815-1914

● Principal cities, with their estimated population in 1860

+++ Railways built by 1860

+-+ Railways under construction in 1860

⊙ Factory development before 1860

⊕ Towns with large factory growth from 1860

■ Industries expanding rapidly from 1860

▓ Centres of the iron and steel production

▧ Sugar factories

PRINCIPAL IMPORTS: Cotton, machine tools, alcohol, dyes, fruit and nuts, wool, tea, olive and vegetable oil, silk, sugar, zinc, steel, iron, copper, horses, cattle, poultry, salt. Over 80% of all imports and exports went through the ports of St. Petersburg and Odessa

PRINCIPAL EXPORTS: Wheat, rye, cereals, flour, flax, hemp, wool, animal fat, lard, seeds, wood, wood products, paper

56

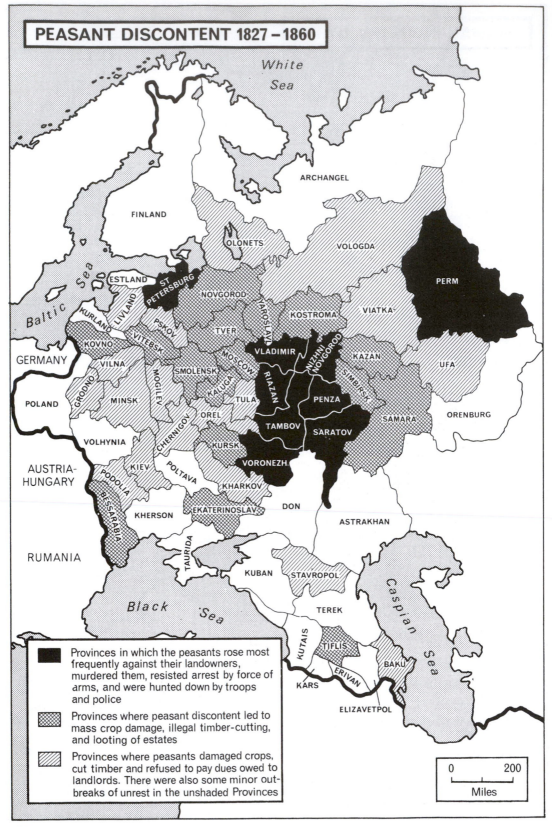

PEASANT DISCONTENT 1827–1860

White Sea

ARCHANGEL

FINLAND

OLONETS

VOLOGDA

PERM

ESTLAND

ST PETERSBURG

NOVGOROD

Baltic Sea

KURLAND

LIVLAND

PSKOV

YAROSLAVL

KOSTROMA

VIATKA

KOVNO

VITEBSK

TVER

VLADIMIR

NIZHNI NOVGOROD

KAZAN

UFA

GERMANY

VILNA

MOSCOW

SIMBIRSK

GRODNO

MOGILEV

SMOLENSK

KALUGA

RIAZAN

PENZA

POLAND

MINSK

OREL

TULA

SAMARA

ORENBURG

VOLHYNIA

CHERNIGOV

KURSK

TAMBOV

SARATOV

AUSTRIA-HUNGARY

KIEV

POLTAVA

VORONEZH

PODOLIA

BESSARABIA

KHARKOV

DON

ASTRAKHAN

EKATERINOSLAV

KHERSON

RUMANIA

TAURIDA

KUBAN

STAVROPOL

Caspian Sea

Black Sea

TEREK

KUTAIS

TIFLIS

BAKU

KARS

ERIVAN

ELIZAVETPOL

■ Provinces in which the peasants rose most frequently against their landowners, murdered them, resisted arrest by force of arms, and were hunted down by troops and police

▨ Provinces where peasant discontent led to mass crop damage, illegal timber-cutting, and looting of estates

▨ Provinces where peasants damaged crops, cut timber and refused to pay dues owed to landlords. There were also some minor outbreaks of unrest in the unshaded Provinces

0   200
Miles

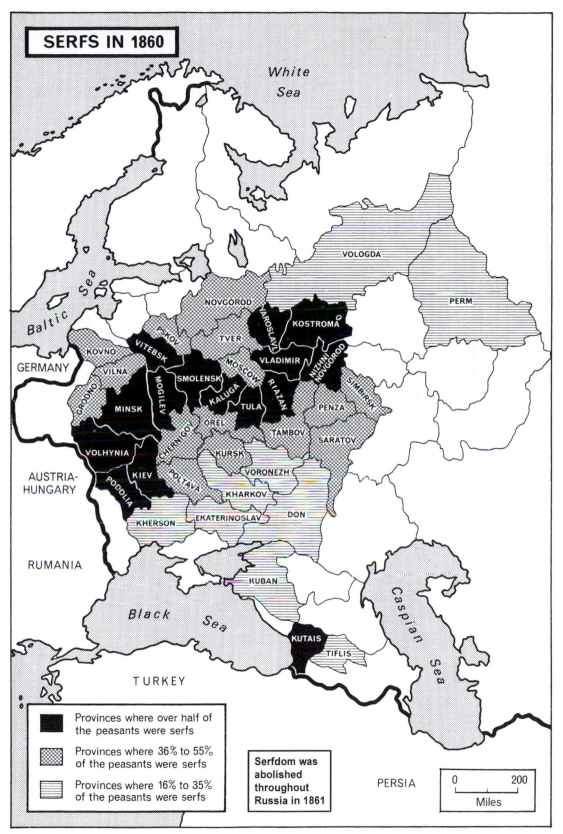

SERFS IN 1860

White Sea

Baltic Sea

GERMANY

VOLOGDA

PERM

NOVGOROD

PSKOV

VITEBSK

KOVNO

VILNA

TVER

YAROSLAVL

KOSTROMA

VLADIMIR

NIZHNI NOVGOROD

MOSCOW

SIMBIRSK

GRODNO

MOGILEV

SMOLENSK

KALUGA

RIAZAN

MINSK

TULA

PENZA

OREL

TAMBOV

SARATOV

CHERNIGOV

VOLHYNIA

KIEV

KURSK

VORONEZH

PODOLIA

POLTAVA

KHARKOV

DON

AUSTRIA-HUNGARY

EKATERINOSLAV

KHERSON

RUMANIA

KUBAN

Black Sea

Caspian Sea

KUTAIS

TIFLIS

TURKEY

Provinces where over half of
the peasants were serfs

Provinces where 36% to 55%
of the peasants were serfs

Provinces where 16% to 35%
of the peasants were serfs

**Serfdom was
abolished
throughout
Russia in 1861**

PERSIA

0   200

Miles

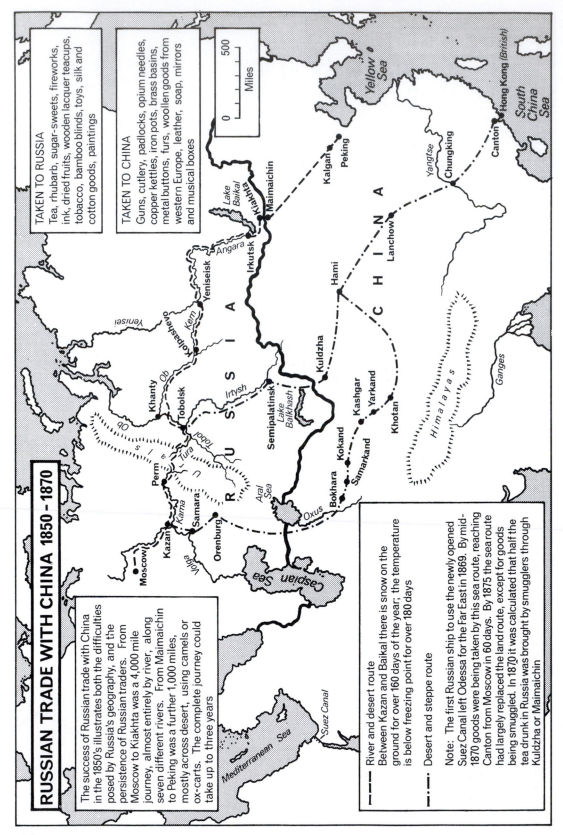

RUSSIAN TRADE WITH CHINA 1850 – 1870

The success of Russian trade with China in the 1850's illustrates both the difficulties posed by Russia's geography, and the persistence of Russian traders. From Moscow to Kiakhta was a 4,000 mile journey, almost entirely by river, along seven different rivers. From Maimaichin to Peking was a further 1,000 miles, mostly across desert, using camels or ox-carts. The complete journey could take up to three years

TAKEN TO RUSSIA
Tea, rhubarb, sugar-sweets, fireworks, ink, dried fruits, wooden lacquer teacups, tobacco, bamboo blinds, toys, silk and cotton goods, paintings

TAKEN TO CHINA
Guns, cutlery, padlocks, opium needles, copper kettles, iron pots, brass basins, metal buttons, furs, woollen goods from western Europe, leather, soap, mirrors and musical boxes

0   500
Miles

- - - River and desert route
Between Kazan and Baikal there is snow on the ground for over 160 days of the year; the temperature is below freezing point for over 180 days

-·-·- Desert and steppe route

Note: The first Russian ship to use the newly opened Suez Canal left Odessa for the Far East in 1869. By mid-1870 goods were being taken by this sea route, reaching Canton from Moscow in 60 days. By 1875 the sea route had largely replaced the land route, except for goods being smuggled. In 1870 it was calculated that half the tea drunk in Russia was brought by smugglers through Kuldzha or Maimaichin

59

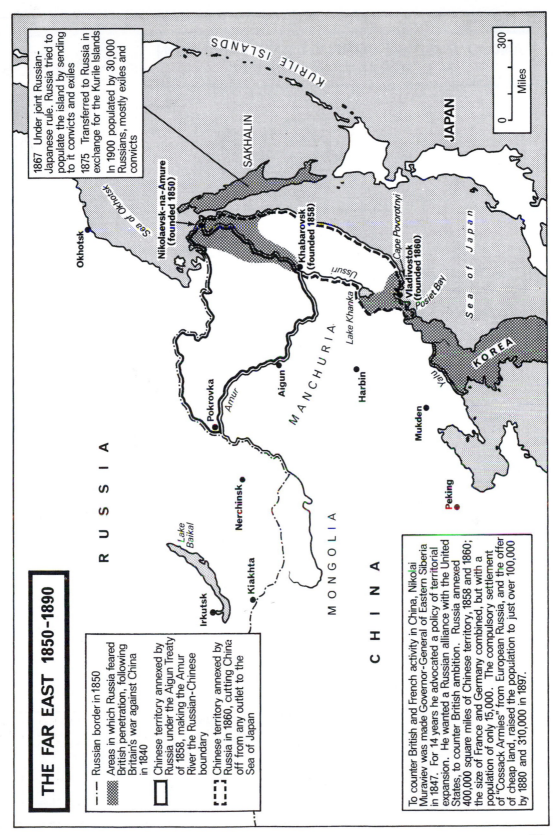

THE FAR EAST 1850-1890

Legend:
- Russian border in 1850
- Areas in which Russia feared British penetration, following Britain's war against China in 1840
- Chinese territory annexed by Russia under the Aigun Treaty of 1858, making the Amur River the Russian-Chinese boundary
- Chinese territory annexed by Russia in 1860, cutting China off from any outlet to the Sea of Japan

To counter British and French activity in China, Nikolai Muraviev was made Governor-General of Eastern Siberia in 1847. For 14 years he advocated a policy of territorial expansion. He wanted a Russian alliance with the United States, to counter British ambition. Russia annexed 400,000 square miles of Chinese territory, 1858 and 1860; the size of France and Germany combined, but with a population of only 15,000. The compulsory settlement of "Cossack Armies" from European Russia, and the offer of cheap land, raised the population to just over 100,000 by 1880 and 310,000 in 1897.

1867 Under joint Russian-Japanese rule. Russia tried to populate the island by sending to it convicts and exiles

1875 Transferred to Russia in exchange for the Kurile Islands In 1900 populated by 30,000 Russians, mostly exiles and convicts

KURILE ISLANDS

SAKHALIN

JAPAN

Sea of Okhotsk

Okhotsk

Nikolaevsk-na-Amure (founded 1850)

Khabarovsk (founded 1858)

Cape Povorotnyi

Vladivostok (founded 1860)

Possiet Bay

Sea of Japan

KOREA

Ussuri

Lake Khanka

Yalu

R U S S I A

M A N C H U R I A

Pokrovka

Aigun

Harbin

Mukden

Amur

Lake Baikal

Nerchinsk

Irkutsk

Kiakhta

M O N G O L I A

C H I N A

Peking

0   300
Miles

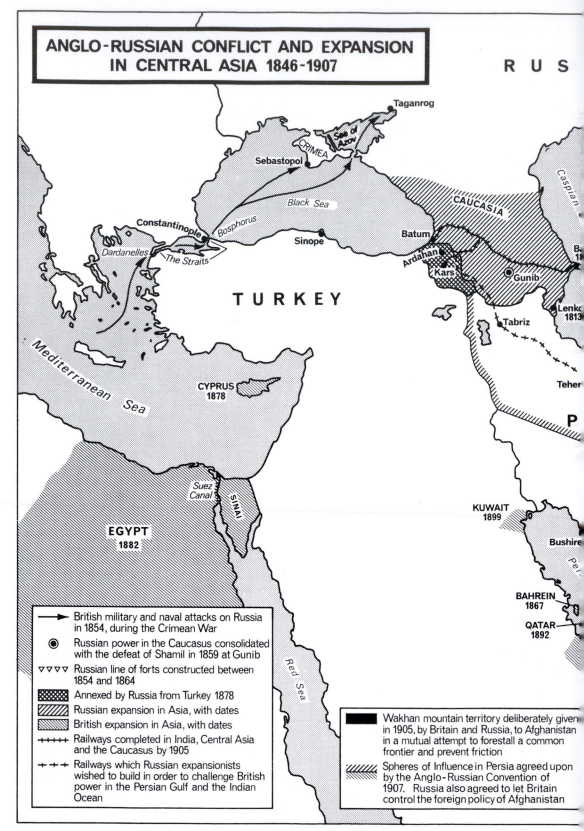

ANGLO-RUSSIAN CONFLICT AND EXPANSION IN CENTRAL ASIA 1846-1907

RUS

Taganrog

Sea of Azov

CRIMEA

Sebastopol

Black Sea

CAUCASIA

Caspian

Constantinople

Bosphorus

Batum

B. 18

Dardanelles

The Straits

Sinope

Ardahan

Kars

Gunib

Lenk 1813

TURKEY

Tabriz

Teher

Mediterranean Sea

CYPRUS 1878

P

Suez Canal

SINAI

KUWAIT 1899

EGYPT 1882

Bushire

Pe

Red Sea

BAHREIN 1867

QATAR 1892

→ British military and naval attacks on Russia in 1854, during the Crimean War

⊙ Russian power in the Caucasus consolidated with the defeat of Shamil in 1859 at Gunib

▽▽▽▽ Russian line of forts constructed between 1854 and 1864

▨ Annexed by Russia from Turkey 1878

▨ Russian expansion in Asia, with dates

▨ British expansion in Asia, with dates

+++++ Railways completed in India, Central Asia and the Caucasus by 1905

+ + + Railways which Russian expansionists wished to build in order to challenge British power in the Persian Gulf and the Indian Ocean

■ Wakhan mountain territory deliberately given in 1905, by Britain and Russia, to Afghanistan in a mutual attempt to forestall a common frontier and prevent friction

▨ Spheres of Influence in Persia agreed upon by the Anglo-Russian Convention of 1907. Russia also agreed to let Britain control the foreign policy of Afghanistan

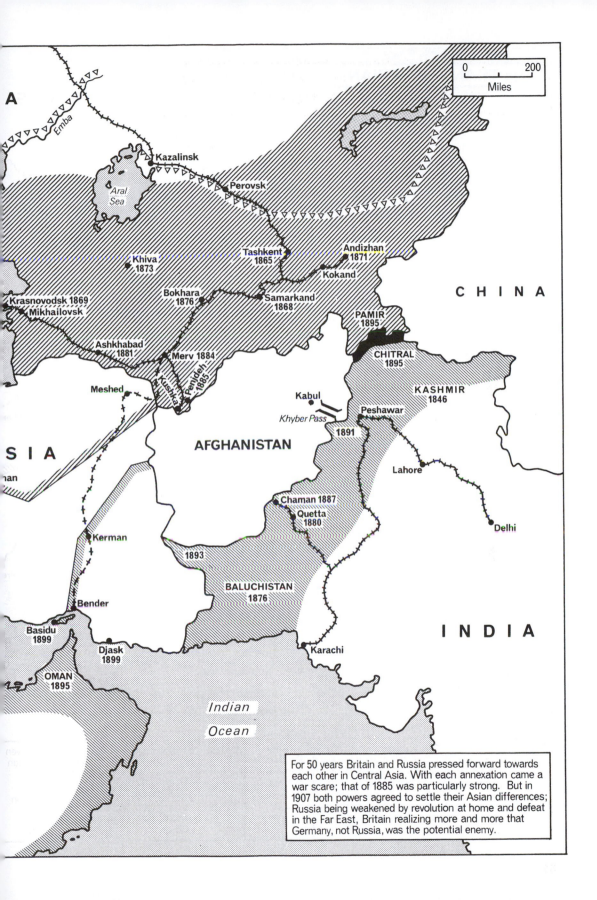

A

Emba

Kazalinsk

Aral
Sea

Perovsk

Khiva
1873

Tashkent
1865

Andizhan
1871

Kokand

CHINA

Krasnovodsk 1869
Mikhailovsk

Bokhara
1876

Samarkand
1868

PAMIR
1895

Ashkhabad
1881

Merv 1884

CHITRAL
1875

Penjdeh
1885

Kushka

SIA

Meshed

Kabul

Khyber Pass

Peshawar

KASHMIR
1846

AFGHANISTAN

1891

Lahore

Kerman

Chaman 1887

Quetta
1880

Delhi

1893

Bender

BALUCHISTAN
1876

INDIA

Basidu
1899

Djask
1899

Karachi

OMAN
1895

Indian

Ocean

For 50 years Britain and Russia pressed forward towards
each other in Central Asia. With each annexation came a
war scare; that of 1885 was particularly strong. But in
1907 both powers agreed to settle their Asian differences;
Russia being weakened by revolution at home and defeat
in the Far East, Britain realizing more and more that
Germany, not Russia, was the potential enemy.

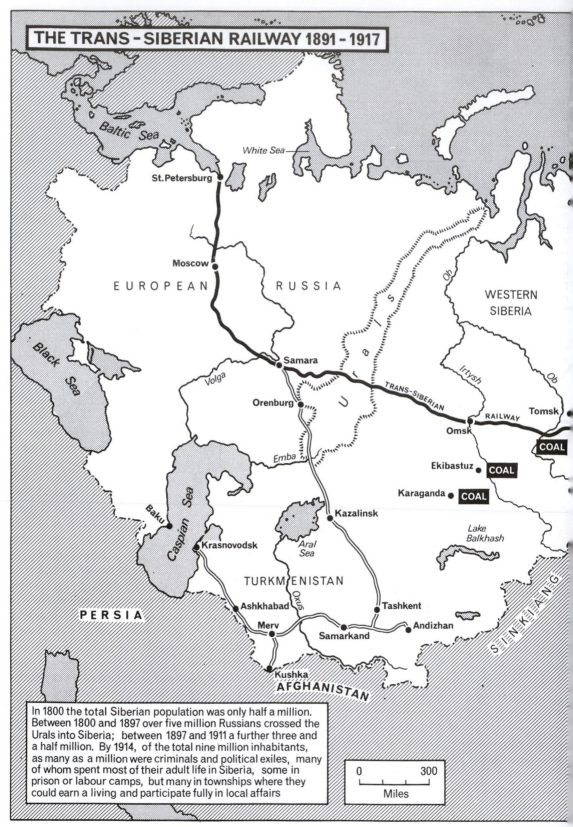

THE TRANS-SIBERIAN RAILWAY 1891-1917

Baltic Sea

White Sea

St.Petersburg

Moscow

EUROPEAN RUSSIA

WESTERN SIBERIA

Black Sea

Samara

Volga

Orenburg

Urals

Irtysh

Ob

TRANS-SIBERIAN

RAILWAY

Omsk

Tomsk

COAL

Emba

Ekibastuz **COAL**

Karaganda **COAL**

Baku

Caspian Sea

Kazalinsk

Aral Sea

Lake Balkhash

Krasnovodsk

TURKMENISTAN

PERSIA

Ashkhabad

Oxus

Tashkent

SINKIANG

Merv

Samarkand

Andizhan

Kushka

AFGHANISTAN

In 1800 the total Siberian population was only half a million. Between 1800 and 1897 over five million Russians crossed the Urals into Siberia; between 1897 and 1911 a further three and a half million. By 1914, of the total nine million inhabitants, as many as a million were criminals and political exiles, many of whom spent most of their adult life in Siberia, some in prison or labour camps, but many in townships where they could earn a living and participate fully in local affairs

0   300

Miles

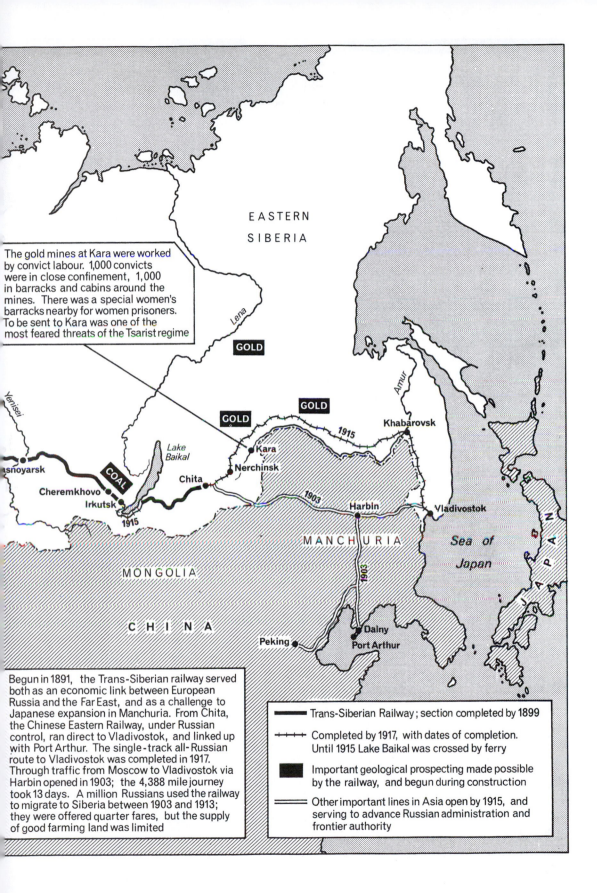

EASTERN SIBERIA

The gold mines at Kara were worked by convict labour. 1,000 convicts were in close confinement, 1,000 in barracks and cabins around the mines. There was a special women's barracks nearby for women prisoners. To be sent to Kara was one of the most feared threats of the Tsarist regime

Lena

GOLD

Yenisei

GOLD

GOLD

Amur

Khabarovsk

1915

Lake Baikal

Kara

Nerchinsk

asnoyarsk

COAL

Chita

1903

Cheremkhovo

Irkutsk

Harbin

Vladivostok

1915

MANCHURIA

Sea of Japan

MONGOLIA

1903

J A P A N

C H I N A

Dalny

Peking

Port Arthur

Begun in 1891, the Trans-Siberian railway served both as an economic link between European Russia and the Far East, and as a challenge to Japanese expansion in Manchuria. From Chita, the Chinese Eastern Railway, under Russian control, ran direct to Vladivostok, and linked up with Port Arthur. The single-track all-Russian route to Vladivostok was completed in 1917. Through traffic from Moscow to Vladivostok via Harbin opened in 1903; the 4,388 mile journey took 13 days. A million Russians used the railway to migrate to Siberia between 1903 and 1913; they were offered quarter fares, but the supply of good farming land was limited

▬▬▬ Trans-Siberian Railway; section completed by 1899

++++ Completed by 1917, with dates of completion. Until 1915 Lake Baikal was crossed by ferry

■ Important geological prospecting made possible by the railway, and begun during construction

═══ Other important lines in Asia open by 1915, and serving to advance Russian administration and frontier authority

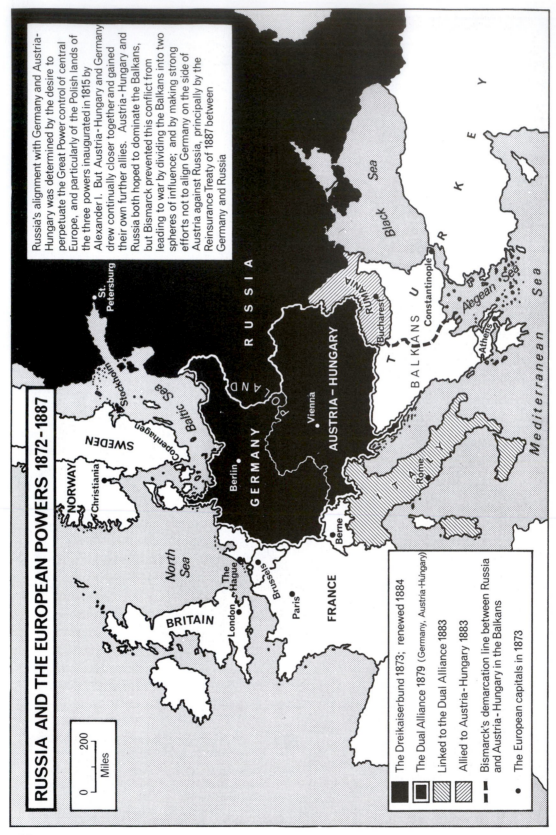

RUSSIA AND THE EUROPEAN POWERS 1872–1887

Russia's alignment with Germany and Austria-Hungary was determined by the desire to perpetuate the Great Power control of central Europe, and particularly of the Polish lands of the three powers inaugurated in 1815 by Alexander I. But Austria-Hungary and Germany drew continually closer together and gained their own further allies. Austria-Hungary and Russia both hoped to dominate the Balkans, but Bismarck prevented this conflict from leading to war by dividing the Balkans into two spheres of influence; and by making strong efforts not to align Germany on the side of Austria against Russia, principally by the Reinsurance Treaty of 1887 between Germany and Russia

The Dreikaiserbund 1873; renewed 1884

The Dual Alliance 1879 (Germany, Austria-Hungary)

Linked to the Dual Alliance 1883

Allied to Austria-Hungary 1883

Bismarck's demarcation line between Russia and Austria-Hungary in the Balkans

The European capitals in 1873

0   200
Miles

63

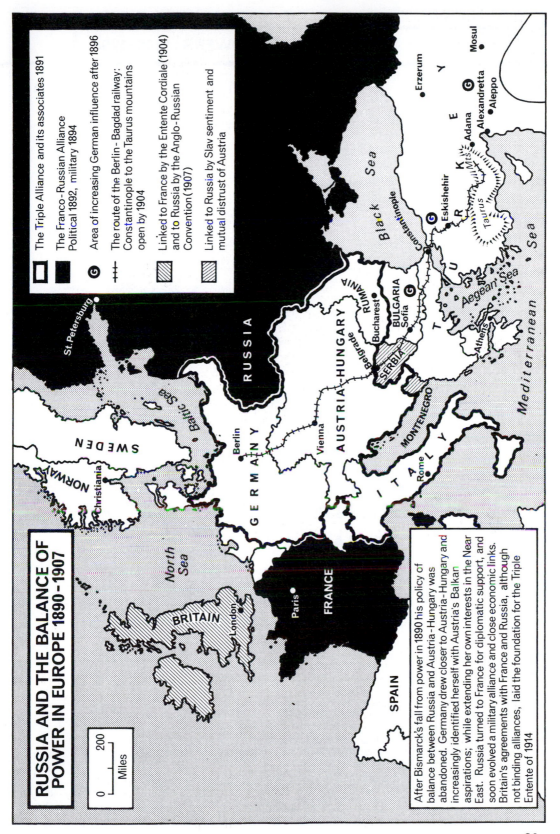

RUSSIA AND THE BALANCE OF POWER IN EUROPE 1890–1907

The Triple Alliance and its associates 1891

The Franco-Russian Alliance Political 1892, military 1894

G Area of increasing German influence after 1896

The route of the Berlin–Bagdad railway: Constantinople to the Taurus mountains open by 1904

Linked to France by the Entente Cordiale (1904) and to Russia by the Anglo-Russian Convention (1907)

Linked to Russia by Slav sentiment and mutual distrust of Austria

After Bismarck's fall from power in 1890 his policy of balance between Russia and Austria-Hungary was abandoned. Germany drew closer to Austria-Hungary and increasingly identified herself with Austria's Balkan aspirations; while extending her own interests in the Near East. Russia turned to France for diplomatic support, and soon evolved a military alliance and close economic links. Britain's agreements with France and Russia, although not binding alliances, laid the foundation for the Triple Entente of 1914

0   200   Miles

NORWAY
Christiania
SWEDEN
St.Petersburg
North Sea
Baltic Sea
RUSSIA
BRITAIN
London
GERMANY
Berlin
Paris
FRANCE
Vienna
AUSTRIA-HUNGARY
SPAIN
ITALY
Rome
MONTENEGRO
SERBIA
Belgrade
RUMANIA
Bucharest
BULGARIA
Sofia
Black Sea
Constantinople
Eskishehir
Erzerum
Mosul
T U R K E Y
Taurus Mts.
Adana
Alexandretta
Aleppo
Athens
Aegean Sea
Mediterranean Sea

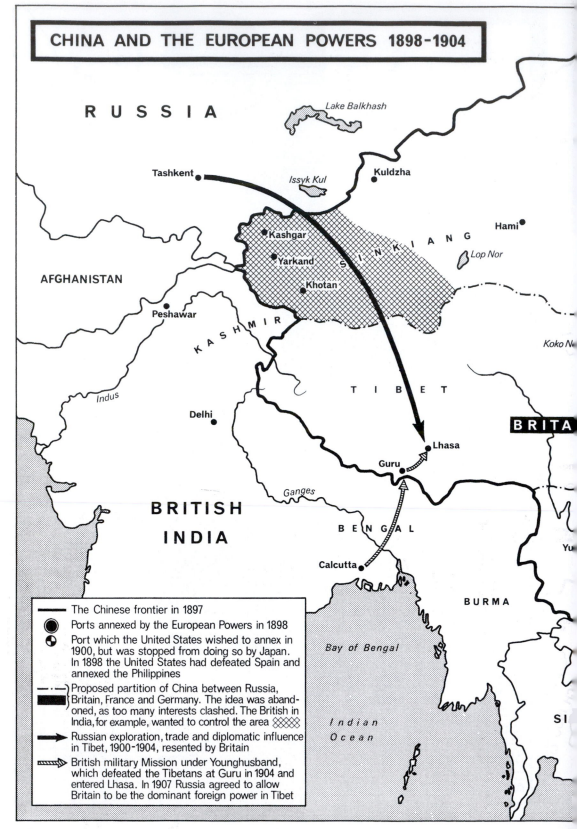

CHINA AND THE EUROPEAN POWERS 1898-1904

RUSSIA

Lake Balkhash

Tashkent

Issyk Kul

Kuldzha

Hami

Kashgar

SINKIANG

Lop Nor

AFGHANISTAN

Yarkand

Khotan

Koko N

Peshawar

KASHMIR

TIBET

Indus

Delhi

Lhasa

BRITA

Guru

Ganges

BRITISH
INDIA

BENGAL

Calcutta

Yu

BURMA

Bay of Bengal

Indian
Ocean

SI

Legend:

— The Chinese frontier in 1897

⬤ Ports annexed by the European Powers in 1898

◔ Port which the United States wished to annex in 1900, but was stopped from doing so by Japan. In 1898 the United States had defeated Spain and annexed the Philippines

⌐·⌐ Proposed partition of China between Russia, Britain, France and Germany. The idea was abandoned, as too many interests clashed. The British in India, for example, wanted to control the area ⊠⊠⊠⊠

➤ Russian exploration, trade and diplomatic influence in Tibet, 1900-1904, resented by Britain

⊳ British military Mission under Younghusband, which defeated the Tibetans at Guru in 1904 and entered Lhasa. In 1907 Russia agreed to allow Britain to be the dominant foreign power in Tibet

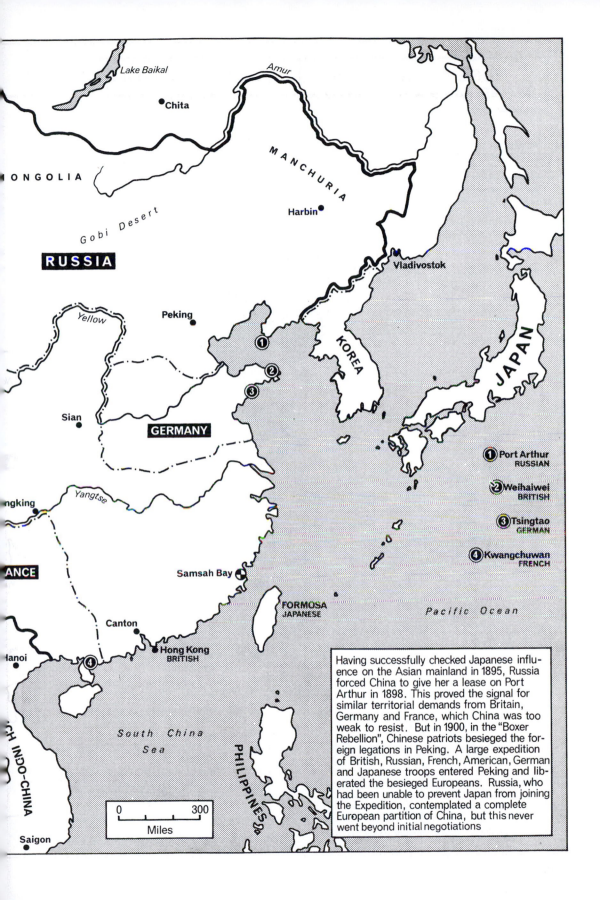

Lake Baikal

●Chita

Amur

M A N C H U R I A

MONGOLIA

Gobi Desert

Harbin ●

RUSSIA

Vladivostok

Yellow

Peking ●

①

②

③

KOREA

JAPAN

Sian ●

GERMANY

Yangtse

ngking ●

① Port Arthur
RUSSIAN

② Weihaiwei
BRITISH

③ Tsingtao
GERMAN

④ Kwangchuwan
FRENCH

ANCE

Samsah Bay

FORMOSA
JAPANESE

Pacific Ocean

Canton ●

Hong Kong
BRITISH

Hanoi ●

④

South China
Sea

PHILIPPINES

CH INDO-CHINA

Saigon ●

0   300
Miles

Having successfully checked Japanese influence on the Asian mainland in 1895, Russia
forced China to give her a lease on Port
Arthur in 1898. This proved the signal for
similar territorial demands from Britain,
Germany and France, which China was too
weak to resist. But in 1900, in the "Boxer
Rebellion", Chinese patriots besieged the foreign legations in Peking. A large expedition
of British, Russian, French, American, German
and Japanese troops entered Peking and liberated the besieged Europeans. Russia, who
had been unable to prevent Japan from joining
the Expedition, contemplated a complete
European partition of China, but this never
went beyond initial negotiations

RUSSIA AND JAPAN IN THE FAR EAST 1860-1895

Kamchatka: part of Russia in 1650. Since 1750 used largely as a place of exile for criminals and political prisoners. Russian schoolboys were often threatened that slackers would be "sent to Kamchatka"– the furthest corner of the classroom. The peninsula has over 20 active volcanoes.

The struggle between Russia and Japan in the Far East was long and bitter. In 1860 Russia acquired an outlet on the Sea of Japan. The Japanese at once adopted a forward policy in China and Korea. When Japan defeated China in 1895 she expected to make wide territorial gains. But Russia, France, Britain and Germany combined to deprive Japan of the fruits of victory. This led to deep anti-Russian resentment throughout Japan. Throughout this period, European penetration in south China continued unabated.

RUSSIA

SIBERIA

KAMCHATKA

Sea of Okhotsk

Petropavlovsk

EASTERN

Nikolaevsk

Amur

SAKHALIN

MANCHURIA

Khabarosvk

KURILE ISLANDS

Sungari

Harbin

Ussuri

Uruppu

Changchun Kirin

Etorofu

Mukden

Vladivostok

Peking

Yalu

Sea of Japan

Pacific

Tientsin

Wonsan

Port Arthur

Seoul

Weihaiwei

Inchon KOREA

JAPAN

Ocean

CHINA

Yellow

Yellow Sea

Pusan

Tsingtao

Nanking

Shanghai

Hankow

0   500

Miles

Yangtse

Oshima

Okinawa

Macao (Portuguese 1557)

RYUKYU ISLANDS

Kowloon (British 1861)

Hongkong (British 1841)

FORMOSA

South China Sea

PHILIPPINES (Spanish 1521)

Legend:

- ■ Territory annexed by Russia from China in 1858–1860
- ⊏_⊐ Islands annexed by Japan from China in 1874
- ⋯ Islands annexed by Japan in return for Russian control of Sakhalin
- ◉ Korean ports open, as the result of Japanese pressure, to Japanese trade 1876–1878
- ⁄⁄⁄ Occupied by Japan during the war with China, 1894–95. Russia, France, Britain and Germany combined to prevent Japan keeping any of this territory
- ▭ Only Chinese territory actually annexed by Japan after the war of 1894–1895

THE RUSSIAN RESPONSE IN THE FAR EAST 1895-1905

0   300
Miles

WAR DEAD 1904-05	
Russian	120,000
Japanese	75,000

RUSSIA

Chita
Nerchinsk
Amur
Argun
MANCHURIA
Hailar
Tsitsihar
Nikolaevsk
Amur
Khabarovsk
SAKHALIN

CHINA

Harbin
Sungari

Mukden
Yalu
Vladivostok

Peking

Port Arthur
Seoul
KOREA

Sea of Japan

Yellow Sea

Tsushima Strait

Tokyo

JAPAN

The Trans-Siberian Railway by 1895

Under increasing Russian control after 1895

Leased by Russia from China in 1898, together with the right to build a railway to Harbin; (completed by 1904)

The Chinese Eastern Railway, controlled by Russia after its completion in 1903

Russian economic penetration. Russia refused to allow Japan a sphere of influence in Korea

Japanese naval and military attacks 1904-1905

Annexed by Japan in 1905

After successfully halting Japanese expansion in 1895, the Russians adopted an active expansionist policy. For 10 years they pressed forward in Manchuria, and discussed the partition of China with the British Government in 1900. But Japan sought revenge for the humiliation of 1895, and in 1902 neutralized Britain by the Anglo-Japanese Alliance. In February 1904, under Russian provocation, Japan attacked Port Arthur. Russia was defeated on land and sea, and a peace treaty was signed in the United States in Sept. 1905. The grave demoralization created by Russia's defeat led to a mass of revolutionary outbreaks in Russia, and to a serious weakening of the Tsarist mystique.

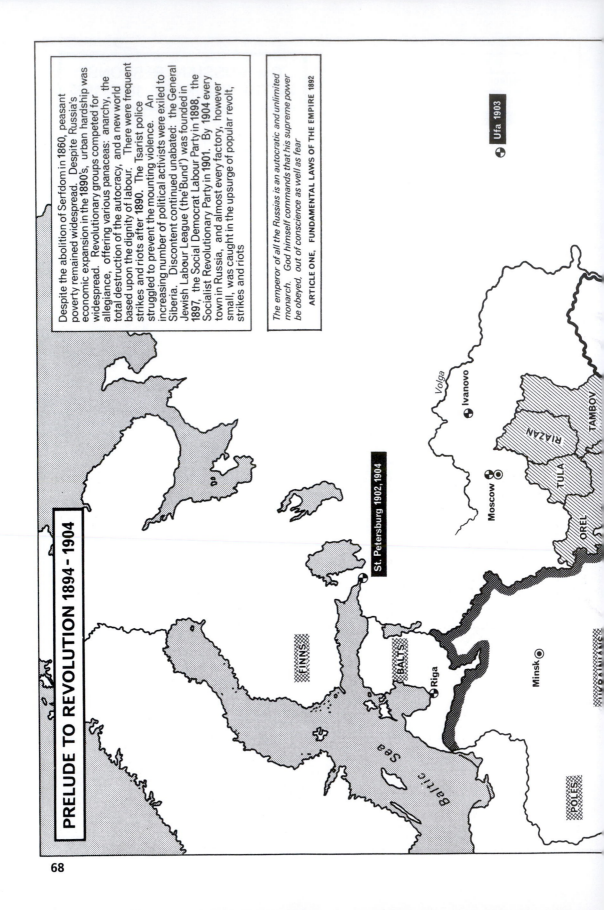

PRELUDE TO REVOLUTION 1894 – 1904

Despite the abolition of Serfdom in 1860, peasant poverty remained widespread. Despite Russia's economic expansion in the 1890's, urban hardship was widespread. Revolutionary groups competed for allegiance, offering various panaceas: anarchy, the total destruction of the autocracy, and a new world based upon the dignity of labour. There were frequent strikes and riots after 1890. The Tsarist police struggled to prevent the mounting violence. An increasing number of political activists were exiled to Siberia. Discontent continued unabated: the General Jewish Labour League (the 'Bund') was founded in 1897, the Social Democrat Labour Party in 1898, the Socialist Revolutionary Party in 1901. By 1904 every town in Russia, and almost every factory, however small, was caught in the upsurge of popular revolt, strikes and riots

The emperor of all the Russias is an autocratic and unlimited monarch. God himself commands that his supreme power be obeyed, out of conscience as well as fear
ARTICLE ONE, FUNDAMENTAL LAWS OF THE EMPIRE 1892

Ufa 1903

Volga

Ivanovo

TAMBOV

RIAZAN

TULA

Moscow

OREL

St. Petersburg 1902, 1904

Baltic Sea

FINNS

BALTS

Riga

Minsk

UKRAINIANS

POLES

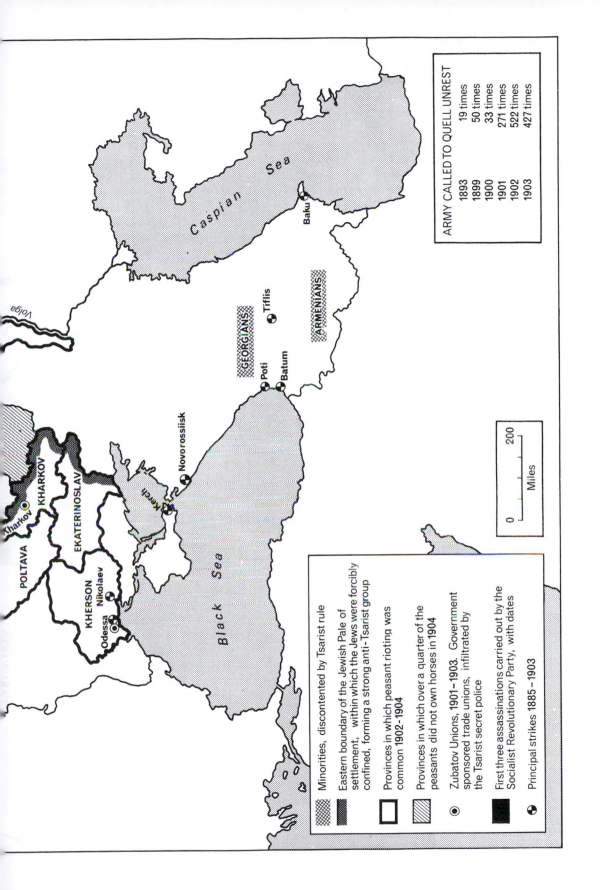

ARMY CALLED TO QUELL UNREST

1893	19 times
1899	50 times
1900	33 times
1901	271 times
1902	522 times
1903	427 times

Caspian Sea

Baku

Volga

Tiflis

GEORGIANS

ARMENIANS

Poti

Batum

Novorossiisk

Kerch

Black Sea

Kharkov

KHARKOV

POLTAVA

EKATERINOSLAV

KHERSON

Nikolaev

Odessa

Miles

0   200

Minorities, discontented by Tsarist rule

Eastern boundary of the Jewish Pale of settlement, within which the Jews were forcibly confined, forming a strong anti-Tsarist group

Provinces in which peasant rioting was common 1902–1904

Provinces in which over a quarter of the peasants did not own horses in 1904

Zubatov Unions, 1901–1903. Government sponsored trade unions, infiltrated by the Tsarist secret police

First three assassinations carried out by the Socialist Revolutionary Party, with dates

Principal strikes 1885–1903

THE JEWS AND THEIR ENEMIES 1648–1917

1903
1906 △ St. Petersburg

Tsarskoye Selo △ 1905

1891. 2,000 Jews deport
many of them in chains

Baltic Sea

Dusiata

Mogilev

Minsk

Starodub

Berlin △
1911

Bialystok

Gomel

Xanten

Sedlits

GERMANY

Lodz

Brest ·
Litovsk

Konotop
Nezhin

Czestochowa

Kiev

Zhitomir

Pereyaslavl

Sme

Elizavetgrad

Balta

Tisza-
Eszlar

Ananay

Nikolaevka

AUSTRIA - HUNGARY

Kishinev

Odessa

RUMANIA

BULGARIA

//// Area in which the Ukrainian peasantry,
led by Bogdan Khmelnitski, massacred
over 100,000 Jews 1648–1656

☐ The Pale of Settlement inside Russia, to
which Russian Jews were confined by law
1815–1917. Of Russia's 5 million Jews
in 1880, only 300,000 had managed to
live outside, mostly illegally

⊙ Principal mob attacks, or "pogroms",
against Jews, 1871–1906

✪ Ritual murder charges, in Russia and
elsewhere, in which Jews were accused
of using the blood of Christian children
to mix with their Passover bread. These
charges led to harsh mob violence
against the Jews

△ Publishing centres before 1917 of the anti-
semitic forgery, "Protocols of Zion", which
claimed to be the Jewish plan for world
domination

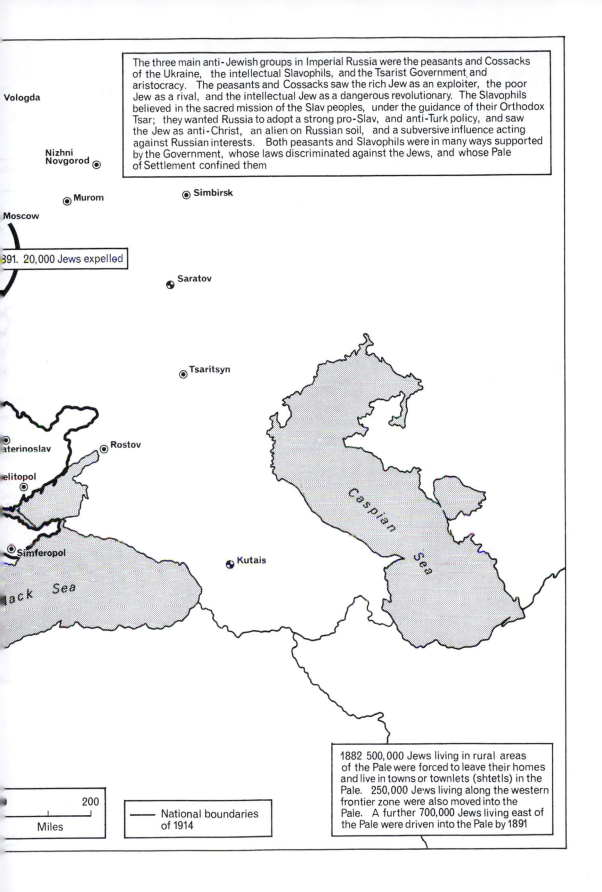

Vologda

The three main anti-Jewish groups in Imperial Russia were the peasants and Cossacks of the Ukraine, the intellectual Slavophils, and the Tsarist Government, and aristocracy. The peasants and Cossacks saw the rich Jew as an exploiter, the poor Jew as a rival, and the intellectual Jew as a dangerous revolutionary. The Slavophils believed in the sacred mission of the Slav peoples, under the guidance of their Orthodox Tsar; they wanted Russia to adopt a strong pro-Slav, and anti-Turk policy, and saw the Jew as anti-Christ, an alien on Russian soil, and a subversive influence acting against Russian interests. Both peasants and Slavophils were in many ways supported by the Government, whose laws discriminated against the Jews, and whose Pale of Settlement confined them

Nizhni
Novgorod ⊙

⊙ Murom   ⊙ Simbirsk

Moscow

891. 20,000 Jews expelled

⊙ Saratov

⊙ Tsaritsyn

aterinoslav   ⊙ Rostov

elitopol
⊙

Caspian Sea

Simferopol   ⊙ Kutais

ack Sea

1882 500,000 Jews living in rural areas of the Pale were forced to leave their homes and live in towns or townlets (shtetls) in the Pale. 250,000 Jews living along the western frontier zone were also moved into the Pale. A further 700,000 Jews living east of the Pale were driven into the Pale by 1891

200

Miles

—— National boundaries of 1914

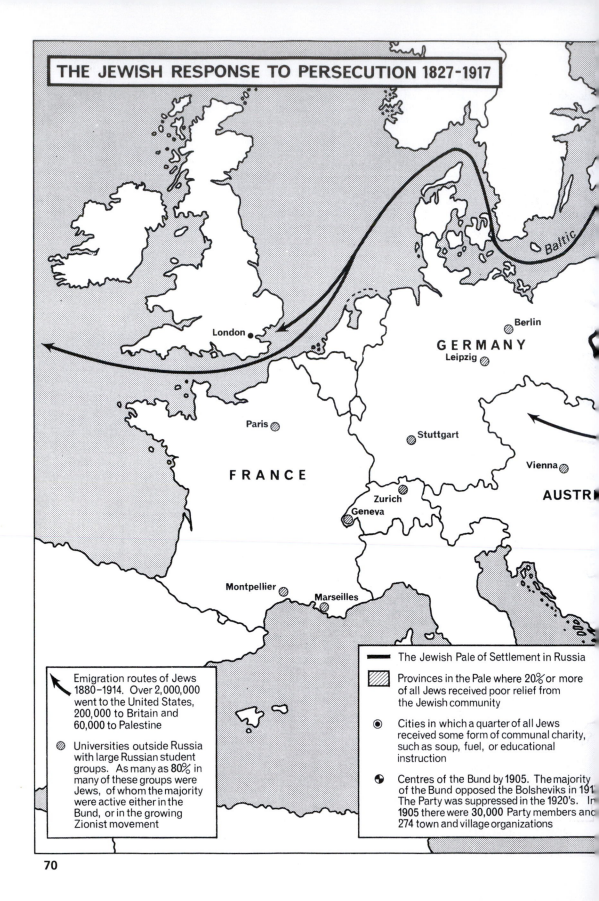

THE JEWISH RESPONSE TO PERSECUTION 1827-1917

Berlin

GERMANY

Leipzig

Baltic

London

Paris

Stuttgart

Vienna

Zurich
Geneva

AUSTRI

FRANCE

Montpellier

Marseilles

Emigration routes of Jews 1880–1914. Over 2,000,000 went to the United States, 200,000 to Britain and 60,000 to Palestine

Universities outside Russia with large Russian student groups. As many as 80% in many of these groups were Jews, of whom the majority were active either in the Bund, or in the growing Zionist movement

The Jewish Pale of Settlement in Russia

Provinces in the Pale where 20% or more of all Jews received poor relief from the Jewish community

Cities in which a quarter of all Jews received some form of communal charity, such as soup, fuel, or educational instruction

Centres of the Bund by 1905. The majority of the Bund opposed the Bolsheviks in 191 The Party was suppressed in the 1920's. In 1905 there were 30,000 Party members and 274 town and village organizations

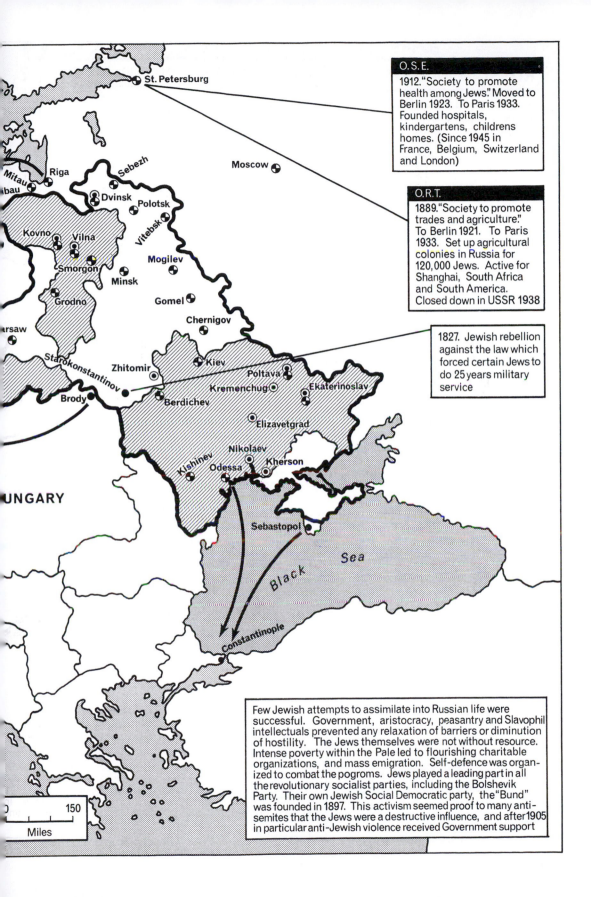

O.S.E.

1912. "Society to promote health among Jews." Moved to Berlin 1923. To Paris 1933. Founded hospitals, kindergartens, childrens homes. (Since 1945 in France, Belgium, Switzerland and London)

O.R.T.

1889. "Society to promote trades and agriculture." To Berlin 1921. To Paris 1933. Set up agricultural colonies in Russia for 120,000 Jews. Active for Shanghai, South Africa and South America. Closed down in USSR 1938

1827. Jewish rebellion against the law which forced certain Jews to do 25 years military service

St. Petersburg

Moscow

Riga
Mitau
Libau
Sebezh
Dvinsk
Polotsk
Kovno
Vilna
Vitebsk
Smorgon
Minsk
Mogilev
Grodno
Gomel
Starokonstantinov
Zhitomir
Chernigov
Brody
Kiev
Berdichev
Poltava
Kremenchug
Ekaterinoslav
Elizavetgrad
Kishinev
Nikolaev
Odessa
Kherson
Sebastopol

arsaw

UNGARY

Black Sea

Constantinople

Few Jewish attempts to assimilate into Russian life were successful. Government, aristocracy, peasantry and Slavophil intellectuals prevented any relaxation of barriers or diminution of hostility. The Jews themselves were not without resource. Intense poverty within the Pale led to flourishing charitable organizations, and mass emigration. Self-defence was organized to combat the pogroms. Jews played a leading part in all the revolutionary socialist parties, including the Bolshevik Party. Their own Jewish Social Democratic party, the "Bund" was founded in 1897. This activism seemed proof to many anti-semites that the Jews were a destructive influence, and after 1905 in particular anti-Jewish violence received Government support

150

Miles

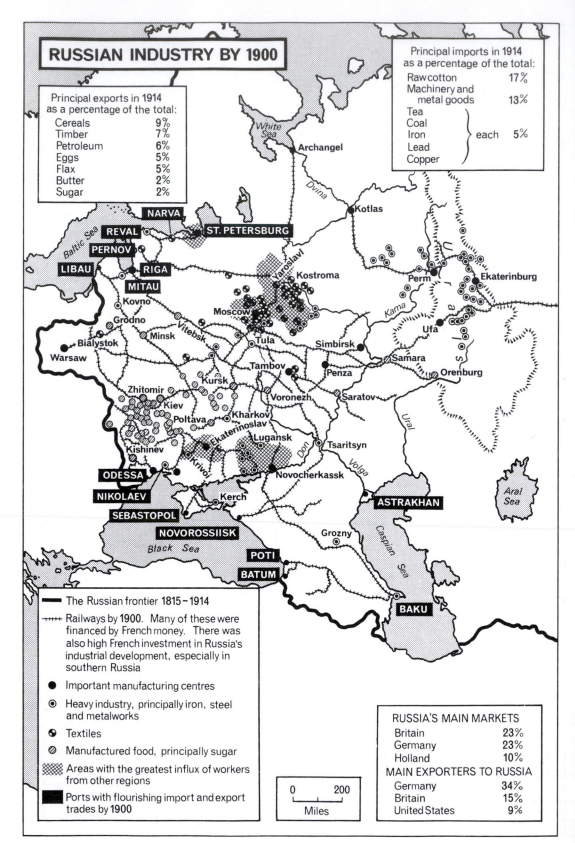

RUSSIAN INDUSTRY BY 1900

Principal exports in 1914
as a percentage of the total:

Cereals	9%
Timber	7%
Petroleum	6%
Eggs	5%
Flax	5%
Butter	2%
Sugar	2%

Principal imports in 1914
as a percentage of the total:

Raw cotton		17%
Machinery and metal goods		13%
Tea		
Coal		
Iron	each	5%
Lead		
Copper		

White Sea

Archangel

Dvina

Kotlas

NARVA

REVAL

PERNOV

ST. PETERSBURG

Baltic Sea

LIBAU

RIGA

MITAU

Kovno

Yaroslavl

Kostroma

Perm

Ekaterinburg

Grodno

Vitebsk

Moscow

Kama

Minsk

Tula

Ufa

Warsaw

Bialystok

Simbirsk

Samara

Orenburg

Zhitomir

Kursk

Tambov

Penza

Kiev

Voronezh

Saratov

Poltava

Kharkov

Ural

Kishinev

Ekaterinoslav

Lugansk

Krivoi

Don

Tsaritsyn

Aral Sea

ODESSA

Novocherkassk

Volga

NIKOLAEV

Kerch

SEBASTOPOL

ASTRAKHAN

NOVOROSSIISK

Black Sea

Grozny

Caspian Sea

POTI

BATUM

BAKU

— The Russian frontier 1815–1914

++++ Railways by 1900. Many of these were
financed by French money. There was
also high French investment in Russia's
industrial development, especially in
southern Russia

● Important manufacturing centres

⊙ Heavy industry, principally iron, steel
and metalworks

✪ Textiles

⊘ Manufactured food, principally sugar

▒ Areas with the greatest influx of workers
from other regions

■ Ports with flourishing import and export
trades by 1900

0	200

Miles

RUSSIA'S MAIN MARKETS

Britain	23%
Germany	23%
Holland	10%

MAIN EXPORTERS TO RUSSIA

Germany	34%
Britain	15%
United States	9%

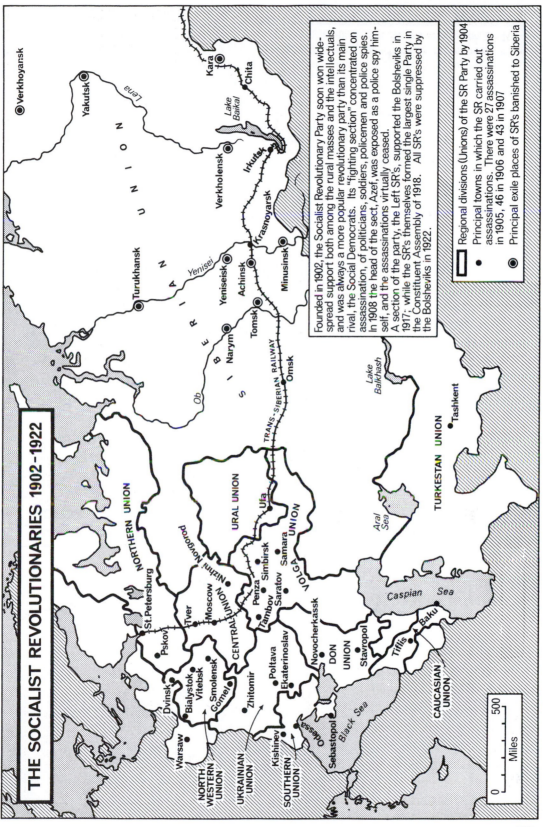

THE SOCIALIST REVOLUTIONARIES 1902-1922

Founded in 1902, the Socialist Revolutionary Party soon won widespread support both among the rural masses and the intellectuals, and was always a more popular revolutionary party than its main rival, the Social Democrats. Its "fighting section" concentrated on assassination, of politicians, soldiers, policemen and police spies. In 1908 the head of the sect, Azef, was exposed as a police spy himself, and the assassinations virtually ceased.
A section of the party, the Left SR's, supported the Bolsheviks in 1917; while the SR's themselves formed the largest single Party in the Constituent Assembly of 1918. All SR's were suppressed by the Bolsheviks in 1922.

□ Regional divisions (Unions) of the SR Party by 1904

● Principal towns in which the SR carried out assassinations. There were 27 assassinations in 1905, 46 in 1906 and 43 in 1907

◉ Principal exile places of SR's banished to Siberia

UNION

SIBERIA

Verkhoyansk
Yakutsk
Lena
Kara
Chita
Lake Baikal
Verkholensk
Irkutsk
Krasnoyarsk
Turukhansk
Yenisei
Yeniseisk
Achinsk
Minusinsk
Narym
Tomsk
TRANS-SIBERIAN RAILWAY
Ob
Omsk

Lake Balkhash

TURKESTAN UNION
Tashkent

Aral Sea

Caspian Sea

NORTHERN UNION
Novgorod
Nizhni Novgorod
URAL UNION
Ufa
St. Petersburg
Tver
Moscow
Pskov
CENTRAL UNION
Penza
Tambov
Simbirsk
Saratov
Samara
VOLGA UNION

Dvinsk
Bialystok
Vitebsk
Smolensk
Gomel
Zhitomir
Poltava
Ekaterinoslav
Novocherkassk
DON UNION
Stavropol

Warsaw
NORTH WESTERN UNION
UKRAINIAN UNION
Kishinev
SOUTHERN UNION
Odessa
Sebastopol
Black Sea

Tiflis
Baku
CAUCASIAN UNION

0   500
Miles

72

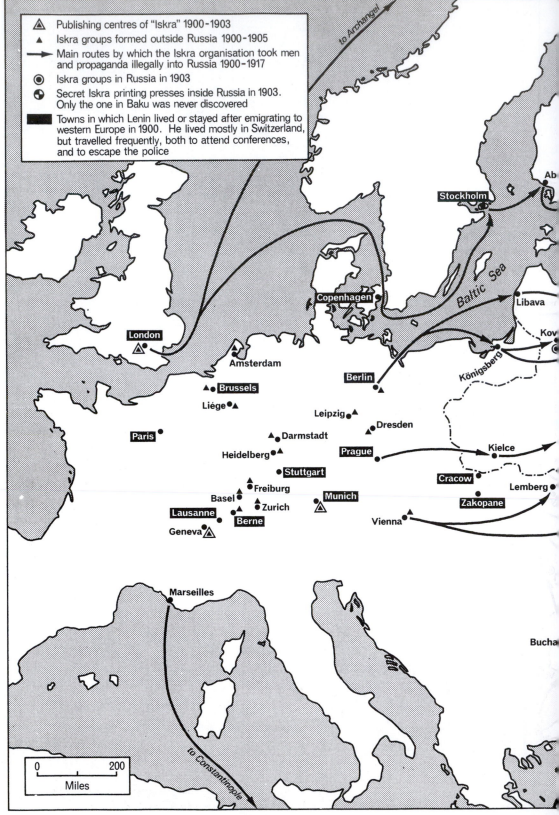

73

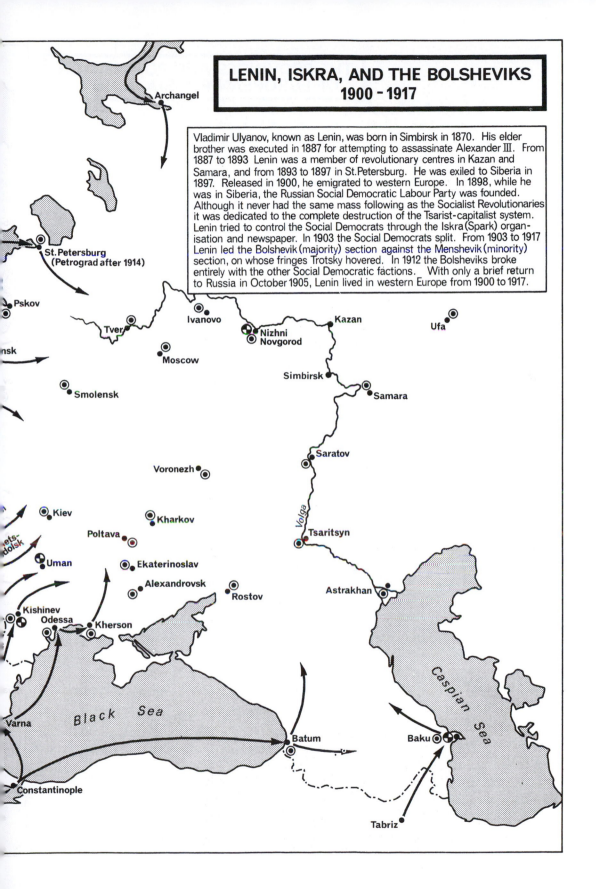

LENIN, ISKRA, AND THE BOLSHEVIKS
1900 - 1917

Vladimir Ulyanov, known as Lenin, was born in Simbirsk in 1870. His elder brother was executed in 1887 for attempting to assassinate Alexander III. From 1887 to 1893 Lenin was a member of revolutionary centres in Kazan and Samara, and from 1893 to 1897 in St.Petersburg. He was exiled to Siberia in 1897. Released in 1900, he emigrated to western Europe. In 1898, while he was in Siberia, the Russian Social Democratic Labour Party was founded. Although it never had the same mass following as the Socialist Revolutionaries it was dedicated to the complete destruction of the Tsarist-capitalist system. Lenin tried to control the Social Democrats through the Iskra (Spark) organisation and newspaper. In 1903 the Social Democrats split. From 1903 to 1917 Lenin led the Bolshevik (majority) section against the Menshevik (minority) section, on whose fringes Trotsky hovered. In 1912 the Bolsheviks broke entirely with the other Social Democratic factions. With only a brief return to Russia in October 1905, Lenin lived in western Europe from 1900 to 1917.

Archangel

St.Petersburg
(Petrograd after 1914)

Pskov

nsk

Tver

Ivanovo

Nizhni
Novgorod

Kazan

Ufa

Moscow

Simbirsk

Smolensk

Samara

Saratov

Voronezh

Volga

Kiev

Kharkov

Poltava

Tsaritsyn

nets-
dolsk

Uman

Ekaterinoslav

Alexandrovsk

Rostov

Astrakhan

Kishinev
Odessa

Kherson

Caspian Sea

Varna

Black Sea

Batum

Baku

Constantinople

Tabriz

THE PROVINCES AND POPULATION OF EUROPEAN RUSSIA IN 1900

NORWAY

SWEDEN

GERMANY

White Sea

ARCHANGEL

FINLAND

OLONETS

VOLOGDA

PERM

Baltic Sea

ESTLAND

ST PETERSBURG

NOVGOROD

KOSTROMA

VIATKA

KURLAND

LIVLAND

PSKOV

TVER

YAROSLAVL

KOVNO

VITEBSK

VLADIMIR

NIZHNI NOVGOROD

KAZAN

UFA

VILNA

MOSCOW

GRODNO

MOGILEV

SMOLENSK

KALUGA

RIAZAN

SIMBIRSK

POLISH PROVINCES

MINSK

TULA

PENZA

ORENBURG

OREL

TAMBOV

SAMARA

VOLHYNIA

CHERNIGOV

KURSK

SARATOV

AUSTRIA-HUNGARY

KIEV

POLTAVA

VORONEZH

PODOLIA

BESSARABIA

KHERSON

EKATERINOSLAV

DON

ASTRAKHAN

RUMANIA

TAURIDA

KUBAN

STAVROPOL

Caspian Sea

TEREK

Black Sea

TURKEY

TRANS-CAUCASIAN PROVINCES

PERSIA

The first official Russian census was held in 1897. The total population was just over 129 million - nearly as large as the combined populations of Britain, France, and Germany. Over 80% of all Russians were peasants. Finland was an autonomous Duchy, and, like Poland, was subdivided into Provinces

MAIN NATIONAL & ETHNIC GROUPS IN EUROPEAN RUSSIA IN 1900	
Russians	55 million
Ukrainians	22 million
Poles	8 million
White Russians	6 million
Jews	5 million
Balts	4 million
Caucasians	3 million
Germans	2 million

THE 1905 REVOLUTION IN THE COUNTRYSIDE

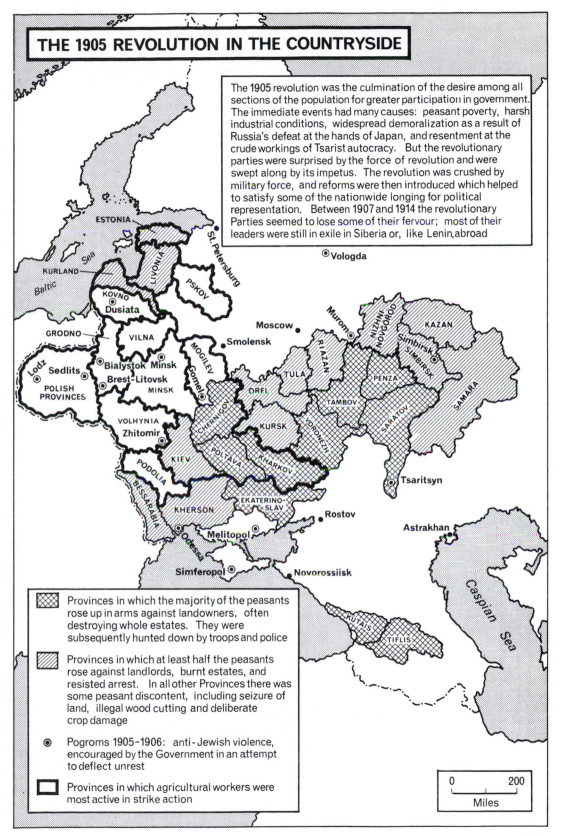

The 1905 revolution was the culmination of the desire among all sections of the population for greater participation in government. The immediate events had many causes: peasant poverty, harsh industrial conditions, widespread demoralization as a result of Russia's defeat at the hands of Japan, and resentment at the crude workings of Tsarist autocracy. But the revolutionary parties were surprised by the force of revolution and were swept along by its impetus. The revolution was crushed by military force, and reforms were then introduced which helped to satisfy some of the nationwide longing for political representation. Between 1907 and 1914 the revolutionary Parties seemed to lose some of their fervour; most of their leaders were still in exile in Siberia or, like Lenin, abroad

Provinces in which the majority of the peasants rose up in arms against landowners, often destroying whole estates. They were subsequently hunted down by troops and police

Provinces in which at least half the peasants rose against landlords, burnt estates, and resisted arrest. In all other Provinces there was some peasant discontent, including seizure of land, illegal wood cutting and deliberate crop damage

Pogroms 1905-1906: anti-Jewish violence, encouraged by the Government in an attempt to deflect unrest

Provinces in which agricultural workers were most active in strike action

0   200
Miles

THE 1905 REVOLUTION IN THE TOWNS

BLOODY SUNDAY : ST. PETERSBURG

200,000 people gathered at the Winter Palace on 9 January 1905. Unarmed, they wished to appeal to Tsar Nicholas II for better working conditions and an end to the war with Japan. Their main plea was for elections based upon universal suffrage. It was a Sunday. Many carried ikons. But the Tsar had left the city, and troops fired on the crowd. As many as 500 people were killed, and over 3,000 wounded

Russian State Expenditure 1903 - 13 (in million roubles)	
The war with Japan	3,016
Railways	886
Defence	455
Bad harvests	403
Redemption of loans before due date	199
Ports	24
Military expeditions (China and Persia)	20

- Principal strike centres, 1905-1906, encouraged by all the revolutionary Parties. By December 1905 every town in Russia had suffered from industrial unrest

- Revolutionary outbreaks in the Army and the Fleet; although these were widespread, the Army remained sufficiently loyal to the Tsar to crush the revolution by the end of 1906

- National groups who wanted a greater degree of autonomy and national recognition, and were particularly active in revolutionary activity. At this time the Ukrainians, for example, were not allowed a single newspaper in their own language

- Uprisings in December 1905, suppressed by armed force

THE BATTLESHIP POTEMKIN

In the late summer of 1905 the crew of the Potemkin seized control of the ship, and for some months terrorized the Black Sea ports, even bombarding Odessa. They finally sought refuge in Rumania, where the ship was interned

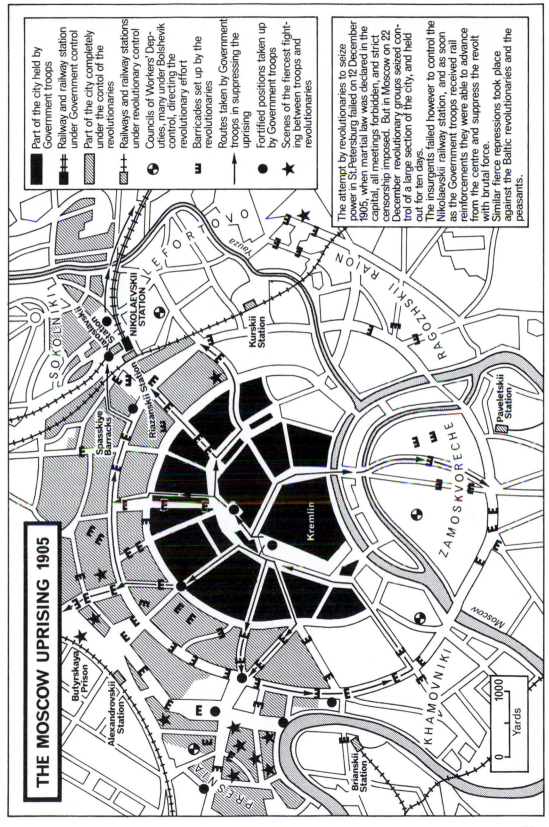

THE MOSCOW UPRISING 1905

Legend

- **Part of the city held by Government troops**
- **Railway and railway station under Government control**
- **Part of the city completely under the control of the revolutionaries**
- **Railways and railway stations under revolutionary control**
- **Councils of Workers' Deputies, many under Bolshevik control, directing the revolutionary effort**
- **Barricades set up by the revolutionaries**
- **Routes taken by Government troops in suppressing the uprising**
- **Fortified positions taken up by Government troops**
- **Scenes of the fiercest fighting between troops and revolutionaries**

The attempt by revolutionaries to seize power in St.Petersburg failed on 12 December 1905, when martial law was declared in the capital, all meetings forbidden, and strict censorship imposed. But in Moscow on 22 December revolutionary groups seized control of a large section of the city, and held out for ten days.

The insurgents failed however to control the Nikolaevskii railway station, and as soon as the Government troops received rail reinforcements they were able to advance from the centre and suppress the revolt with brutal force.

Similar fierce repressions took place against the Baltic revolutionaries and the peasants.

Map labels: LEFORTOVO · Yauza · ROGOZHSKII RAION · SOKOLNIKI · NIKOLAEVSKII STATION · Iaroslavskii Station · Kurskii Station · Riazanskii Station · Spasskiye Barracks · Kremlin · ZAMOSKVORECHE · Paveletskii Station · KHAMOVNIKI · Moscow · Butyrskaya Prison · Alexandrovskii Station · PRESNIA · Brianskii Station · Yards · 0 1000

RUSSIA AND THE BALKANS 1876-1885

0   100
Miles

Russia wanted to drive the Turk from Europe and dominate the
Balkans.   Britain supported Russian protests against Turkish
atrocities against the Bulgarians in 1875, which led Russia to
attack Turkey. After defeating the Turks at Plevna in 1876 Russia
tried to set up a large independent Bulgaria, but Britain and
Austria-Hungary challenged Russia's aspirations, and under
German mediation Russia agreed to the creation of a much
smaller Bulgaria. Austria advanced her own Balkan interests
by occupying the former Turkish province of Bosnia, which she
formally annexed in 1908, and entering Novi Pazar.

RUSSIA

AUSTRIA-HUNGARY

R U M A N I A

Bucharest

Constanza

BOSNIA
Sarajevo

Belgrade

S E R B I A

Danube

Plevna

Silistria

Varna

B U L G A R I A

NOVI PAZAR

Nish

Tirnovo

Cattaro

Sofia

Burgas

EAST RUMELIA

MONTENEGRO

Adriatic Sea

Skopje

Midia

Adrianople

Constantinople

MACEDONIA

Kavalla

Rodosto

San
Stephano

Black Sea

Dedeagatch

Chanak

TURKEY –

IN – ASIA

Aegean Sea

G R E E C E

Athens

- - - —   The boundary of Turkey-in-Europe 1876

Russian proposal for an independent "Big
Bulgaria", agreed to by the Turks at the
Treaty of San Stephano 1878

Bulgaria, autonomous, not independent,
as allowed by Britain and Germany by
the Treaty of Berlin 1878

Turkish territory added to Serbia, Rumania
and Montenegro (who each gained their
independence from Turkey) by the Treaty of
Berlin 1878; and to Greece in 1881

Occupied by Austria-Hungary in 1878

Added to Bulgaria in 1885, when Bulgaria
became fully independent of Turkey

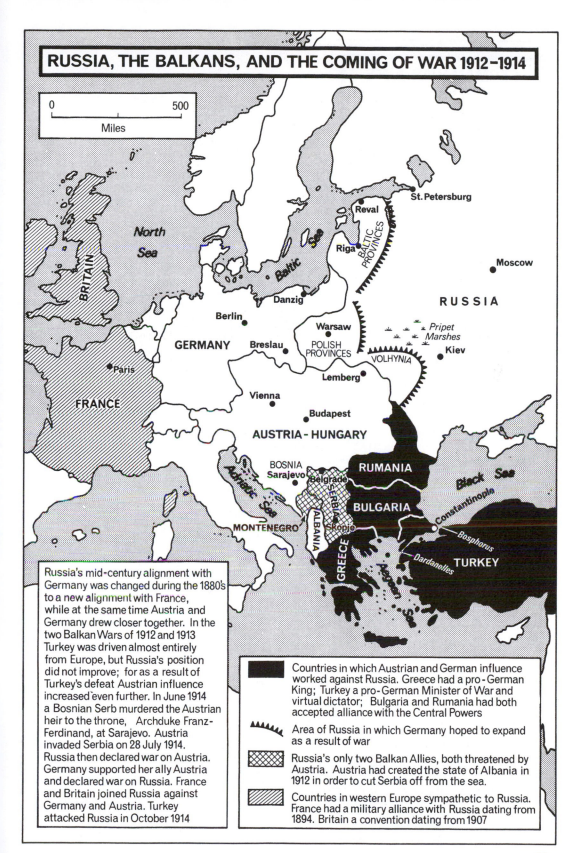

RUSSIA, THE BALKANS, AND THE COMING OF WAR 1912-1914

0 _____ 500
Miles

St. Petersburg

Reval

North Sea

Riga

BALTIC PROVINCES

Moscow

BRITAIN

Baltic

Danzig

RUSSIA

Berlin

Warsaw

Pripet Marshes

GERMANY

Breslau

POLISH PROVINCES

Kiev

VOLHYNIA

Paris

Lemberg

FRANCE

Vienna

Budapest

AUSTRIA - HUNGARY

BOSNIA
Sarajevo

RUMANIA

Adriatic Sea

Belgrade

SERBIA

Black Sea

BULGARIA

MONTENEGRO

ALBANIA

Skopje

Constantinople

Bosphorus

GREECE

Dardanelles

TURKEY

Russia's mid-century alignment with Germany was changed during the 1880's to a new alignment with France, while at the same time Austria and Germany drew closer together. In the two Balkan Wars of 1912 and 1913 Turkey was driven almost entirely from Europe, but Russia's position did not improve; for as a result of Turkey's defeat Austrian influence increased even further. In June 1914 a Bosnian Serb murdered the Austrian heir to the throne, Archduke Franz-Ferdinand, at Sarajevo. Austria invaded Serbia on 28 July 1914. Russia then declared war on Austria. Germany supported her ally Austria and declared war on Russia. France and Britain joined Russia against Germany and Austria. Turkey attacked Russia in October 1914

Countries in which Austrian and German influence worked against Russia. Greece had a pro-German King; Turkey a pro-German Minister of War and virtual dictator; Bulgaria and Rumania had both accepted alliance with the Central Powers

Area of Russia in which Germany hoped to expand as a result of war

Russia's only two Balkan Allies, both threatened by Austria. Austria had created the state of Albania in 1912 in order to cut Serbia off from the sea.

Countries in western Europe sympathetic to Russia. France had a military alliance with Russia dating from 1894. Britain a convention dating from 1907

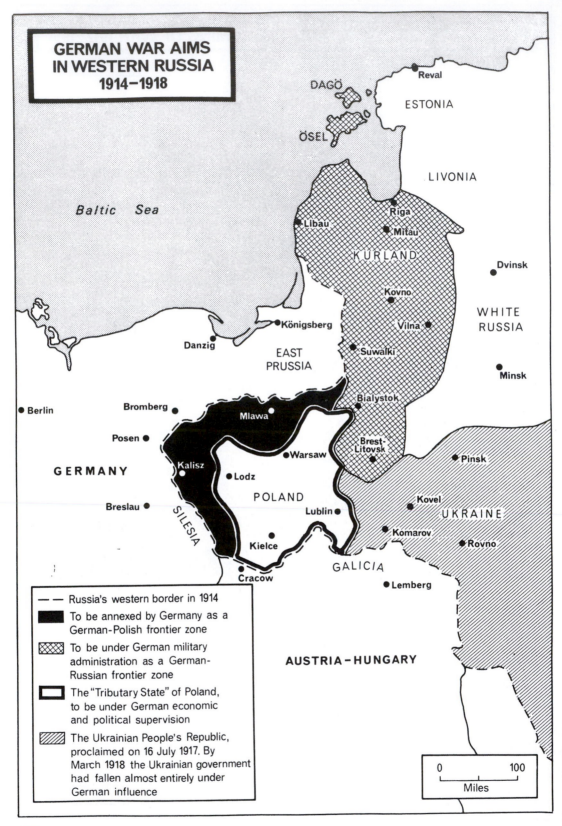

GERMAN WAR AIMS IN WESTERN RUSSIA 1914–1918

Baltic Sea

DAGÖ

ÖSEL

Reval

ESTONIA

LIVONIA

Riga

Libau

Mitau

KURLAND

Dvinsk

Kovno

Königsberg

Vilna

WHITE RUSSIA

Danzig

EAST PRUSSIA

Suwalki

Minsk

Bialystok

Berlin

Bromberg

Mlawa

Brest-Litovsk

Pinsk

Posen

Warsaw

GERMANY

Kalisz

Lodz

Kovel

POLAND

UKRAINE

Breslau

Lublin

SILESIA

Komarov

Rovno

Kielce

GALICIA

Cracow

Lemberg

AUSTRIA–HUNGARY

— — Russia's western border in 1914

To be annexed by Germany as a German-Polish frontier zone

To be under German military administration as a German-Russian frontier zone

The "Tributary State" of Poland, to be under German economic and political supervision

The Ukrainian People's Republic, proclaimed on 16 July 1917. By March 1918 the Ukrainian government had fallen almost entirely under German influence

0   100
Miles

THE EASTERN FRONT 1914

Baltic Sea

GERMANY

Danzig •
• Elbing
• Königsberg
Gumbinnen ⊙
⊕ Vilkoviski

E A S T   P R U S S I A

Vistula

Masurian Lakes ⊙
• Suvalki
• Augustow

• Tannenberg

• Mlawa

• Bialystok

R U S S I A

Plotsk •

• Kutno

Bug

• Warsaw
• Brest–Litovsk

• Kalisz
⊙ Lodz

Vistula

Piotrkow •

• Kielce
• Lublin

S I L E S I A

Novo •
Radomsk
⊙ Krasnik
⊙ Komarov

• Czestochowa

G A L I C I A

Cracow •

• Tarnow

Przemysl ⊙
Lemberg •

Gorlice •

C a r p a t h i a n s

**AUSTRIA-
HUNGARY**

Legend

▨ Russian advance into East Prussia 4-23 August. Between August 26 and September 13 they were defeated at Tannenberg and the Masurian Lakes, and driven back into Russia

■ Russian territory conquered by Germany September 28 - December 31. At the Battle of Lodz, in November, the Germans prevented a Russian advance into Silesia

⇨ Austrian advances into Russia

◀ Russian counter-attacks into Austria

▨ Conquered by Russia from Austria

— The front line on 31 December 1914

| 0 | 50 |
Miles

⊙ Russian victories
⊕ German victories

81

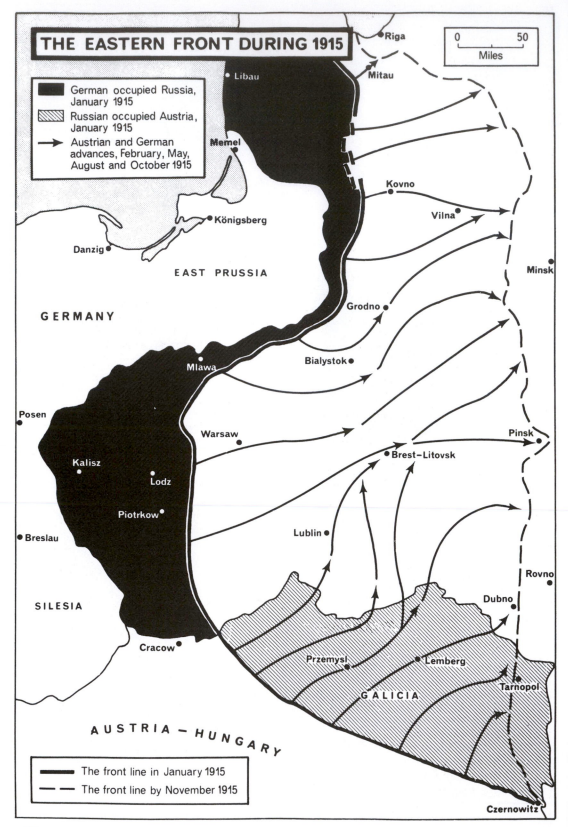

THE EASTERN FRONT DURING 1915

0   50
Miles

■ German occupied Russia, January 1915
▨ Russian occupied Austria, January 1915
→ Austrian and German advances, February, May, August and October 1915

Riga
Libau
Mitau
Memel
Kovno
Vilna
Minsk
Königsberg
Danzig
EAST PRUSSIA
Grodno
GERMANY
Mlawa
Bialystok
Posen
Warsaw
Pinsk
Kalisz
Lodz
Brest–Litovsk
Piotrkow
Breslau
Lublin
Rovno
SILESIA
Dubno
Cracow
Przemysl
Lemberg
Tarnopol
GALICIA
AUSTRIA – HUNGARY
Czernowitz

▬▬▬ The front line in January 1915
- - - The front line by November 1915

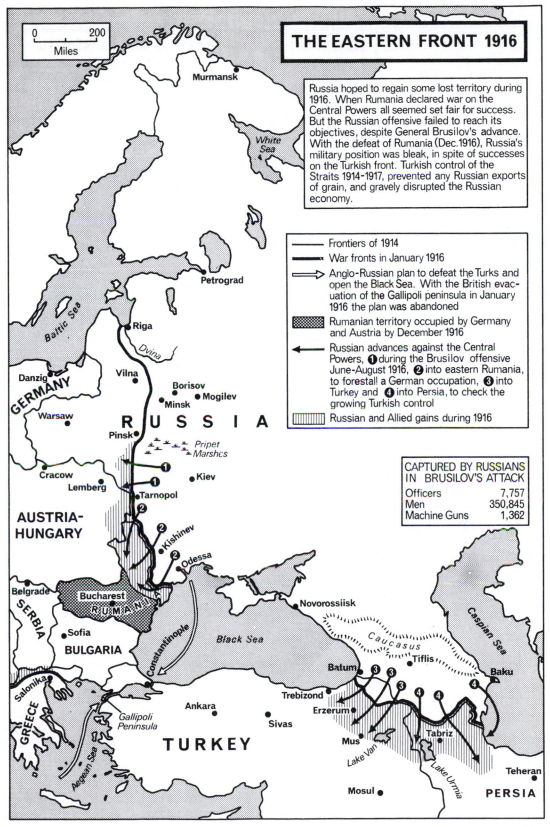

THE EASTERN FRONT 1916

Russia hoped to regain some lost territory during 1916. When Rumania declared war on the Central Powers all seemed set fair for success. But the Russian offensive failed to reach its objectives, despite General Brusilov's advance. With the defeat of Rumania (Dec.1916), Russia's military position was bleak, in spite of successes on the Turkish front. Turkish control of the Straits 1914-1917, prevented any Russian exports of grain, and gravely disrupted the Russian economy.

Frontiers of 1914

War fronts in January 1916

Anglo-Russian plan to defeat the Turks and open the Black Sea. With the British evacuation of the Gallipoli peninsula in January 1916 the plan was abandoned

Rumanian territory occupied by Germany and Austria by December 1916

Russian advances against the Central Powers, **1** during the Brusilov offensive June-August 1916, **2** into eastern Rumania, to forestall a German occupation, **3** into Turkey and **4** into Persia, to check the growing Turkish control

Russian and Allied gains during 1916

CAPTURED BY RUSSIANS IN BRUSILOV'S ATTACK	
Officers	7,757
Men	350,845
Machine Guns	1,362

0 — 200 Miles

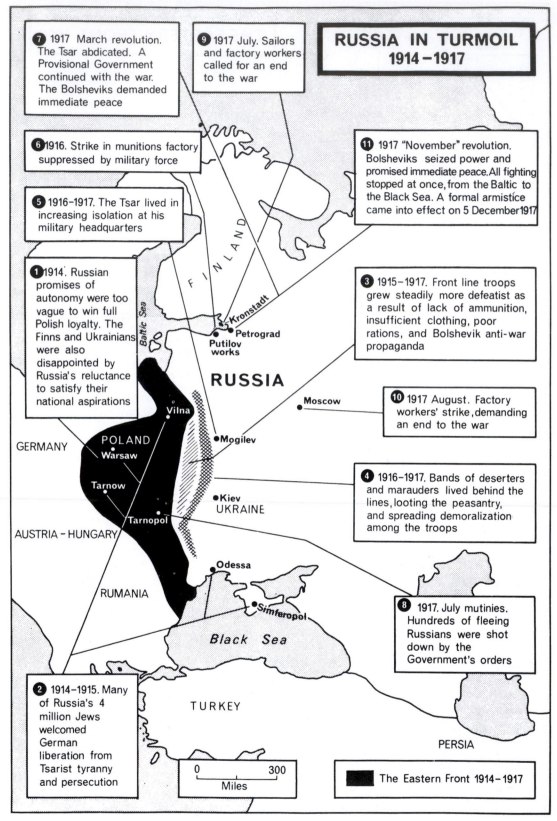

RUSSIA IN TURMOIL 1914–1917

7 1917 March revolution. The Tsar abdicated. A Provisional Government continued with the war. The Bolsheviks demanded immediate peace

9 1917 July. Sailors and factory workers called for an end to the war

6 1916. Strike in munitions factory suppressed by military force

5 1916–1917. The Tsar lived in increasing isolation at his military headquarters

11 1917 "November" revolution. Bolsheviks seized power and promised immediate peace. All fighting stopped at once, from the Baltic to the Black Sea. A formal armistice came into effect on 5 December 1917

1 1914. Russian promises of autonomy were too vague to win full Polish loyalty. The Finns and Ukrainians were also disappointed by Russia's reluctance to satisfy their national aspirations

3 1915–1917. Front line troops grew steadily more defeatist as a result of lack of ammunition, insufficient clothing, poor rations, and Bolshevik anti-war propaganda

10 1917 August. Factory workers' strike, demanding an end to the war

4 1916–1917. Bands of deserters and marauders lived behind the lines, looting the peasantry, and spreading demoralization among the troops

8 1917. July mutinies. Hundreds of fleeing Russians were shot down by the Government's orders

2 1914–1915. Many of Russia's 4 million Jews welcomed German liberation from Tsarist tyranny and persecution

FINLAND

Baltic Sea

Kronstadt
Petrograd
Putilov works

RUSSIA

Moscow

Mogilev

GERMANY

POLAND
Warsaw

Vilna

Tarnow

Tarnopol

Kiev
UKRAINE

AUSTRIA – HUNGARY

RUMANIA

Odessa

Simferopol

Black Sea

TURKEY

PERSIA

0   300
Miles

■ The Eastern Front 1914–1917

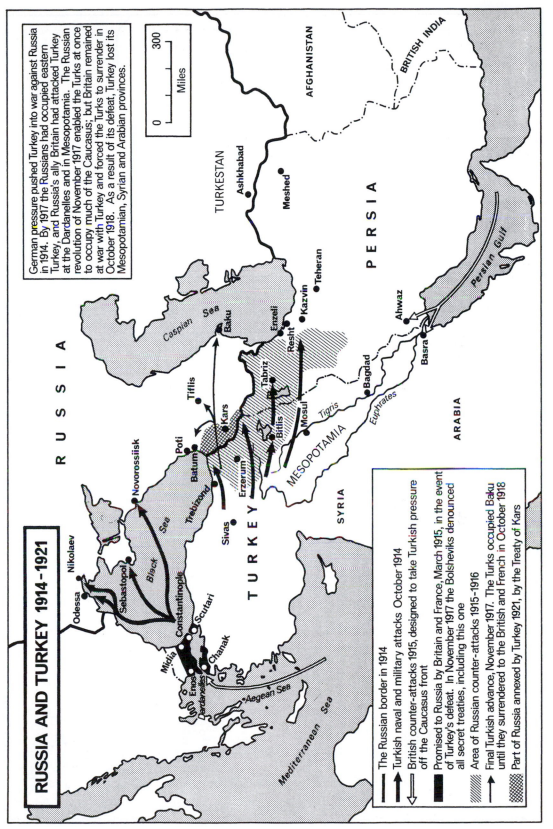

RUSSIA AND TURKEY 1914–1921

German pressure pushed Turkey into war against Russia in 1914. By 1917 the Russians had occupied eastern Turkey, and Russia's ally Britain had attacked Turkey at the Dardanelles and in Mesopotamia. The Russian revolution of November 1917 enabled the Turks at once to occupy much of the Caucasus; but Britain remained at war with Turkey and forced the Turks to surrender in October 1918. As a result of its defeat, Turkey lost its Mesopotamian, Syrian and Arabian provinces.

300

Miles

0

RUSSIA

TURKESTAN

AFGHANISTAN

BRITISH INDIA

Ashkhabad

Meshed

PERSIA

Caspian Sea

Baku

Enzeli

Resht

Kazvin

Teheran

Tabriz

Ahwaz

Persian Gulf

Tiflis

Kars

Mosul

Bagdad

Basra

Bitlis

Tigris

Euphrates

Poti

Batum

Erzerum

MESOPOTAMIA

ARABIA

Novorossiisk

Trebizond

SYRIA

Black Sea

Sivas

Sebastopol

TURKEY

Odessa

Nikolaev

Constantinople

Scutari

Midia

Enos

Chanak

Dardanelles

Aegean Sea

Mediterranean Sea

The Russian border in 1914

Turkish naval and military attacks October 1914

British counter-attacks 1915, designed to take Turkish pressure off the Caucasus front

Promised to Russia by Britain and France, March 1915, in the event of Turkey's defeat. In November 1917 the Bolsheviks denounced all secret treaties, including this one

Area of Russian counter-attacks 1915–1916

Final Turkish advance, November 1917. The Turks occupied Baku until they surrendered to the British and French in October 1918

Part of Russia annexed by Turkey 1921, by the Treaty of Kars

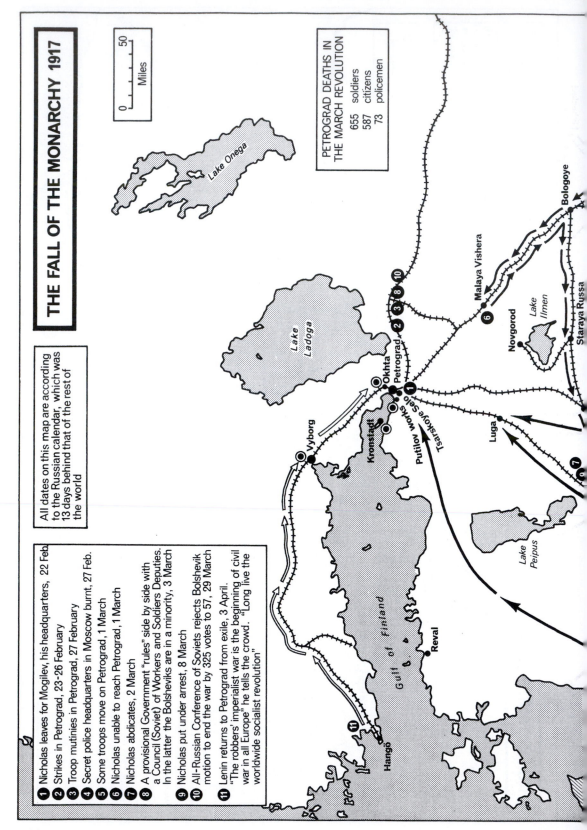

THE FALL OF THE MONARCHY 1917

0 — 50 Miles

Lake Onega

PETROGRAD DEATHS IN
THE MARCH REVOLUTION

655 soldiers
587 citizens
73 policemen

All dates on this map are according
to the Russian calendar, which was
13 days behind that of the rest of
the world

1. Nicholas leaves for Mogilev, his headquarters, 22 Feb.
2. Strikes in Petrograd, 23-26 February
3. Troop mutinies in Petrograd, 27 February
4. Secret police headquarters in Moscow burnt, 27 Feb.
5. Some troops move on Petrograd, 1 March
6. Nicholas unable to reach Petrograd, 1 March
7. Nicholas abdicates, 2 March
8. A provisional Government "rules" side by side with a Council (Soviet) of Workers and Soldiers Deputies. In the latter the Bolsheviks are in a minority, 3 March
9. Nicholas put under arrest, 8 March
10. All-Russian Conference of Soviets rejects Bolshevik motion to end the war by 325 votes to 57, 29 March
11. Lenin returns to Petrograd from exile, 3 April. "The robbers' imperialist war is the beginning of civil war in all Europe" he tells the crowd. "Long live the worldwide socialist revolution"

Lake Ladoga

Okhta
Petrograd
Vyborg
Kronstadt
Putilov works
Tsarskoye Selo

Malaya Vishera
Bologoye
Novgorod
Lake Ilmen
Staraya Russa
Luga

Gulf of Finland

Hangö
Reval
Lake Peipus

86

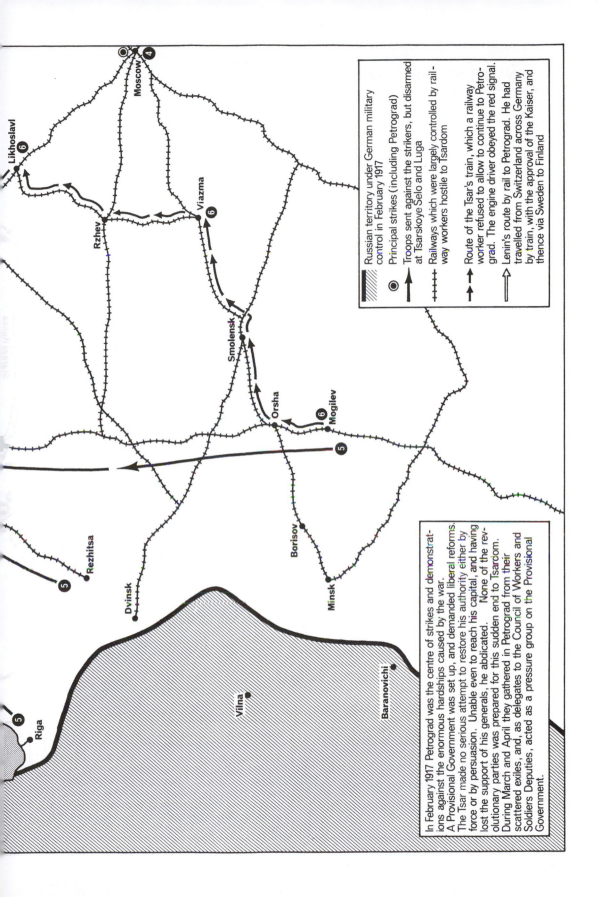

Moscow

Likhoslavl ⑥

Viazma ⑥

Rzhev

Smolensk

Orsha

Mogilev ⑥

⑤

Borisov

Minsk

Rezhitsa ⑤

Dvinsk

⑤

Vilna

Baranovichi

Riga ⑤

— Russian territory under German military control in February 1917

◉ Principal strikes (including Petrograd)

→ Troops sent against the strikers, but disarmed at Tsarskoye Selo and Luga

╫ Railways which were largely controlled by railway workers hostile to Tsardom

↑ Route of the Tsar's train, which a railway worker refused to allow to continue to Petrograd. The engine driver obeyed the red signal.

⇨ Lenin's route by rail to Petrograd. He had travelled from Switzerland across Germany by train, with the approval of the Kaiser, and thence via Sweden to Finland

In February 1917 Petrograd was the centre of strikes and demonstrations against the enormous hardships caused by the war. A Provisional Government was set up, and demanded liberal reforms. The Tsar made no serious attempt to restore his authority either by force or by persuasion. Unable even to reach his capital, and having lost the support of his generals, he abdicated. None of the revolutionary parties was prepared for this sudden end to Tsardom. During March and April they gathered in Petrograd from their scattered exiles, and, as delegates to the Council of Workers and Soldiers Deputies, acted as a pressure group on the Provisional Government.

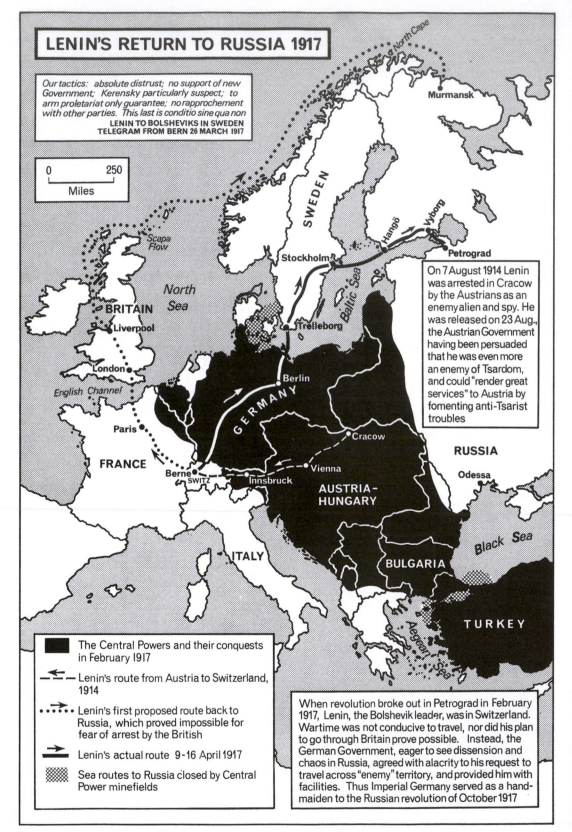

LENIN'S RETURN TO RUSSIA 1917

Our tactics: absolute distrust; no support of new Government; Kerensky particularly suspect; to arm proletariat only guarantee; no rapprochement with other parties. This last is conditio sine qua non
LENIN TO BOLSHEVIKS IN SWEDEN
TELEGRAM FROM BERN 26 MARCH 1917

0   250
Miles

Murmansk

North Cape

SWEDEN

Vyborg

Hangö

Petrograd

Stockholm

North Sea

BRITAIN

Liverpool

Baltic Sea

Trelleborg

London

English Channel

Berlin

GERMANY

Paris

FRANCE

Berne
SWITZ.

Innsbruck

Vienna

Cracow

AUSTRIA-HUNGARY

RUSSIA

Odessa

ITALY

BULGARIA

Black Sea

Aegean Sea

TURKEY

On 7 August 1914 Lenin was arrested in Cracow by the Austrians as an enemy alien and spy. He was released on 23 Aug., the Austrian Government having been persuaded that he was even more an enemy of Tsardom, and could "render great services" to Austria by fomenting anti-Tsarist troubles

■ The Central Powers and their conquests in February 1917

⊢--◄--⊣ Lenin's route from Austria to Switzerland, 1914

••••►•• Lenin's first proposed route back to Russia, which proved impossible for fear of arrest by the British

───► Lenin's actual route 9-16 April 1917

▨ Sea routes to Russia closed by Central Power minefields

When revolution broke out in Petrograd in February 1917, Lenin, the Bolshevik leader, was in Switzerland. Wartime was not conducive to travel, nor did his plan to go through Britain prove possible. Instead, the German Government, eager to see dissension and chaos in Russia, agreed with alacrity to his request to travel across "enemy" territory, and provided him with facilities. Thus Imperial Germany served as a handmaiden to the Russian revolution of October 1917

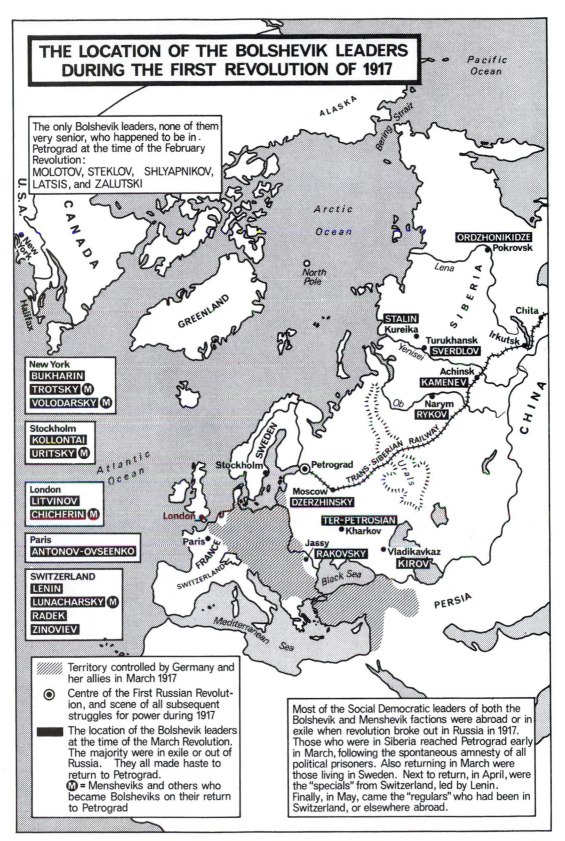

THE LOCATION OF THE BOLSHEVIK LEADERS DURING THE FIRST REVOLUTION OF 1917

The only Bolshevik leaders, none of them very senior, who happened to be in Petrograd at the time of the February Revolution:
MOLOTOV, STEKLOV, SHLYAPNIKOV, LATSIS, and ZALUTSKI

New York
BUKHARIN
TROTSKY Ⓜ
VOLODARSKY Ⓜ

Stockholm
KOLLONTAI
URITSKY Ⓜ

London
LITVINOV
CHICHERIN Ⓜ

Paris
ANTONOV-OVSEENKO

SWITZERLAND
LENIN
LUNACHARSKY Ⓜ
RADEK
ZINOVIEV

ORDZHONIKIDZE
● Pokrovsk

STALIN
Kureika

Turukhansk
SVERDLOV

Achinsk
KAMENEV

Narym
RYKOV

● Chita

Irkutsk

Petrograd

Moscow
DZERZHINSKY

TER-PETROSIAN
● Kharkov

Jassy
RAKOVSKY

● Vladikavkaz
KIROV

////// Territory controlled by Germany and her allies in March 1917

◎ Centre of the First Russian Revolution, and scene of all subsequent struggles for power during 1917

▬ The location of the Bolshevik leaders at the time of the March Revolution. The majority were in exile or out of Russia. They all made haste to return to Petrograd.
Ⓜ = Mensheviks and others who became Bolsheviks on their return to Petrograd

Most of the Social Democratic leaders of both the Bolshevik and Menshevik factions were abroad or in exile when revolution broke out in Russia in 1917. Those who were in Siberia reached Petrograd early in March, following the spontaneous amnesty of all political prisoners. Also returning in March were those living in Sweden. Next to return, in April, were the "specials" from Switzerland, led by Lenin. Finally, in May, came the "regulars" who had been in Switzerland, or elsewhere abroad.

THE WAR AND REVOLUTION JULY AND AUGUST 1917

In March 1917 the Provisional Government assured Britain and France that it would continue the war against the Central Powers. But the offensive launched on 1 July ended two weeks later in mutiny and failure. Mass demonstrations in Petrograd on 16 and 17 July, though leaderless, showed how much the war had become, and the Bolsheviks soon dominated the Soviets by their cry of "Bread and Peace". The Provisional Government then published evidence of financial dealings between the Bolsheviks and German agents, forced Lenin to go into hiding in Finland, and arrested Trotsky. In August General Kornilov led an army against Petrograd, intending to crush the Soviets and stiffen the Provisional Government against concessions. The Bolsheviks took a leading part in the defence of the city, and greatly increased their military power, having been armed by the Provisional Government. They also gained support among the masses, who feared the return of autocracy

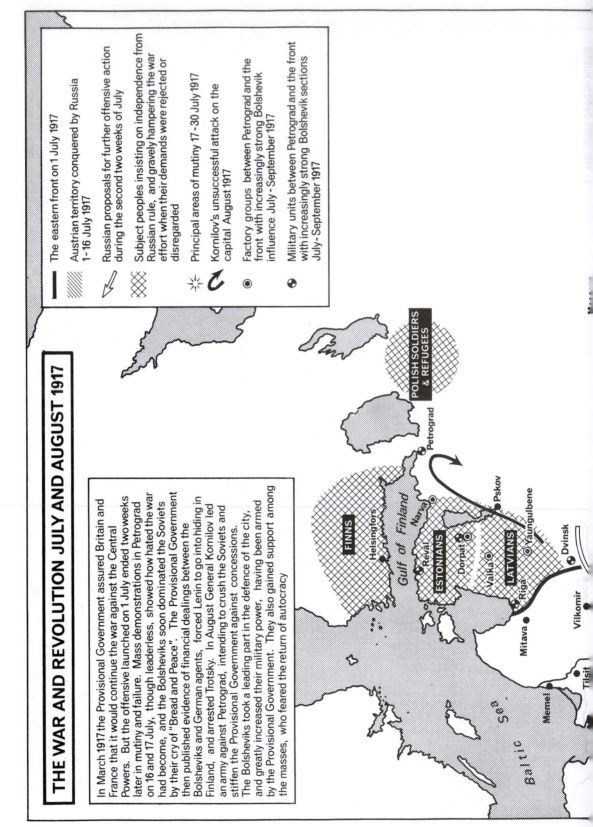

Legend:

▬ The eastern front on 1 July 1917

▨ Austrian territory conquered by Russia 1-16 July 1917

⇗ Russian proposals for further offensive action during the second two weeks of July

▨ Subject peoples insisting on independence from Russian rule, and gravely hampering the war effort when their demands were rejected or disregarded

☼ Principal areas of mutiny 17-30 July 1917

↻ Kornilov's unsuccessful attack on the capital August 1917

◉ Factory groups between Petrograd and the front with increasingly strong Bolshevik influence July-September 1917

◓ Military units between Petrograd and the front with increasingly strong Bolshevik sections July-September 1917

POLISH SOLDIERS & REFUGEES

Petrograd

FINNS

Helsingfors

Gulf of Finland

Narva

Reval

ESTONIANS

Dorpat

Valka

Pskov

Yaungulbene

LATVIANS

Riga

Dvinsk

Mitava

Vilkomir

Tilsit

Memel

Baltic Sea

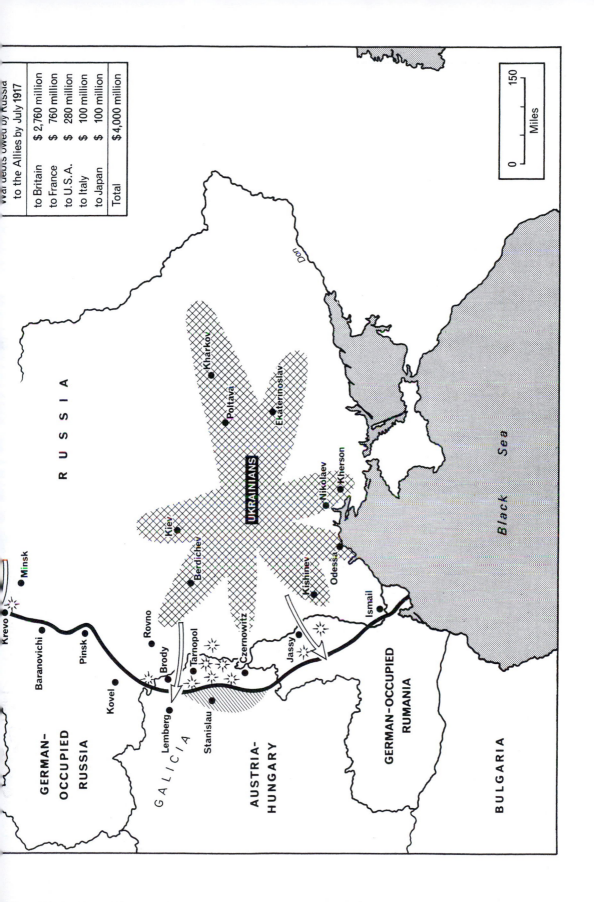

War debts owed by Russia to the Allies by July 1917	
to Britain	$ 2,760 million
to France	$ 760 million
to U.S.A.	$ 280 million
to Italy	$ 100 million
to Japan	$ 100 million
Total	$ 4,000 million

RUSSIA

GERMAN-OCCUPIED RUSSIA

GALICIA

AUSTRIA-HUNGARY

GERMAN-OCCUPIED RUMANIA

BULGARIA

Black Sea

Don

Minsk

Krevo

Baranovichi

Pinsk

Kovel

Rovno

Brody

Tarnopol

Lemberg

Stanislau

Czernowitz

Jassy

Berdichev

Kiev

Kishinev

Odessa

Nikolaev

Kherson

Ismail

UKRAINIANS

Kharkov

Poltava

Ekaterinoslav

0   150
Miles

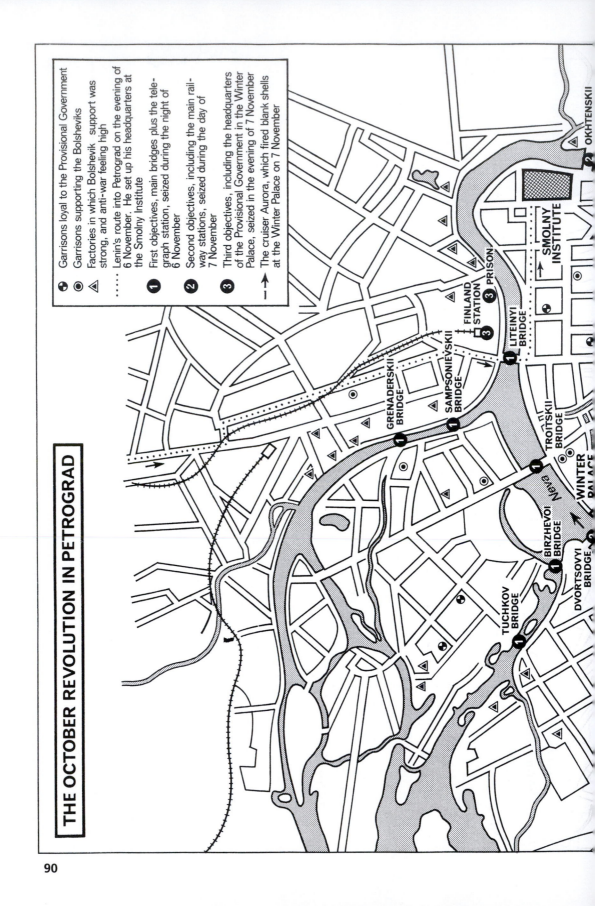

THE OCTOBER REVOLUTION IN PETROGRAD

Garrisons loyal to the Provisional Government

Garrisons supporting the Bolsheviks

Factories in which Bolshevik support was strong, and anti-war feeling high

Lenin's route into Petrograd on the evening of 6 November. He set up his headquarters at the Smolny Institute

1 First objectives, main bridges plus the telegraph station, seized during the night of 6 November

2 Second objectives, including the main railway stations, seized during the day of 7 November

3 Third objectives, including the headquarters of the Provisional Government in the Winter Palace, seized in the evening of 7 November

The cruiser Aurora, which fired blank shells at the Winter Palace on 7 November

OKHTENSKII

SMOLNY INSTITUTE

PRISON

FINLAND STATION

LITEINYI BRIDGE

GRENADERSKII BRIDGE

SAMPSONIEVSKII BRIDGE

TROITSKII BRIDGE

Neva

WINTER PALACE

BIRZHEVOI BRIDGE

TUCHKOV BRIDGE

DVORTSOVYI BRIDGE

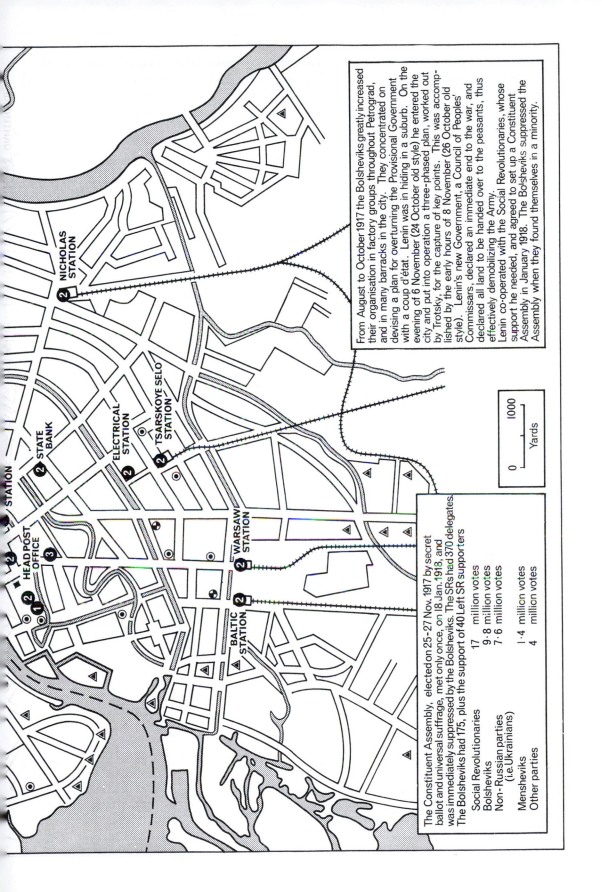

NICHOLAS
STATION

2

STATION

STATE
BANK

2

ELECTRICAL
STATION

2

TSARSKOYE SELO
STATION

2

HEAD POST
OFFICE

2

3

2

2

1

WARSAW
STATION

2

BALTIC
STATION

2

0   1000

Yards

The Constituent Assembly, elected on 25-27 Nov. 1917 by secret ballot and universal suffrage, met only once, on 18 Jan. 1918, and was immediately suppressed by the Bolsheviks. The SRs had 370 delegates. The Bolsheviks had 175, plus the support of 40 Left SR supporters

Social Revolutionaries	17	million votes
Bolsheviks	9·8	million votes
Non-Russian parties (i.e. Ukrainians)	7·6	million votes
Mensheviks	1·4	million votes
Other parties	4	million votes

From August to October 1917 the Bolsheviks greatly increased their organisation in factory groups throughout Petrograd, and in many barracks in the city. They concentrated on devising a plan for overturning the Provisional Government with a coup d'état. Lenin was in hiding in a suburb. On the evening of 6 November (24 October old style) he entered the city and put into operation a three-phased plan, worked out by Trotsky, for the capture of key points. This was accomplished by the early hours of 8 November (26 October old style). Lenin's new Government, a Council of Peoples' Commissars, declared an immediate end to the war, and declared all land to be handed over to the peasants, thus effectively demobilizing the Army.
Lenin co-operated with the Social Revolutionaries, whose support he needed, and agreed to set up a Constituent Assembly in January 1918. The Bolsheviks suppressed the Assembly when they found themselves in a minority.

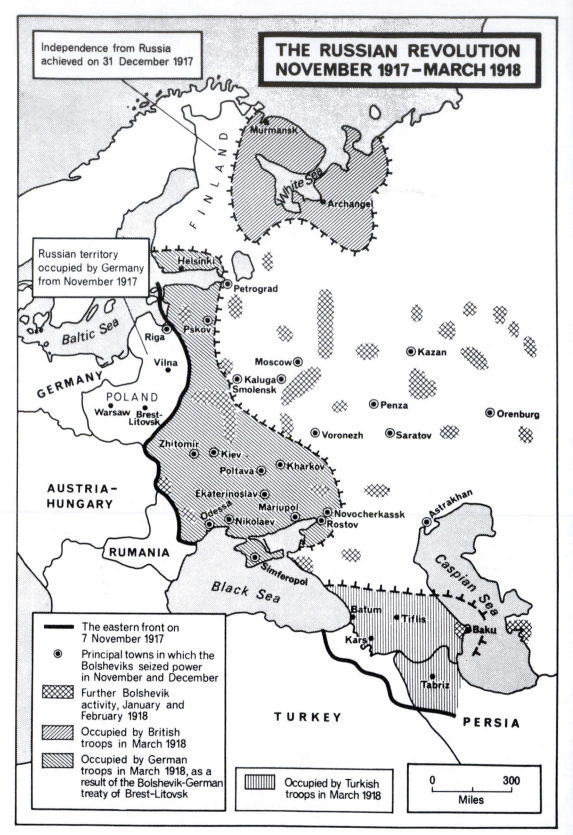

Independence from Russia
achieved on 31 December 1917

THE RUSSIAN REVOLUTION
NOVEMBER 1917 – MARCH 1918

FINLAND

Murmansk

White Sea

Archangel

Russian territory
occupied by Germany
from November 1917

Helsinki

Baltic Sea

Petrograd

Riga · Pskov

Vilna

GERMANY

Moscow

Kazan

POLAND

Kaluga
Smolensk

Penza

Orenburg

Warsaw · Brest-
Litovsk

Zhitomir

Kiev

Voronezh

Saratov

AUSTRIA-
HUNGARY

Poltava

Kharkov

Ekaterinoslav

Mariupol

Odessa · Nikolaev

Novocherkassk
Rostov

Astrakhan

RUMANIA

Simferopol

Black Sea

Caspian Sea

Batum

Tiflis

Baku

Kars

The eastern front on
7 November 1917

Principal towns in which the
Bolsheviks seized power
in November and December

Further Bolshevik
activity, January and
February 1918

Occupied by British
troops in March 1918

Occupied by German
troops in March 1918, as a
result of the Bolshevik-German
treaty of Brest-Litovsk

Tabriz

TURKEY

PERSIA

Occupied by Turkish
troops in March 1918

0   300
Miles

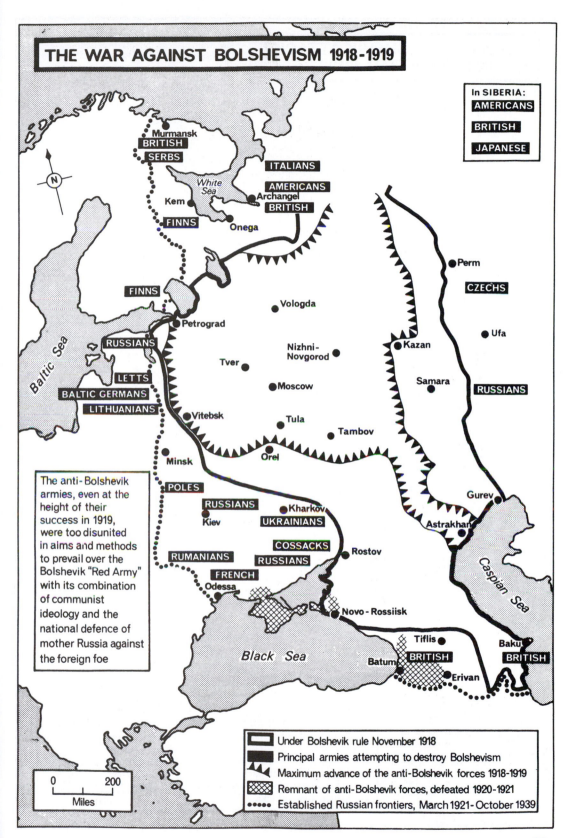

THE WAR AGAINST BOLSHEVISM 1918-1919

In SIBERIA:
AMERICANS
BRITISH
JAPANESE

Murmansk
BRITISH
SERBS

White Sea

Kem
Onega
FINNS

ITALIANS
AMERICANS
Archangel
BRITISH

Perm

CZECHS

FINNS

Vologda

Petrograd

Kazan

Ufa

RUSSIANS

Nizhni-Novgorod

Tver

Samara

Baltic Sea

LETTS
BALTIC GERMANS
LITHUANIANS

Moscow

RUSSIANS

Vitebsk

Tula

Tambov

Minsk

Orel

POLES

RUSSIANS

Kharkov

Gurev

The anti-Bolshevik armies, even at the height of their success in 1919, were too disunited in aims and methods to prevail over the Bolshevik "Red Army" with its combination of communist ideology and the national defence of mother Russia against the foreign foe

Kiev

UKRAINIANS

Astrakhan

RUMANIANS

COSSACKS
RUSSIANS

Rostov

FRENCH

Odessa

Caspian Sea

Novo - Rossiisk

Tiflis

Baku
BRITISH

Black Sea

Batum
BRITISH

Erivan

0   200
Miles

☐ Under Bolshevik rule November 1918
■ Principal armies attempting to destroy Bolshevism
◣ Maximum advance of the anti-Bolshevik forces 1918-1919
▨ Remnant of anti-Bolshevik forces, defeated 1920-1921
••• Established Russian frontiers, March 1921- October 1939

92

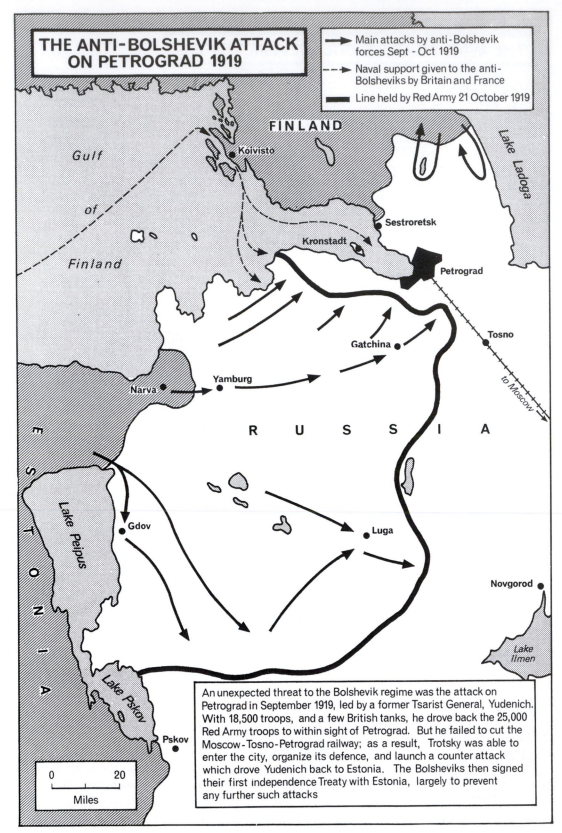

THE ANTI-BOLSHEVIK ATTACK ON PETROGRAD 1919

→ Main attacks by anti-Bolshevik forces Sept - Oct 1919

--→ Naval support given to the anti-Bolsheviks by Britain and France

▬ Line held by Red Army 21 October 1919

FINLAND

Gulf

of

Finland

Koivisto

Sestroretsk

Kronstadt

Petrograd

Tosno

to Moscow

Gatchina

Yamburg

Narva

R U S S I A

Lake Ladoga

E
S
T
O
N
I
A

Lake Peipus

Gdov

Luga

Novgorod

Lake
Ilmen

Lake
Pskov

Pskov

An unexpected threat to the Bolshevik regime was the attack on Petrograd in September 1919, led by a former Tsarist General, Yudenich. With 18,500 troops, and a few British tanks, he drove back the 25,000 Red Army troops to within sight of Petrograd. But he failed to cut the Moscow-Tosno-Petrograd railway; as a result, Trotsky was able to enter the city, organize its defence, and launch a counter attack which drove Yudenich back to Estonia. The Bolsheviks then signed their first independence Treaty with Estonia, largely to prevent any further such attacks

0   20
Miles

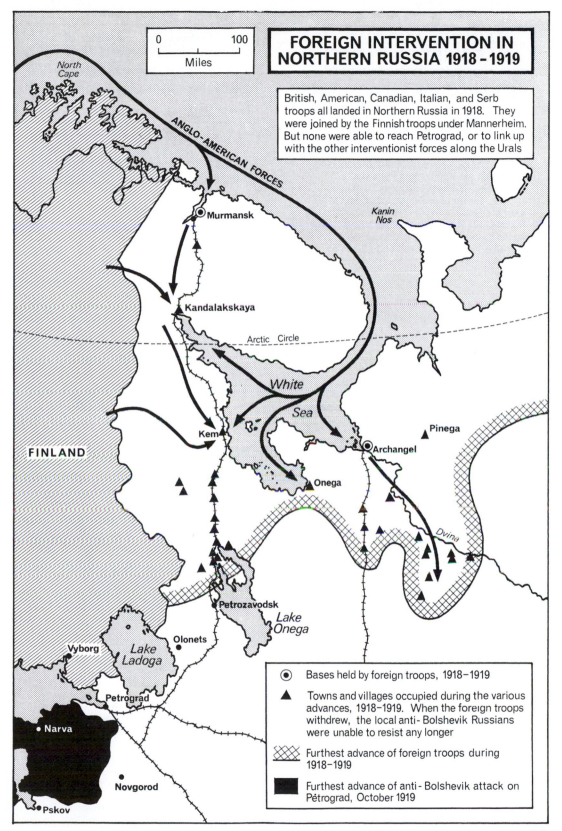

FOREIGN INTERVENTION IN NORTHERN RUSSIA 1918-1919

British, American, Canadian, Italian, and Serb
troops all landed in Northern Russia in 1918. They
were joined by the Finnish troops under Mannerheim.
But none were able to reach Petrograd, or to link up
with the other interventionist forces along the Urals

0   100
Miles

*North
Cape*

ANGLO-AMERICAN FORCES

⊙ Murmansk

*Kanin
Nos*

▲ Kandalakskaya

Arctic   Circle

White

Sea

▲ Pinega

Kem ▲

⊙ Archangel

FINLAND

▲ Onega

Dvina

Petrozavodsk

*Lake
Onega*

Olonets

Vyborg

*Lake
Ladoga*

Petrograd

● **Narva**

⊙   Bases held by foreign troops, 1918–1919

▲   Towns and villages occupied during the various
     advances, 1918–1919. When the foreign troops
     withdrew, the local anti- Bolshevik Russians
     were unable to resist any longer

⬚   Furthest advance of foreign troops during
     1918–1919

■   Furthest advance of anti- Bolshevik attack on
     Pétrograd, October 1919

Novgorod

● **Pskov**

94

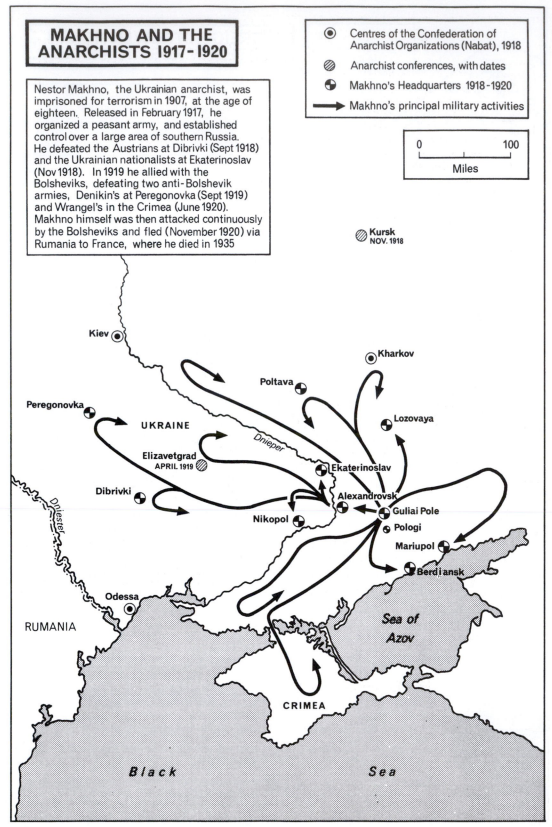

MAKHNO AND THE ANARCHISTS 1917-1920

Nestor Makhno, the Ukrainian anarchist, was imprisoned for terrorism in 1907, at the age of eighteen. Released in February 1917, he organized a peasant army, and established control over a large area of southern Russia. He defeated the Austrians at Dibrivki (Sept 1918) and the Ukrainian nationalists at Ekaterinoslav (Nov 1918). In 1919 he allied with the Bolsheviks, defeating two anti-Bolshevik armies, Denikin's at Peregonovka (Sept 1919) and Wrangel's in the Crimea (June 1920). Makhno himself was then attacked continuously by the Bolsheviks and fled (November 1920) via Rumania to France, where he died in 1935

Centres of the Confederation of Anarchist Organizations (Nabat), 1918

Anarchist conferences, with dates

Makhno's Headquarters 1918-1920

Makhno's principal military activities

0   100

Miles

Kursk
NOV. 1918

Kiev

Kharkov

Poltava

Peregonovka

Lozovaya

UKRAINE

Dnieper

Elizavetgrad
APRIL 1919

Dibrivki

Ekaterinoslav

Alexandrovsk

Nikopol

Guliai Pole

Pologi

Mariupol

Berdiansk

Odessa

RUMANIA

Sea of Azov

Dniester

CRIMEA

Black   Sea

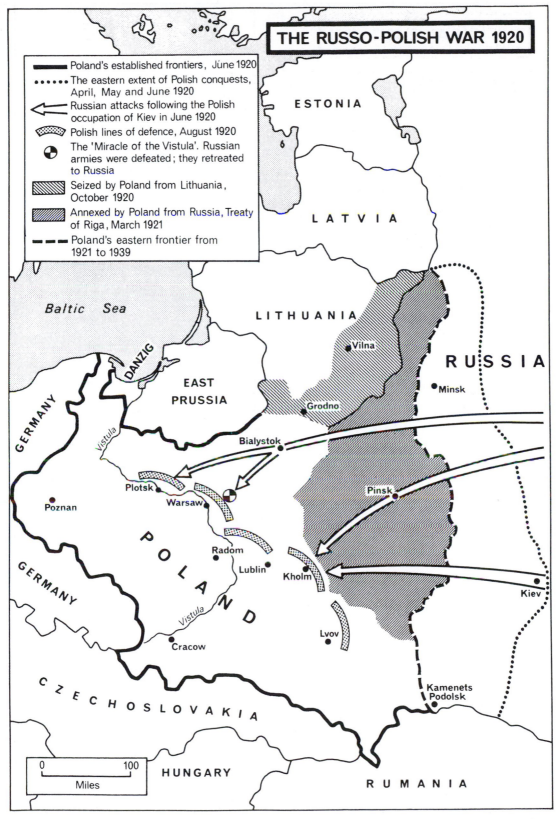

THE RUSSO-POLISH WAR 1920

Poland's established frontiers, June 1920

The eastern extent of Polish conquests, April, May and June 1920

Russian attacks following the Polish occupation of Kiev in June 1920

Polish lines of defence, August 1920

The 'Miracle of the Vistula'. Russian armies were defeated; they retreated to Russia

Seized by Poland from Lithuania, October 1920

Annexed by Poland from Russia, Treaty of Riga, March 1921

Poland's eastern frontier from 1921 to 1939

ESTONIA

LATVIA

LITHUANIA

RUSSIA

Baltic Sea

DANZIG

EAST PRUSSIA

GERMANY

Vilna

Minsk

Grodno

Bialystok

Plotsk

Warsaw

Poznan

POLAND

Radom

Lublin

Kholm

Pinsk

Kiev

Vistula

Vistula

Cracow

Lvov

GERMANY

CZECHOSLOVAKIA

Kamenets Podolsk

0   100
Miles

HUNGARY

RUMANIA

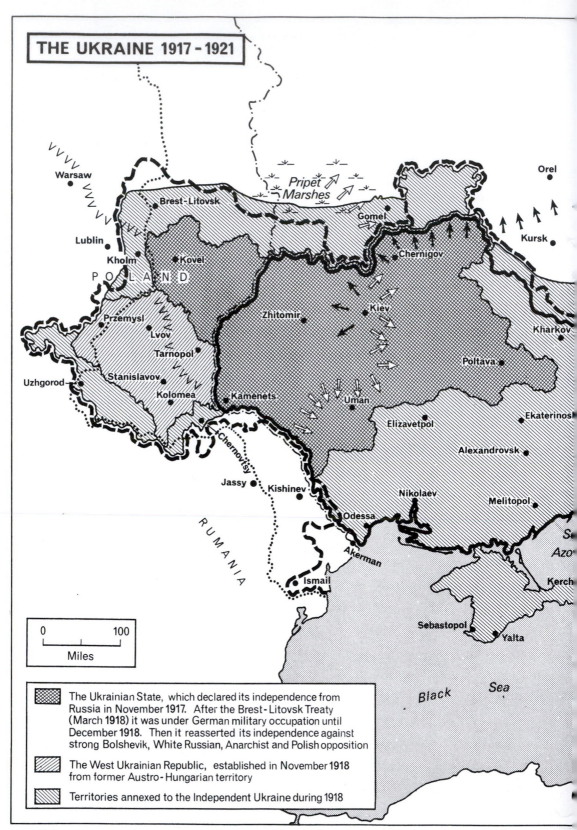

THE UKRAINE 1917 - 1921

Orel

Warsaw

Pripet
Marshes

Brest-Litovsk

Gomel

Kursk

Lublin

Kholm

Chernigov

Kovel

P O L A N D

Zhitomir

Kiev

Kharkov

Przemysl

Lvov

Tarnopol

Poltava

Uzhgorod

Stanislavov

Kamenets

Uman

Kolomea

Elizavetpol

Ekaterinos

Chernovtsy

Alexandrovsk

Jassy

Kishinev

Nikolaev

Melitopol

R U M A N I A

Odessa

S.
Azo

Akerman

Kerch

Ismail

Sebastopol

Yalta

0   100

Miles

Black   Sea

The Ukrainian State, which declared its independence from
Russia in November 1917. After the Brest-Litovsk Treaty
(March 1918) it was under German military occupation until
December 1918. Then it reasserted its independence against
strong Bolshevik, White Russian, Anarchist and Polish opposition

The West Ukrainian Republic, established in November 1918
from former Austro-Hungarian territory

Territories annexed to the Independent Ukraine during 1918

Territory claimed by the Ukrainian nationalists as part of the "ethnographic" Ukraine

Boundary of the Ukrainian Soviet Socialist Republic 1921

Western boundary of the Soviet Union 1921–1939

Western boundary of the Soviet Union since 1945

Furthest northern advance of Denikin's anti-Bolshevik armies, November 1919. Denikin's Great Russian policies failed to gain him much Ukrainian support

Furthest eastern advance of the Polish Army in June 1920

Furthest western advance of the Red Army by August 1920

Voronezh

Buturlinovka

Lugansk

Taganrog

Rostov

Mariupol

Astrakhan

Ekaterinodar

Stavropol

Armavir

Novorossiisk

Mineralnye Vody

Mozdok

Tuapse

Sochi

Causasus

Batum

Caspian Sea

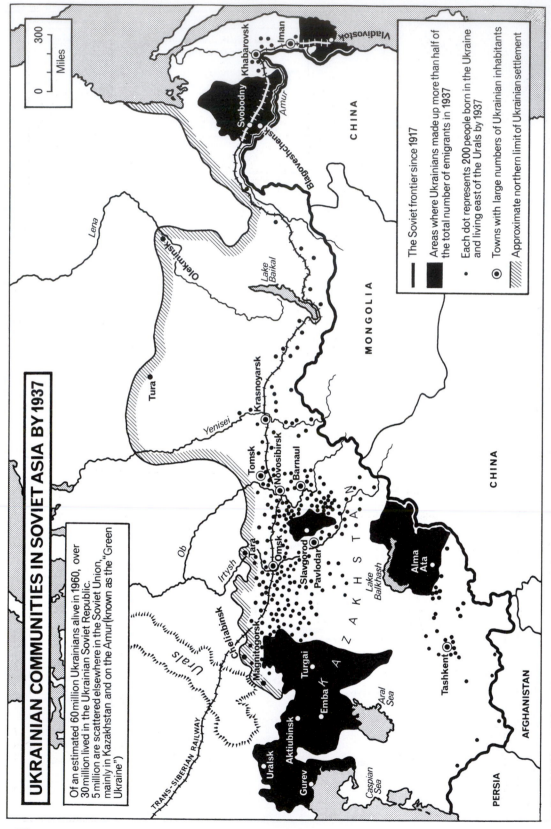

UKRAINIAN COMMUNITIES IN SOVIET ASIA BY 1937

Of an estimated 60 million Ukrainians alive in 1960, over 30 million lived in the Ukrainian Soviet Republic. 5 million are scattered elsewhere in the Soviet Union, mainly in Kazakhstan and on the Amur (known as the "Green Ukraine")

The Soviet frontier since 1917

Areas where Ukrainians made up more than half of the total number of emigrants in 1937

Each dot represents 200 people born in the Ukraine and living east of the Urals by 1937

Towns with large numbers of Ukrainian inhabitants

Approximate northern limit of Ukrainian settlement

300 Miles
0

CHINA

MONGOLIA

CHINA

KAZAKHSTAN

PERSIA

AFGHANISTAN

Vladivostok
Iman
Khabarovsk
Svobodny
Blagoveshchensk
Amur

Olekminsk
Lena

Lake Baikal

Tura

Krasnoyarsk
Yenisei

Tomsk
Novosibirsk
Barnaul

Ob

Irtysh
Tara
Omsk
Slavgrod
Pavlodar

Lake Balkhash

Alma Ata

Tashkent

Cheliabinsk
Magnitogorsk
Urals

Turgai

Emba

Aral Sea

Uralsk
Aktiubinsk
Gurev
Caspian Sea

TRANS-SIBERIAN RAILWAY

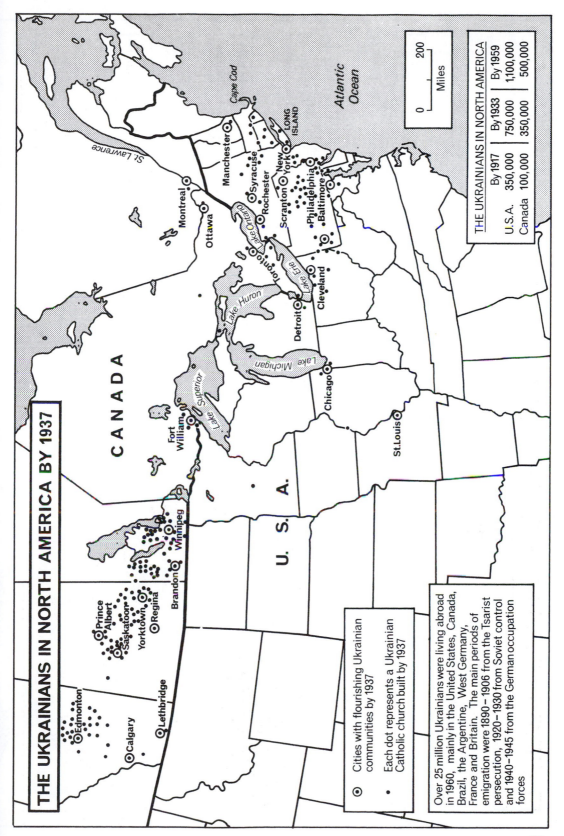

THE UKRAINIANS IN NORTH AMERICA BY 1937

CANADA

U. S. A.

Atlantic Ocean

Cape Cod

St. Lawrence

LONG ISLAND

Manchester
Syracuse
Rochester
New York
Scranton
Philadelphia
Baltimore

Montreal
Ottawa

Lake Ontario
Toronto
Lake Erie
Cleveland

Lake Huron

Detroit

Lake Michigan

Chicago

St. Louis

Lake Superior

Fort William

Winnipeg

Brandon

Prince Albert
Saskatoon
Yorkton
Regina

Edmonton

Calgary

Lethbridge

THE UKRAINIANS IN NORTH AMERICA			
	By 1917	By 1933	By 1959
U.S.A.	350,000	750,000	1,100,000
Canada	100,000	350,000	500,000

0   200
Miles

⊙ Cities with flourishing Ukrainian communities by 1937

· Each dot represents a Ukrainian Catholic church built by 1937

Over 25 million Ukrainians were living abroad in 1960, mainly in the United States, Canada, Brazil, the Argentine, West Germany, France and Britain. The main periods of emigration were 1890–1906 from the Tsarist persecution, 1920–1930 from Soviet control and 1940–1945 from the German occupation forces

THE BORDER STATES 1919–1920

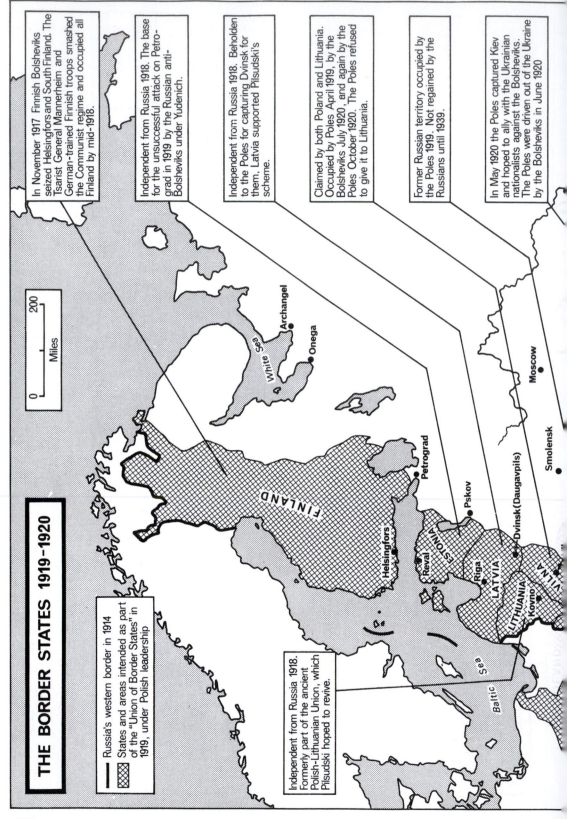

— Russia's western border in 1914

▨ States and areas intended as part of the "Union of Border States" in 1919, under Polish leadership

0 ——— 200
Miles

Independent from Russia 1918. Formerly part of the ancient Polish-Lithuanian Union, which Pilsudski hoped to revive.

In November 1917 Finnish Bolsheviks seized Helsingfors and South Finland. The Tsarist General Mannerheim and German-trained Finnish troops smashed the Communist regime and occupied all Finland by mid-1918.

Independent from Russia 1918. The base for the unsuccessful attack on Petrograd in 1919 by the Russian anti-Bolsheviks under Yudenich.

Independent from Russia 1918. Beholden to the Poles for capturing Dvinsk for them. Latvia supported Pilsudski's scheme.

Claimed by both Poland and Lithuania. Occupied by Poles April 1919, by the Bolsheviks July 1920, and again by the Poles October 1920. The Poles refused to give it to Lithuania.

Former Russian territory occupied by the Poles 1919. Not regained by the Russians until 1939.

In May 1920 the Poles captured Kiev and hoped to ally with the Ukrainian nationalists against the Bolsheviks. The Poles were driven out of the Ukraine by the Bolsheviks in June 1920

Archangel
Onega
White Sea
FINLAND
Petrograd
Pskov
Helsingfors
Reval
ESTONIA
Riga
LATVIA
Dvinsk (Daugavpils)
LITHUANIA
Kovno
Moscow
Smolensk
Baltic Sea

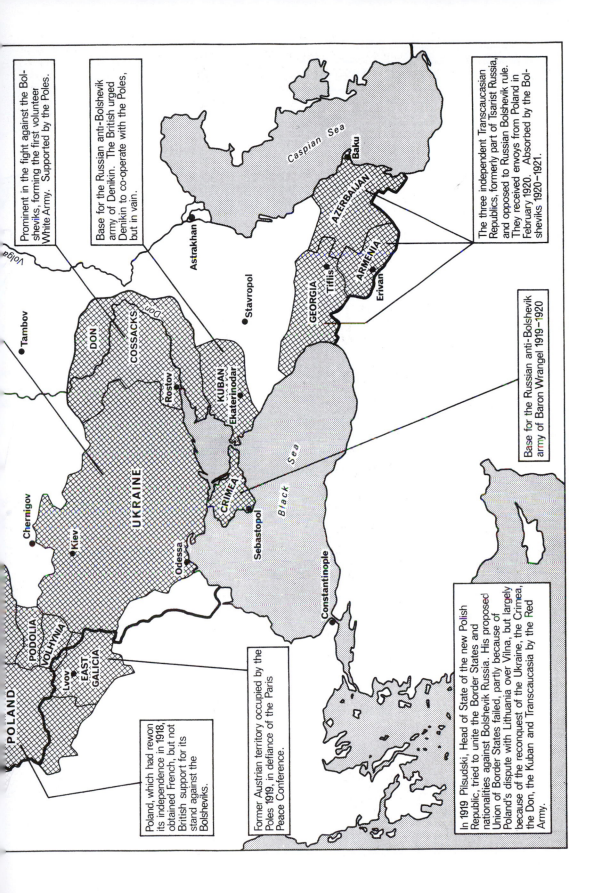

Prominent in the fight against the Bolsheviks, forming the first volunteer White Army. Supported by the Poles.

Base for the Russian anti-Bolshevik army of Denikin. The British urged Denikin to co-operate with the Poles, but in vain.

The three independent Transcaucasian Republics, formerly part of Tsarist Russia, and opposed to Russian Bolshevik rule. They received envoys from Poland in February 1920. Absorbed by the Bolsheviks 1920–1921.

Base for the Russian anti-Bolshevik army of Baron Wrangel 1919–1920

Poland, which had rewon its independence in 1918, obtained French, but not British support for its stand against the Bolsheviks.

Former Austrian territory occupied by the Poles 1919, in defiance of the Paris Peace Conference.

In 1919 Pilsudski, Head of State of the new Polish Republic, tried to unite the Border States and nationalities against Bolshevik Russia. His proposed Union of Border States failed, partly because of Poland's dispute with Lithuania over Vilna, but largely because of the reconquest of the Ukraine, the Crimea, the Don, the Kuban and Transcaucasia by the Red Army.

Caspian Sea

Baku

Astrakhan

AZERBAIJAN

ARMENIA

GEORGIA

Tiflis

Erivan

Volga

Tambov

DON

COSSACKS

Don

Stavropol

Rostov

KUBAN

Ekaterinodar

UKRAINE

Chernigov

Kiev

CRIMEA

Odessa

Sebastopol

Black Sea

Constantinople

POLAND

PODOLIA

VOLHYNIA

Lvov

EAST GALICIA

SOVIET DIPLOMACY 1920-1940

North Sea

Bay of Biscay

Baltic Sea

Mediterranean Sea

NORWAY

FINLAND

BRITAIN

London

GERMANY

Berlin

POLAND

Warsaw

ESTONIA

LATVIA

Leningrad

Smole

FLYING SCHOO

FRANCE

Paris

CZECHO SLOVAKIA

AUSTRIA

ITALY

RUMANIA

San Sebastian

Madrid

Barcelona

SPAIN

10,000 VEHICLES
4,500 TONS MUNITIONS

0, 200 TANKS
3,300 MACHINE GUNS

1,000 OFFICERS & MEN

1,000 OFFICERS & MEN
1,300 TRUCKS
1,300 RIFLES & GUNS
242 AEROPLANES

0   400
Miles

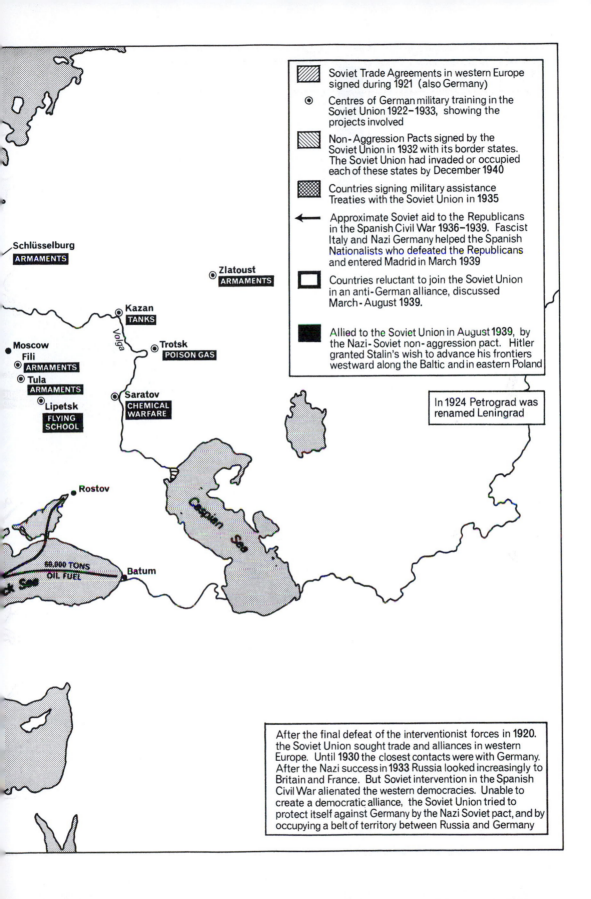

Soviet Trade Agreements in western Europe signed during 1921 (also Germany)

Centres of German military training in the Soviet Union 1922–1933, showing the projects involved

Non-Aggression Pacts signed by the Soviet Union in 1932 with its border states. The Soviet Union had invaded or occupied each of these states by December 1940

Countries signing military assistance Treaties with the Soviet Union in 1935

Approximate Soviet aid to the Republicans in the Spanish Civil War 1936–1939. Fascist Italy and Nazi Germany helped the Spanish Nationalists who defeated the Republicans and entered Madrid in March 1939

Countries reluctant to join the Soviet Union in an anti-German alliance, discussed March-August 1939.

Allied to the Soviet Union in August 1939, by the Nazi-Soviet non-aggression pact. Hitler granted Stalin's wish to advance his frontiers westward along the Baltic and in eastern Poland

Schlüsselburg
ARMAMENTS

Zlatoust
ARMAMENTS

Kazan
TANKS

Volga

Moscow
Fili
ARMAMENTS

Trotsk
POISON GAS

Tula
ARMAMENTS

Lipetsk
FLYING
SCHOOL

Saratov
CHEMICAL
WARFARE

In 1924 Petrograd was renamed Leningrad

Rostov

Caspian Sea

50,000 TONS
OIL FUEL

Batum

Black Sea

After the final defeat of the interventionist forces in 1920. the Soviet Union sought trade and alliances in western Europe. Until 1930 the closest contacts were with Germany. After the Nazi success in 1933 Russia looked increasingly to Britain and France. But Soviet intervention in the Spanish Civil War alienated the western democracies. Unable to create a democratic alliance, the Soviet Union tried to protect itself against Germany by the Nazi Soviet pact, and by occupying a belt of territory between Russia and Germany

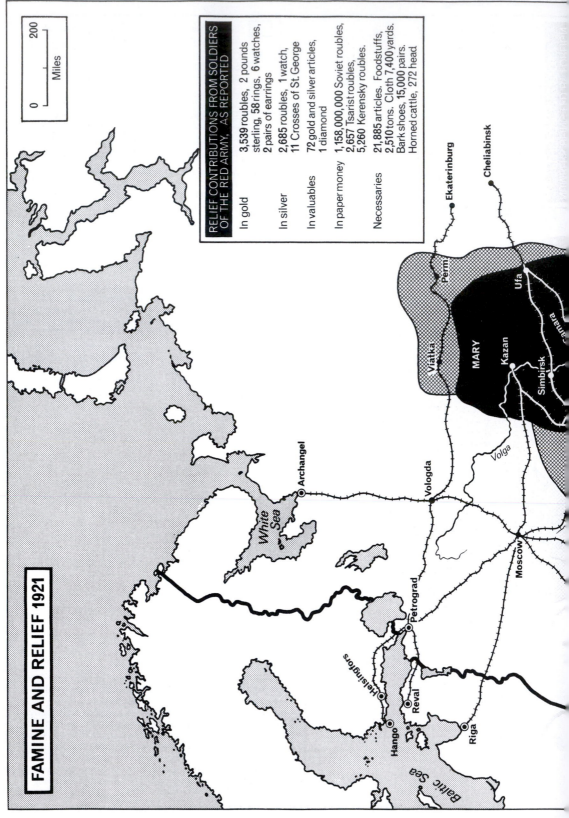

FAMINE AND RELIEF 1921

RELIEF CONTRIBUTIONS FROM SOLDIERS OF THE RED ARMY, AS REPORTED

In gold	3,539 roubles, 2 pounds sterling, 58 rings. 6 watches, 2 pairs of earrings
In silver	2,685 roubles, 1 watch, 11 Crosses of St. George
In valuables	72 gold and silver articles, 1 diamond
In paper money	1,158,000,000 Soviet roubles, 2,657 Tsarist roubles, 5,260 Kerensky roubles.
Necessaries	21,885 articles. Foodstuffs, 2,510 tons. Cloth 7,400 yards. Bark shoes, 15,000 pairs. Horned cattle, 272 head

0 — 200 Miles

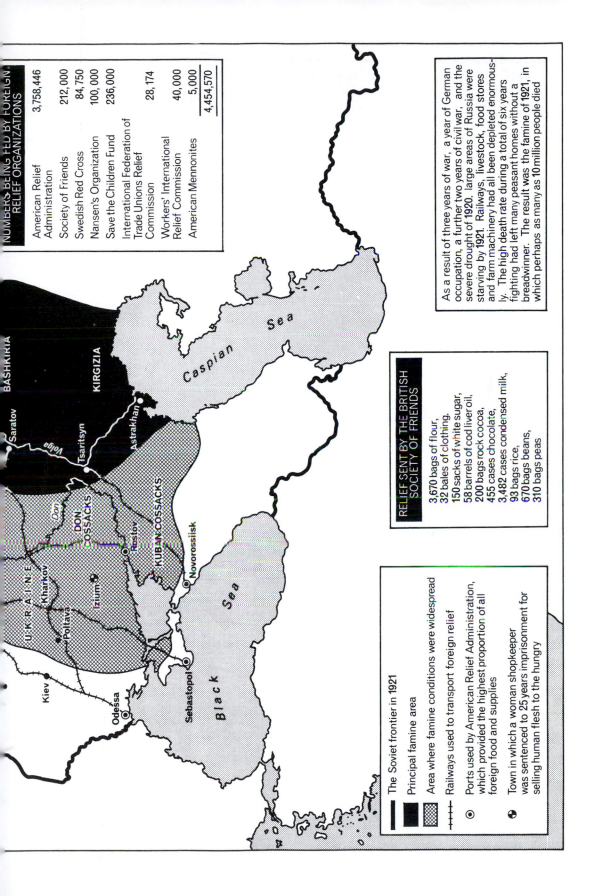

NUMBERS BEING FED BY FOREIGN RELIEF ORGANIZATIONS	
American Relief Administration	3,758,446
Society of Friends	212,000
Swedish Red Cross	84,750
Nansen's Organization	100,000
Save the Children Fund	236,000
International Federation of Trade Unions Relief Commission	28,174
Workers' International Relief Commission	40,000
American Mennonites	5,000
	4,454,570

As a result of three years of war, a year of German occupation, a further two years of civil war, and the severe drought of 1920, large areas of Russia were starving by 1921. Railways, livestock, food stores and farm machinery had all been depleted enormously. The high death rate during a total of six years fighting had left many peasant homes without a breadwinner. The result was the famine of 1921, in which perhaps as many as 10 million people died

RELIEF SENT BY THE BRITISH SOCIETY OF FRIENDS

3,670 bags of flour,
32 bales of clothing,
150 sacks of white sugar,
58 barrels of cod liver oil,
200 bags rock cocoa,
455 cases chocolate,
3,482 cases condensed milk,
93 bags rice,
670 bags beans,
310 bags peas

BASHKIRIA

KIRGIZIA

Caspian Sea

Saratov

KIRGIZIA

Tsaritsyn

Volga

Astrakhan

UKRAINE

Kharkov

Don

DON COSSACKS

Rostov

KUBAN COSSACKS

Poltava

Izium

Novorossiisk

Kiev

Odessa

Sebastopol

Black Sea

━━━ The Soviet frontier in 1921

▓▓▓ Principal famine area

▒▒▒ Area where famine conditions were widespread

┼┼┼ Railways used to transport foreign relief

◉ Ports used by American Relief Administration, which provided the highest proportion of all foreign food and supplies

◖ Town in which a woman shopkeeper was sentenced to 25 years imprisonment for selling human flesh to the hungry

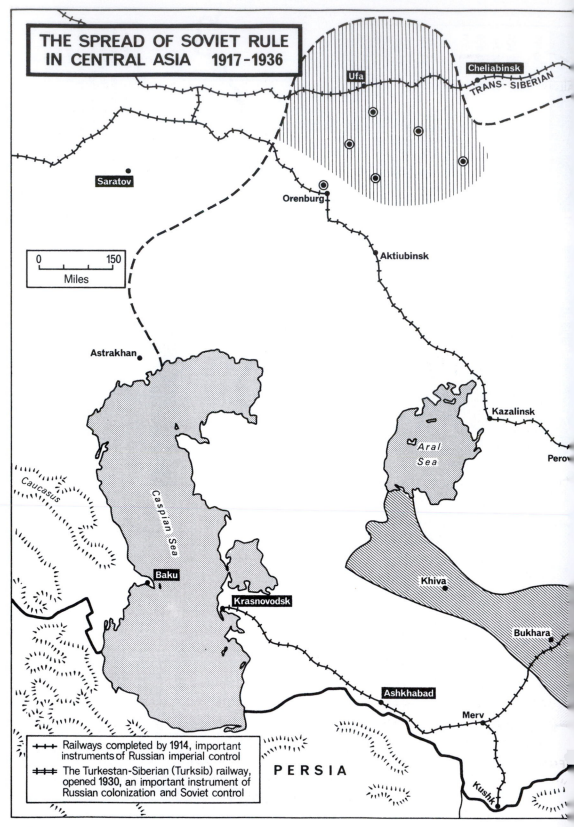

THE SPREAD OF SOVIET RULE
IN CENTRAL ASIA   1917–1936

Ufa

Cheliabinsk

TRANS - SIBERIAN

Saratov

Orenburg

Aktiubinsk

0   150
Miles

Astrakhan

Kazalinsk

Aral
Sea

Perov

Caucasus

Caspian Sea

Khiva

Baku

Krasnovodsk

Bukhara

Ashkhabad

Merv

Railways completed by 1914, important
instruments of Russian imperial control

The Turkestan-Siberian (Turksib) railway,
opened 1930, an important instrument of
Russian colonization and Soviet control

P E R S I A

Kushk

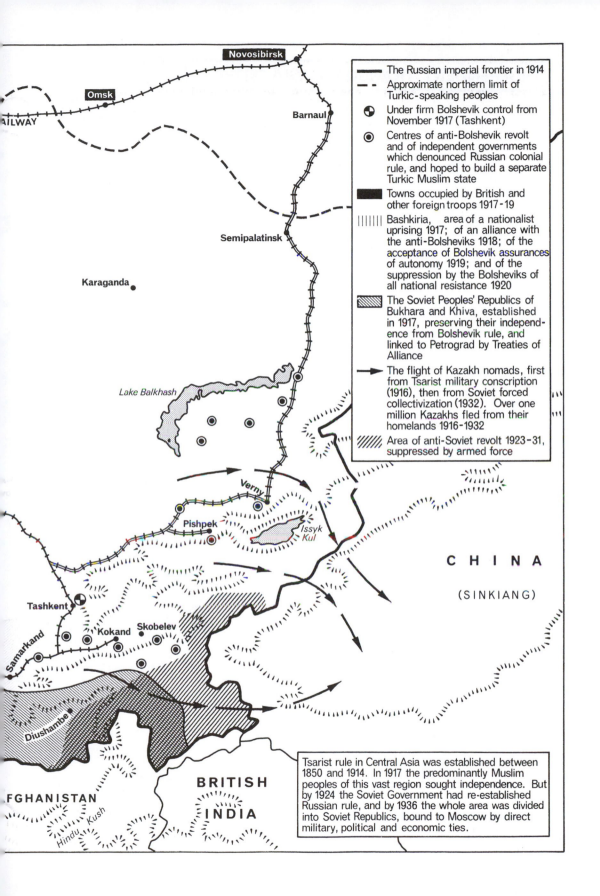

The Russian imperial frontier in 1914

Approximate northern limit of Turkic-speaking peoples

Under firm Bolshevik control from November 1917 (Tashkent)

Centres of anti-Bolshevik revolt and of independent governments which denounced Russian colonial rule, and hoped to build a separate Turkic Muslim state

Towns occupied by British and other foreign troops 1917-19

Bashkiria, area of a nationalist uprising 1917; of an alliance with the anti-Bolsheviks 1918; of the acceptance of Bolshevik assurances of autonomy 1919; and of the suppression by the Bolsheviks of all national resistance 1920

The Soviet Peoples' Republics of Bukhara and Khiva, established in 1917, preserving their independence from Bolshevik rule, and linked to Petrograd by Treaties of Alliance

The flight of Kazakh nomads, first from Tsarist military conscription (1916), then from Soviet forced collectivization (1932). Over one million Kazakhs fled from their homelands 1916-1932

Area of anti-Soviet revolt 1923-31, suppressed by armed force

Novosibirsk

Omsk

AILWAY

RAILWAY

Barnaul

Semipalatinsk

Karaganda

Lake Balkhash

Verny

Pishpek

Issyk Kul

CHINA

(SINKIANG)

Tashkent

Samarkand

Kokand

Skobelev

Diushambe

FGHANISTAN

Hindu Kush

BRITISH

INDIA

Tsarist rule in Central Asia was established between 1850 and 1914. In 1917 the predominantly Muslim peoples of this vast region sought independence. But by 1924 the Soviet Government had re-established Russian rule, and by 1936 the whole area was divided into Soviet Republics, bound to Moscow by direct military, political and economic ties.

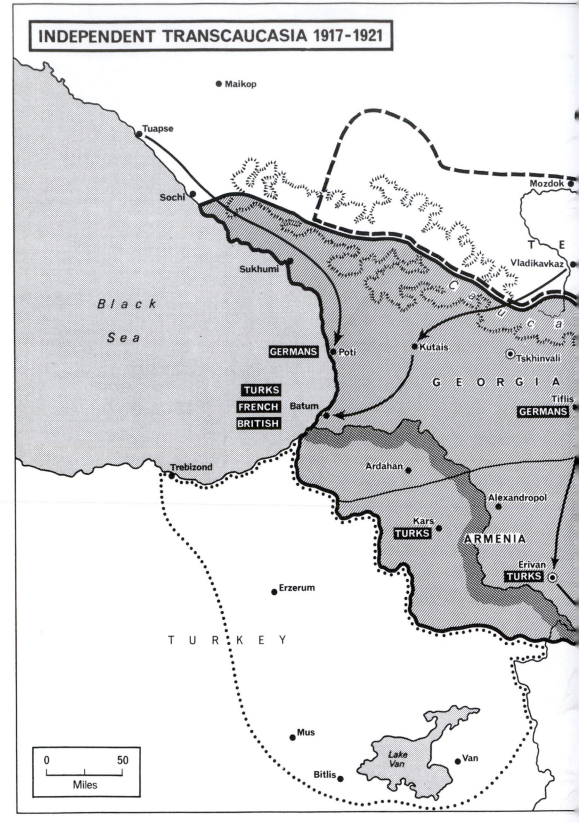

INDEPENDENT TRANSCAUCASIA 1917-1921

Maikop

Tuapse

Sochi

Sukhumi

Black

Sea

GERMANS Poti

Kutais

Mozdok

T E

Vladikavkaz

C

a u c a

Tskhinvali

TURKS
FRENCH Batum
BRITISH

G E O R G I A

Tiflis
GERMANS

Trebizond

Ardahan

Alexandropol

Kars
TURKS

A R M E N I A

Erivan
TURKS

Erzerum

T U R K E Y

Mus

Bitlis

*Lake
Van*

Van

0   50

Miles

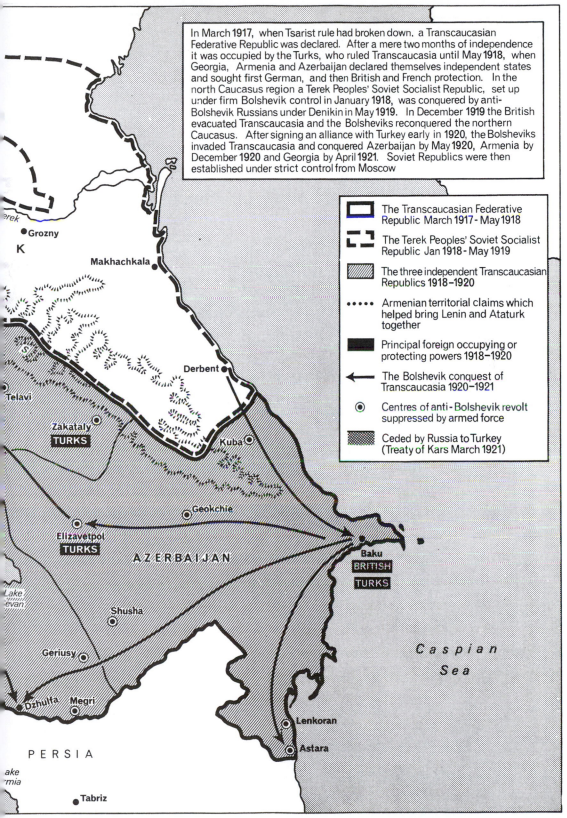

In March 1917, when Tsarist rule had broken down, a Transcaucasian Federative Republic was declared. After a mere two months of independence it was occupied by the Turks, who ruled Transcaucasia until May 1918, when Georgia, Armenia and Azerbaijan declared themselves independent states and sought first German, and then British and French protection. In the north Caucasus region a Terek Peoples' Soviet Socialist Republic, set up under firm Bolshevik control in January 1918, was conquered by anti-Bolshevik Russians under Denikin in May 1919. In December 1919 the British evacuated Transcaucasia and the Bolsheviks reconquered the northern Caucasus. After signing an alliance with Turkey early in 1920, the Bolsheviks invaded Transcaucasia and conquered Azerbaijan by May 1920, Armenia by December 1920 and Georgia by April 1921. Soviet Republics were then established under strict control from Moscow

The Transcaucasian Federative Republic March 1917 - May 1918

The Terek Peoples' Soviet Socialist Republic Jan 1918 - May 1919

The three independent Transcaucasian Republics 1918–1920

Armenian territorial claims which helped bring Lenin and Ataturk together

Principal foreign occupying or protecting powers 1918–1920

The Bolshevik conquest of Transcaucasia 1920–1921

Centres of anti-Bolshevik revolt suppressed by armed force

Ceded by Russia to Turkey (Treaty of Kars March 1921)

Grozny

Makhachkala

Derbent

Telavi

Zakataly
TURKS

Kuba

Geokchie

Elizavetpol
TURKS

AZERBAIJAN

Baku
BRITISH
TURKS

Lake evan

Shusha

Caspian Sea

Geriusy

Dzhulfa   Megri

Lenkoran

Astara

PERSIA

ake rmia

Tabriz

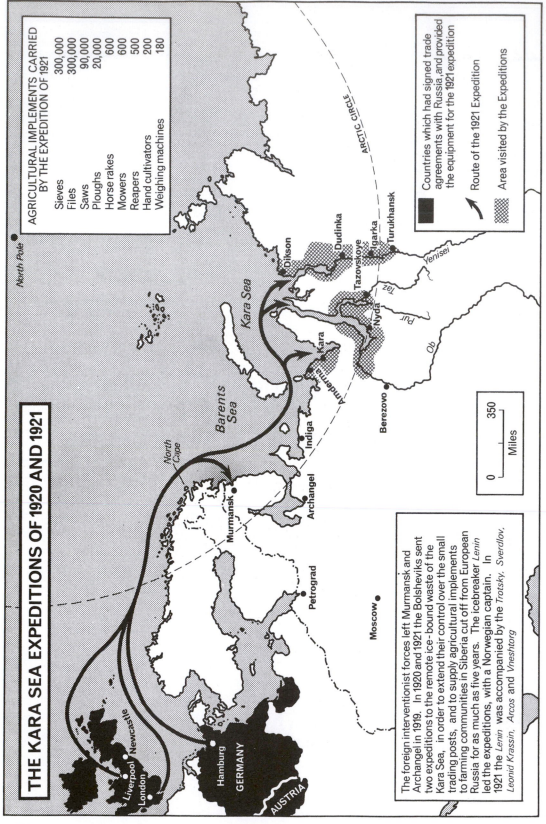

THE KARA SEA EXPEDITIONS OF 1920 AND 1921

AGRICULTURAL IMPLEMENTS CARRIED BY THE EXPEDITION OF 1921	
Sieves	300,000
Files	300,000
Saws	90,000
Ploughs	20,000
Horse rakes	600
Mowers	600
Reapers	500
Hand cultivators	200
Weighing machines	180

Countries which had signed trade agreements with Russia, and provided the equipment for the 1921 expedition

Route of the 1921 Expedition

Area visited by the Expeditions

The foreign interventionist forces left Murmansk and Archangel in 1919. In 1920 and 1921 the Bolsheviks sent two expeditions to the remote ice-bound waste of the Kara Sea, in order to extend their control over the small trading posts, and to supply agricultural implements to farming communities in Siberia cut off from European Russia for as much as five years. The icebreaker *Lenin* led the expeditions, with a Norwegian captain. In 1921 the *Lenin* was accompanied by the *Trotsky, Sverdlov, Leonid Krassin, Arcos* and *Vneshtorg.*

North Pole

Kara Sea

Barents Sea

ARCTIC CIRCLE

Dikson

Dudinka

Igarka

Turukhansk

Tazovskoye

Nyda

Kara

Amderma

Yenisei

Taz

Pur

Ob

Berezovo

Indiga

North Cape

Archangel

Murmansk

Petrograd

Moscow

Newcastle

Liverpool

London

Hamburg

GERMANY

AUSTRIA

0   350

Miles

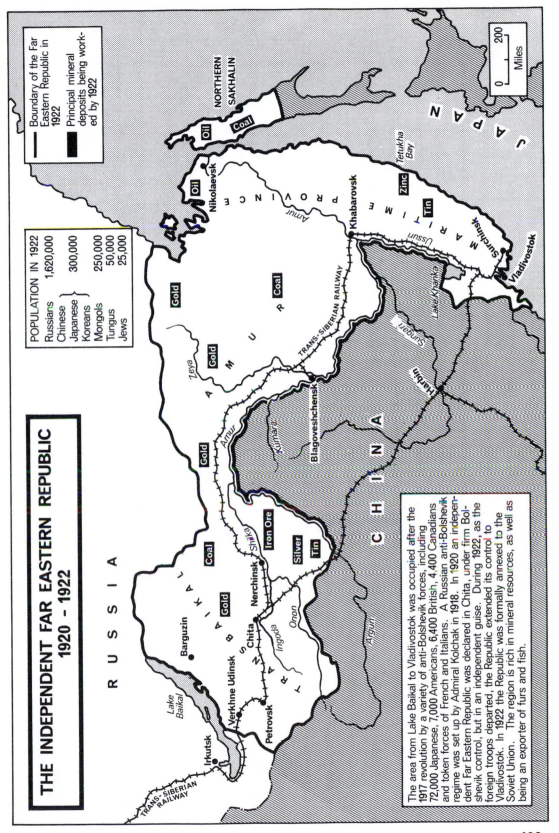

THE INDEPENDENT FAR EASTERN REPUBLIC 1920 – 1922

Boundary of the Far Eastern Republic in 1922

Principal mineral deposits being worked by 1922

POPULATION IN 1922	
Russians	1,620,000
Chinese	300,000
Japanese	
Koreans	250,000
Mongols	50,000
Tungus	25,000
Jews	

200 Miles
0

NORTHERN SAKHALIN

JAPAN

Oil

Coal

Oil

Nikolaevsk

Zinc

Tetukha Bay

Tin

Khabarovsk

Suchinsk

MARITIME PROVINCE

AMUR PROVINCE

Amur

Coal

Gold

Ussuri

Vladivostok

Lake Khanka

Gold

Zeya

Gold

TRANS-SIBERIAN RAILWAY

Blagoveshchensk

Kumara

Sungari

Harbin

Gold

Amur

CHINA

RUSSIA

Lake Baikal

Irkutsk

TRANS-SIBERIAN RAILWAY

Verkhne Udinsk

Petrovsk

Barguzin

BAIKAL

Gold

Coal

TRANS

Chita

Nerchinsk

Iron Ore

Silver

Tin

Shilka

Ingoda

Onon

Argun

The area from Lake Baikal to Vladivostok was occupied after the 1917 revolution by a variety of anti-Bolshevik forces, including 72,000 Japanese, 7,000 Americans, 6,400 British, 4,400 Canadians and token forces of French and Italians. A Russian anti-Bolshevik regime was set up by Admiral Kolchak in 1918. In 1920 an independent Far Eastern Republic was declared in Chita, under firm Bolshevik control, but in an independent guise. During 1922, as the foreign troops departed, the Republic extended its control to Vladivostok. In 1922 the Republic was formally annexed to the Soviet Union. The region is rich in mineral resources, as well as being an exporter of furs and fish.

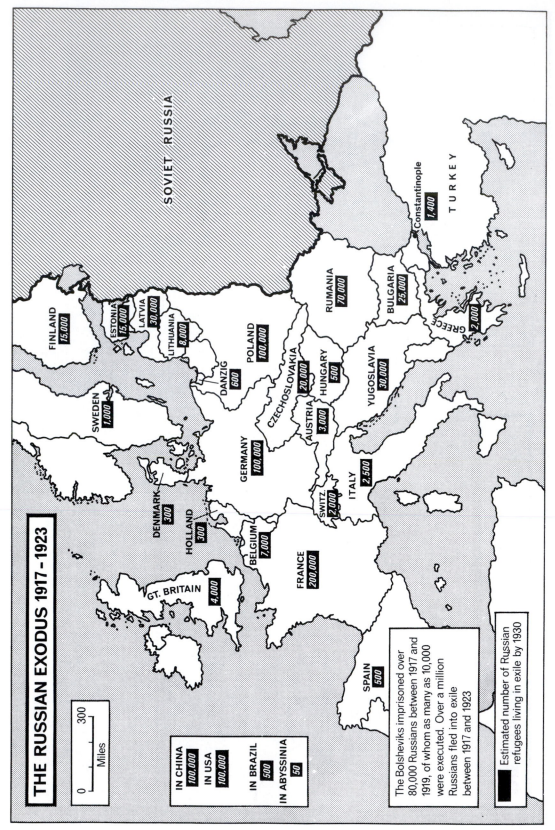

THE RUSSIAN EXODUS 1917–1923

SOVIET RUSSIA

TURKEY

Constantinople | 1,400

GREECE | 2,000

RUMANIA | 70,000

BULGARIA | 25,000

FINLAND | 15,000

ESTONIA | 15,000

LATVIA | 30,000

LITHUANIA | 8,000

POLAND | 100,000

DANZIG | 600

CZECHOSLOVAKIA | 20,000

HUNGARY | 500

YUGOSLAVIA | 30,000

SWEDEN | 1,000

GERMANY | 100,000

AUSTRIA | 3,000

SWITZ. | 2,000

ITALY | 2,500

DENMARK | 300

HOLLAND | 300

BELGIUM | 7,000

FRANCE | 200,000

GT. BRITAIN | 4,000

SPAIN | 500

300

0

Miles

IN CHINA | 100,000
IN USA | 100,000
IN BRAZIL | 500
IN ABYSSINIA | 50

The Bolsheviks imprisoned over 80,000 Russians between 1917 and 1919, of whom as many as 10,000 were executed. Over a million Russians fled into exile between 1917 and 1923

Estimated number of Russian refugees living in exile by 1930

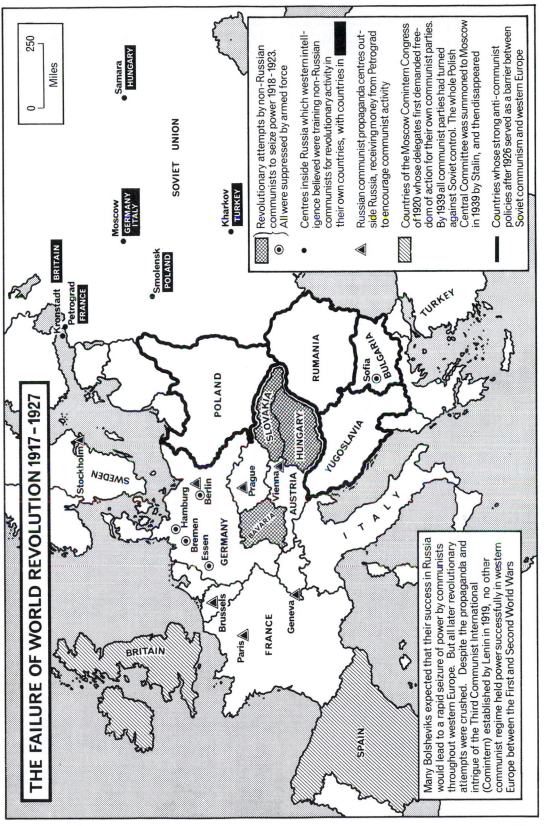

THE FAILURE OF WORLD REVOLUTION 1917–1927

Many Bolsheviks expected that their success in Russia would lead to a rapid seizure of power by communists throughout western Europe. But all later revolutionary attempts were crushed. Despite the propaganda and intrigue of the Third Communist International (Comintern) established by Lenin in 1919, no other communist regime held power successfully in western Europe between the First and Second World Wars

Revolutionary attempts by non-Russian communists to seize power 1918 - 1923. All were suppressed by armed force

Centres inside Russia which western intelligence believed were training non-Russian communists for revolutionary activity in their own countries, with countries in

Russian communist propaganda centres outside Russia, receiving money from Petrograd to encourage communist activity

Countries of the Moscow Comintern Congress of 1920 whose delegates first demanded freedom of action for their own communist parties. By 1939 all communist parties had turned against Soviet control. The whole Polish Central Committee was summoned to Moscow in 1939 by Stalin, and then disappeared

Countries whose strong anti-communist policies after 1926 served as a barrier between Soviet communism and western Europe

SOVIET UNION

BRITAIN
FRANCE
SWEDEN
GERMANY
POLAND
FRANCE
SPAIN
ITALY
AUSTRIA
HUNGARY
SLOVAKIA
BAVARIA
YUGOSLAVIA
RUMANIA
BULGARIA
TURKEY

Kronstadt
Petrograd
Stockholm
Hamburg
Bremen
Berlin
Essen
Brussels
Prague
Vienna
Paris
Geneva
Sofia

Samara HUNGARY
Moscow GERMANY ITALY
Smolensk POLAND
Kharkov TURKEY

0   250
Miles

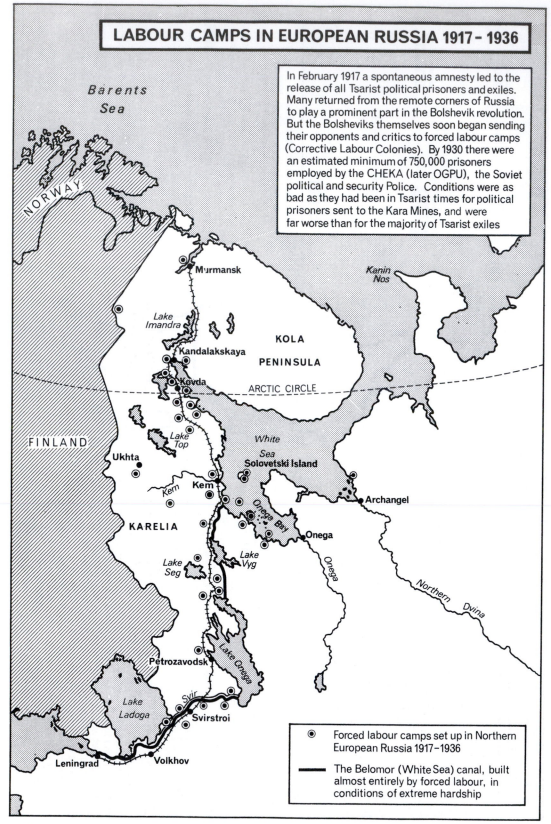

LABOUR CAMPS IN EUROPEAN RUSSIA 1917 – 1936

In February 1917 a spontaneous amnesty led to the release of all Tsarist political prisoners and exiles. Many returned from the remote corners of Russia to play a prominent part in the Bolshevik revolution. But the Bolsheviks themselves soon began sending their opponents and critics to forced labour camps (Corrective Labour Colonies). By 1930 there were an estimated minimum of 750,000 prisoners employed by the CHEKA (later OGPU), the Soviet political and security Police. Conditions were as bad as they had been in Tsarist times for political prisoners sent to the Kara Mines, and were far worse than for the majority of Tsarist exiles

Barents Sea

NORWAY

Murmansk

Kanin Nos

Lake Imandra

Kandalakskaya

KOLA

PENINSULA

Kovda

ARCTIC CIRCLE

FINLAND

Lake Top

White Sea

Solovetski Island

Ukhta

Kem **Kem**

Archangel

Onega Bay

KARELIA

Onega

Lake Vyg

Lake Seg

Onega

Northern Dvina

Lake Onega

Petrozavodsk

Svir

Lake Ladoga

Svirstroi

Leningrad   **Volkhov**

⊚ Forced labour camps set up in Northern European Russia 1917–1936

▬ The Belomor (White Sea) canal, built almost entirely by forced labour, in conditions of extreme hardship

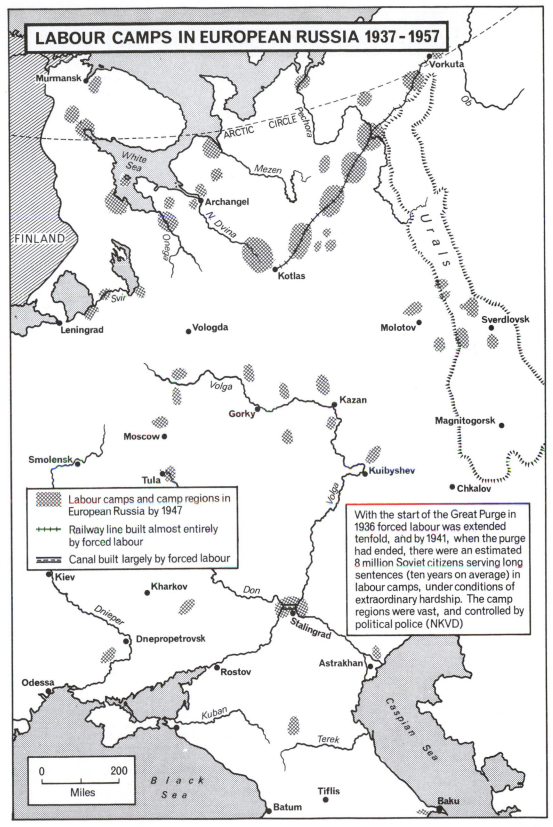

LABOUR CAMPS IN EUROPEAN RUSSIA 1937 - 1957

Murmansk

Vorkuta

ARCTIC CIRCLE

Pechora

Ob

White Sea

Mezen

Archangel

Onega

N Dvina

FINLAND

Svir

Kotlas

U r a l s

Leningrad

Vologda

Molotov

Sverdlovsk

Volga

Gorky

Kazan

Magnitogorsk

Moscow

Smolensk

Kuibyshev

Tula

Volga

Chkalov

Labour camps and camp regions in European Russia by 1947

Railway line built almost entirely by forced labour

Canal built largely by forced labour

With the start of the Great Purge in 1936 forced labour was extended tenfold, and by 1941, when the purge had ended, there were an estimated 8 million Soviet citizens serving long sentences (ten years on average) in labour camps, under conditions of extraordinary hardship. The camp regions were vast, and controlled by political police (NKVD)

Kiev

Kharkov

Don

Dnieper

Stalingrad

Dnepropetrovsk

Rostov

Astrakhan

Odessa

Kuban

Caspian Sea

0   200

Miles

Black Sea

Terek

Tiflis

Baku

Batum

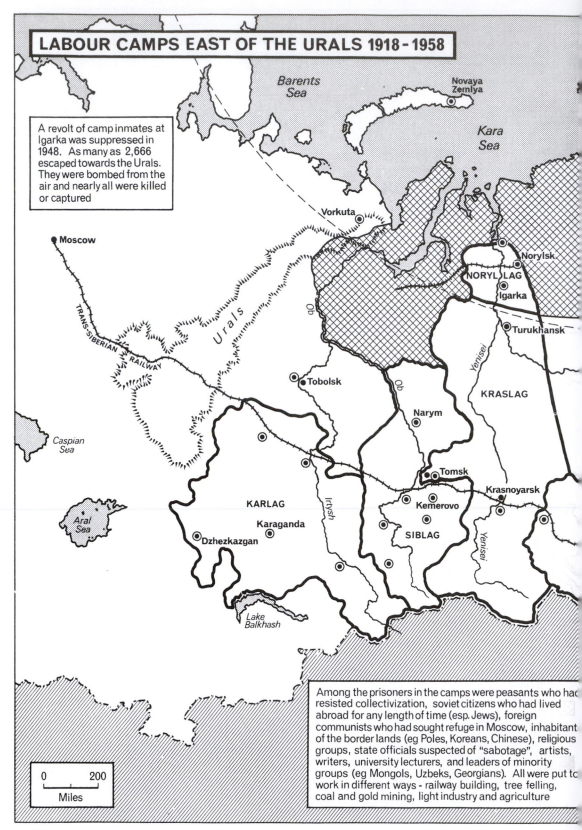

LABOUR CAMPS EAST OF THE URALS 1918-1958

Barents Sea

Novaya Zemlya

Kara Sea

A revolt of camp inmates at Igarka was suppressed in 1948. As many as 2,666 escaped towards the Urals. They were bombed from the air and nearly all were killed or captured

● Moscow

Vorkuta

● Norylsk

NORYL LAG

● Igarka

Ob

● Turukhansk

Yenisei

U r a l s

Ob

KRASLAG

TRANS-SIBERIAN RAILWAY

● Tobolsk

Narym

Caspian Sea

Irtysh

● Tomsk

Krasnoyarsk

KARLAG

Kemerovo

Aral Sea

Karaganda

SIBLAG

● Dzhezkazgan

Yenisei

Lake Balkhash

Among the prisoners in the camps were peasants who had resisted collectivization, soviet citizens who had lived abroad for any length of time (esp. Jews), foreign communists who had sought refuge in Moscow, inhabitant of the border lands (eg Poles, Koreans, Chinese), religious groups, state officials suspected of "sabotage", artists, writers, university lecturers, and leaders of minority groups (eg Mongols, Uzbeks, Georgians). All were put to work in different ways - railway building, tree felling, coal and gold mining, light industry and agriculture

0   200
Miles

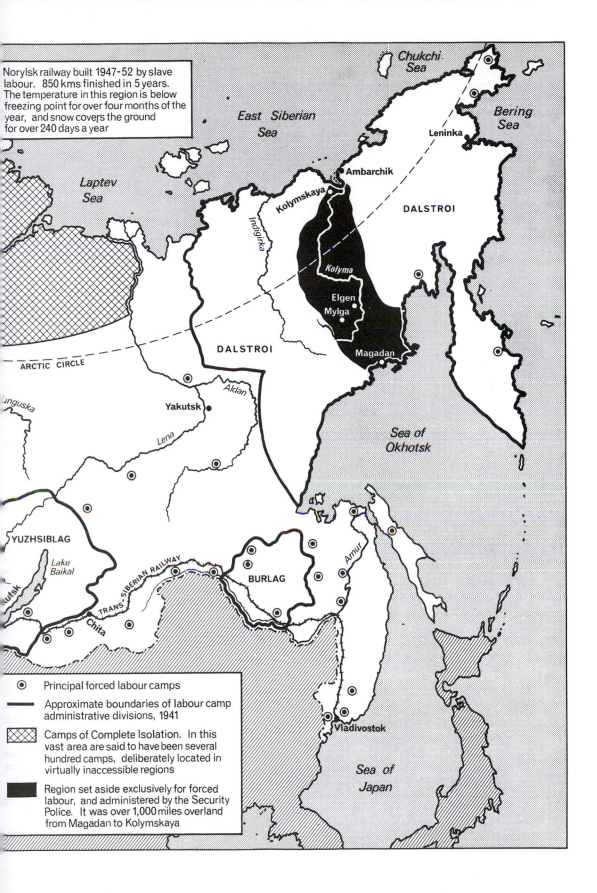

Norylsk railway built 1947-52 by slave labour. 850 kms finished in 5 years. The temperature in this region is below freezing point for over four months of the year, and snow covers the ground for over 240 days a year

Chukchi Sea

East Siberian Sea

Bering Sea

Leninka

Laptev Sea

Ambarchik

Kolymskaya

DALSTROI

Indigirka

Kolyma

Elgen
Mylga

DALSTROI

Magadan

ARCTIC CIRCLE

Aldan

Sea of Okhotsk

Tunguska

Yakutsk

Lena

YUZHSIBLAG

Lake Baikal

TRANS-SIBERIAN RAILWAY

Amur

BURLAG

Chita

kutsk

Vladivostok

Sea of Japan

◉ Principal forced labour camps

── Approximate boundaries of labour camp administrative divisions, 1941

▨ Camps of Complete Isolation. In this vast area are said to have been several hundred camps, deliberately located in virtually inaccessible regions

▰ Region set aside exclusively for forced labour, and administered by the Security Police. It was over 1,000 miles overland from Magadan to Kolymskaya

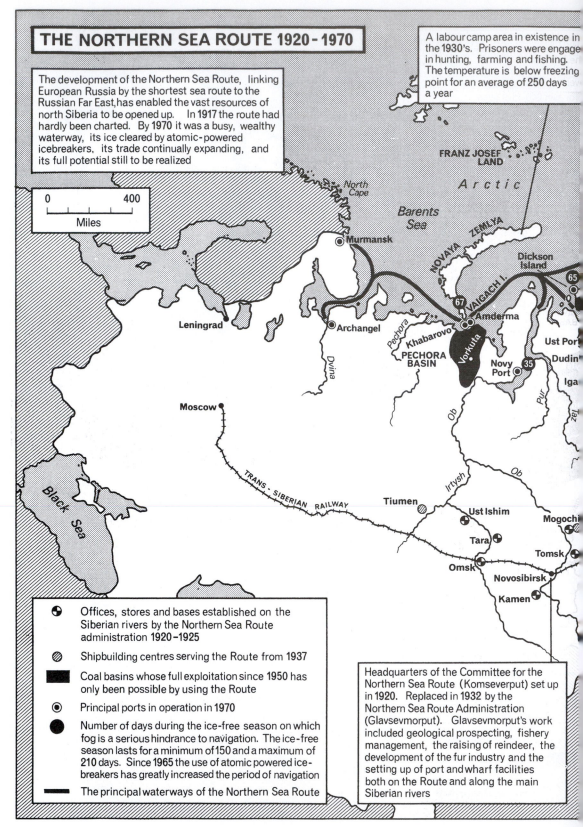

THE NORTHERN SEA ROUTE 1920-1970

The development of the Northern Sea Route, linking European Russia by the shortest sea route to the Russian Far East, has enabled the vast resources of north Siberia to be opened up. In 1917 the route had hardly been charted. By 1970 it was a busy, wealthy waterway, its ice cleared by atomic-powered icebreakers, its trade continually expanding, and its full potential still to be realized

A labour camp area in existence in the 1930's. Prisoners were engaged in hunting, farming and fishing. The temperature is below freezing point for an average of 250 days a year

FRANZ JOSEF LAND

Arctic

Barents Sea

North Cape

NOVAYA ZEMLYA

Murmansk

Dickson Island

65

67 VAIGACH I.

Amderma

Pechora

Ust Port

Archangel

Khabarovo

PECHORA BASIN

Vorkuta

Dudin

Novy Port

35

Iga

Leningrad

Dvina

Ob

Pur

Taz

Moscow

Iga

TRANS - SIBERIAN RAILWAY

Irtysh

Ob

Black Sea

Tiumen

Ust Ishim

Mogochi

Tara

Tomsk

Omsk

Novosibirsk

Kamen

0 — 400
Miles

Offices, stores and bases established on the Siberian rivers by the Northern Sea Route administration 1920–1925

Shipbuilding centres serving the Route from 1937

Coal basins whose full exploitation since 1950 has only been possible by using the Route

Principal ports in operation in 1970

Number of days during the ice-free season on which fog is a serious hindrance to navigation. The ice-free season lasts for a minimum of 150 and a maximum of 210 days. Since 1965 the use of atomic powered ice-breakers has greatly increased the period of navigation

The principal waterways of the Northern Sea Route

Headquarters of the Committee for the Northern Sea Route (Komseverput) set up in 1920. Replaced in 1932 by the Northern Sea Route Administration (Glavsevmorput). Glavsevmorput's work included geological prospecting, fishery management, the raising of reindeer, the development of the fur industry and the setting up of port and wharf facilities both on the Route and along the main Siberian rivers

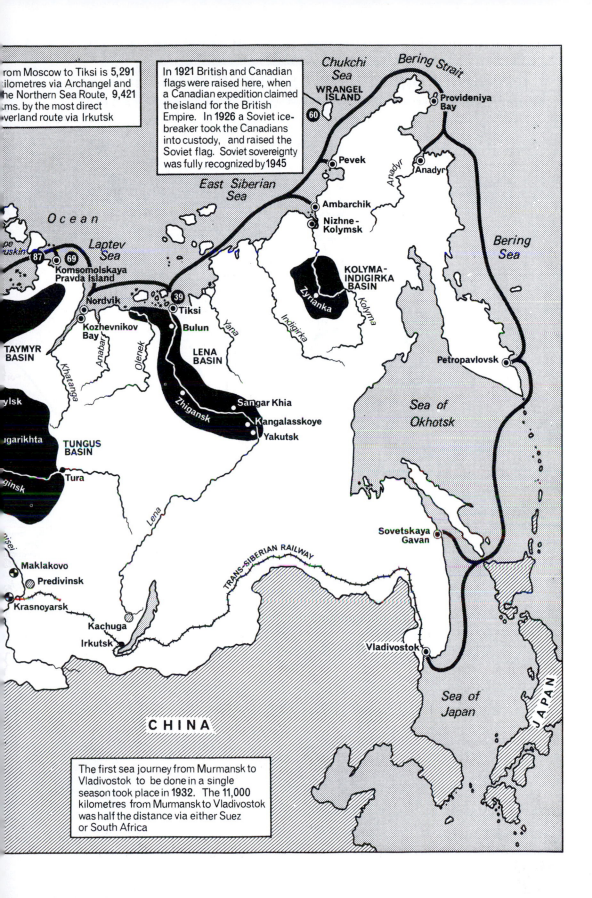

From Moscow to Tiksi is 5,291 kilometres via Archangel and the Northern Sea Route, 9,421 kms. by the most direct overland route via Irkutsk

In 1921 British and Canadian flags were raised here, when a Canadian expedition claimed the island for the British Empire. In 1926 a Soviet ice-breaker took the Canadians into custody, and raised the Soviet flag. Soviet sovereignty was fully recognized by 1945

The first sea journey from Murmansk to Vladivostok to be done in a single season took place in 1932. The 11,000 kilometres from Murmansk to Vladivostok was half the distance via either Suez or South Africa

Chukchi Sea
Bering Strait
WRANGEL ISLAND
60
Providaniya Bay
Pevek
Anadyr
East Siberian Sea
Ambarchik
Nizhne-Kolymsk
Bering Sea
Ocean
Laptev Sea
87
69
Komsomolskaya Pravda Island
KOLYMA-INDIGIRKA BASIN
Zyrianka
Nordvik
39
Tiksi
Bulun
Kozhevnikov Bay
TAYMYR BASIN
Yana
LENA BASIN
Indigirka
Kolyma
Petropavlovsk
ylsk
Khatanga
Anabar
Olenek
Zhigansk
Sangar Khia
Kangalasskoye
Yakutsk
Sea of Okhotsk
ugarikhta
TUNGUS BASIN
Tura
Lena
giinsk
nisei
Maklakovo
Predivinsk
Krasnoyarsk
TRANS-SIBERIAN RAILWAY
Sovetskaya Gavan
Kachuga
Irkutsk
Vladivostok
CHINA
Sea of Japan
JAPAN

THE SOVIET UNION UNDER STALIN 1922-1953

Arct

Barer

North
Sea

NORWAY

SWEDEN

FINLAND

London

DENMARK

FRANCE

WEST GERMANY

Rhine

Berlin

Potsdam
1945

Prague

Warsaw

Leningrad

100

Volga

Moscow
1942
1944

200

AUSTRIA

Vienna

Budapest

100

Kiev

Kuibysh

ITALY

Adriatic Sea

Danube

Belgrade

Kharkov

Saratov

Urals

Bucharest

400

DONBASS

Sofia

GREECE

Yalta
1945

Black Sea

Prinkipo

Caucasus

Caspian Sea

Mediterranean Sea

TURKEY

Tabriz

Tehera
1943

PERSIA

0   300
Miles

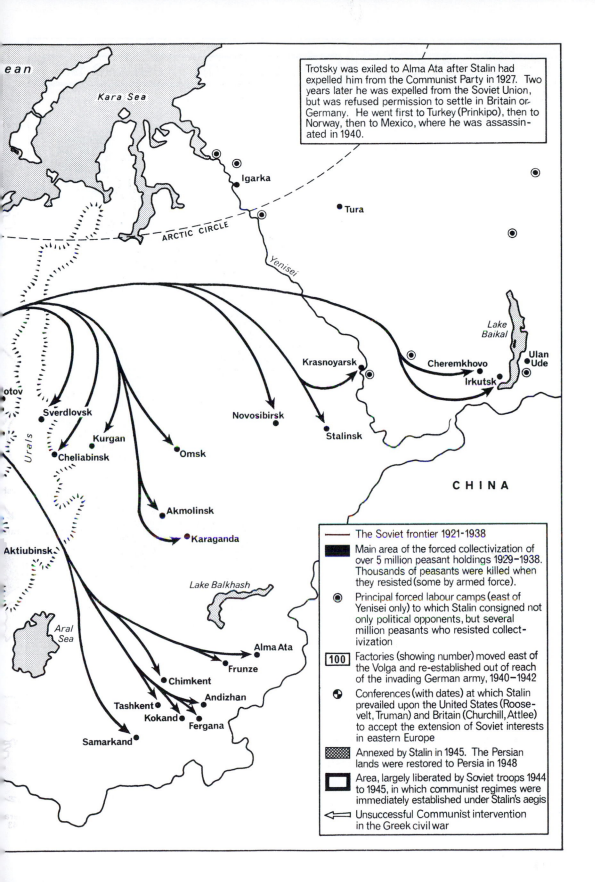

Trotsky was exiled to Alma Ata after Stalin had expelled him from the Communist Party in 1927. Two years later he was expelled from the Soviet Union, but was refused permission to settle in Britain or Germany. He went first to Turkey (Prinkipo), then to Norway, then to Mexico, where he was assassinated in 1940.

Kara Sea

ean

Igarka

ARCTIC CIRCLE

Yenisei

Tura

Lake Baikal

Krasnoyarsk

Cheremkhovo

Ulan Ude

Irkutsk

...otov

Sverdlovsk

Kurgan

Cheliabinsk

Urals

Omsk

Novosibirsk

Stalinsk

CHINA

Akmolinsk

Karaganda

Aktiubinsk

Lake Balkhash

Aral Sea

Alma Ata

Frunze

Chimkent

Andizhan

Tashkent

Kokand

Fergana

Samarkand

The Soviet frontier 1921-1938

Main area of the forced collectivization of over 5 million peasant holdings 1929-1938. Thousands of peasants were killed when they resisted (some by armed force).

Principal forced labour camps (east of Yenisei only) to which Stalin consigned not only political opponents, but several million peasants who resisted collectivization

100 Factories (showing number) moved east of the Volga and re-established out of reach of the invading German army, 1940-1942

Conferences (with dates) at which Stalin prevailed upon the United States (Roosevelt, Truman) and Britain (Churchill, Attlee) to accept the extension of Soviet interests in eastern Europe

Annexed by Stalin in 1945. The Persian lands were restored to Persia in 1948

Area, largely liberated by Soviet troops 1944 to 1945, in which communist regimes were immediately established under Stalin's aegis

Unsuccessful Communist intervention in the Greek civil war

THE PARTITION OF POLAND 1939

The destruction of Poland was principally a German action. 1,700,000 German troops soon defeated the 600,000 Polish soldiers. German air attack destroyed the centres of the main Polish cities. The Poles hoped to make a final stand in the Pripet marsh area, but the Russian advance destroyed all chance of further Polish resistance

Baltic Sea

LITHUANIA

Königsberg

EAST PRUSSIA

Vilna

Suvalki

Augustov

Grodno

Minsk

Lomza

Bialystok

Posnan

Warsaw

Brest-Litovsk

Pinsk

Pripet

Marshes

R U S S I A

P O L A N D

Lublin

S O V I E T

Lodz

Lutsk

Sokal

Rovno

GERMANY

Tarnov

Cracow

Yaroslav

Lvov

Tarnopol

Przemysl

Stanislavov

Kamenets Podolsk

SLOVAKIA

H U N G A R Y

RUMANIA

⟹ German advance against Poland from 3 September 1939

⟸ Russian advance against Poland from 17 September 1939

▬ Dividing line between the German and Russian zones of occupation, agreed upon in advance by the Russo-German Pact of 23 August 1939

◼ Annexed by the Soviet Union in October 1939

▨ Annexed by Germany

▧ Annexed by Lithuania

0   100

Miles

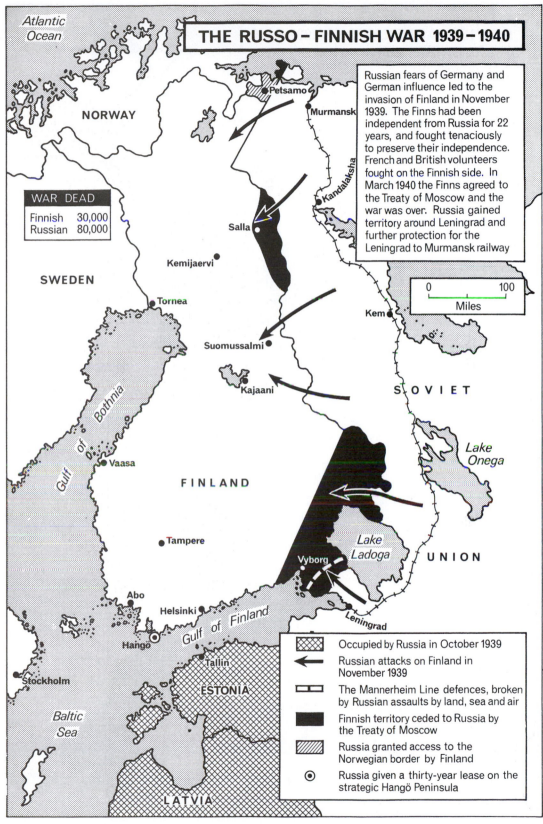

THE RUSSO – FINNISH WAR 1939 – 1940

Russian fears of Germany and German influence led to the invasion of Finland in November 1939. The Finns had been independent from Russia for 22 years, and fought tenaciously to preserve their independence. French and British volunteers fought on the Finnish side. In March 1940 the Finns agreed to the Treaty of Moscow and the war was over. Russia gained territory around Leningrad and further protection for the Leningrad to Murmansk railway

WAR DEAD

Finnish 30,000
Russian 80,000

0 — 100
Miles

Atlantic Ocean

NORWAY

Petsamo

Murmansk

Kandalaksha

Salla

Kemijaervi

SWEDEN

Tornea

Kem

Suomussalmi

Kajaani

S O V I E T

Lake Onega

Gulf of Bothnia

Vaasa

F I N L A N D

Tampere

Lake Ladoga

Vyborg

U N I O N

Abo

Helsinki

Gulf of Finland

Leningrad

Hango

Tallin

Stockholm

ESTONIA

Baltic Sea

LATVIA

Occupied by Russia in October 1939

Russian attacks on Finland in November 1939

The Mannerheim Line defences, broken by Russian assaults by land, sea and air

Finnish territory ceded to Russia by the Treaty of Moscow

Russia granted access to the Norwegian border by Finland

Russia given a thirty-year lease on the strategic Hangö Peninsula

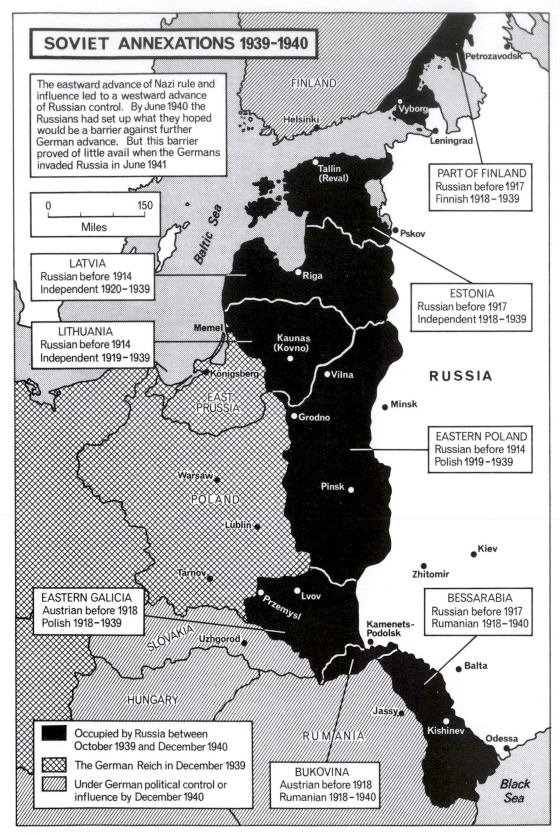

SOVIET ANNEXATIONS 1939-1940

The eastward advance of Nazi rule and influence led to a westward advance of Russian control. By June 1940 the Russians had set up what they hoped would be a barrier against further German advance. But this barrier proved of little avail when the Germans invaded Russia in June 1941

```
0          150
    Miles
```

FINLAND

Petrozavodsk

Helsinki

Vyborg

Leningrad

Tallin (Reval)

PART OF FINLAND
Russian before 1917
Finnish 1918–1939

Pskov

Baltic Sea

LATVIA
Russian before 1914
Independent 1920–1939

Riga

ESTONIA
Russian before 1917
Independent 1918–1939

Memel

LITHUANIA
Russian before 1914
Independent 1919–1939

Kaunas (Kovno)

Königsberg

EAST PRUSSIA

Vilna

RUSSIA

Minsk

Grodno

EASTERN POLAND
Russian before 1914
Polish 1919–1939

Warsaw

POLAND

Pinsk

Lublin

Kiev

Tarnov

Zhitomir

EASTERN GALICIA
Austrian before 1918
Polish 1918–1939

Przemysl

Lvov

Kamenets-Podolsk

BESSARABIA
Russian before 1917
Rumanian 1918–1940

SLOVAKIA

Uzhgorod

Balta

HUNGARY

Jassy

Kishinev

Odessa

■ Occupied by Russia between October 1939 and December 1940

▨ The German Reich in December 1939

▧ Under German political control or influence by December 1940

RUMANIA

BUKOVINA
Austrian before 1918
Rumanian 1918–1940

Black Sea

EUROPE ON 22 JUNE 1941

Archangel

NORWAY

SWEDEN

FINLAND

Hango

Leningrad

Riga

Kovno

Vilna

Moscow

DENMARK

Danzig

SOVIET
UNION

EIRE

BRITAIN

London

HOLLAND

Berlin

Brest-Litovsk

Warsaw

GREATER
GERMANY

Cologne

Cracow

Lvov

BELGIUM

Prague

Munich

Vienna

SLOVAKIA

Kishinev

FRANCE

SWITZ

HUNGARY

Odessa

RUMANIA

SPAIN

YUGOSLAVIA

BULGARIA

ITALY

ALBANIA

TURKEY

GREECE

The German Reich on 22 June 1941,
the day of the German invasion of Russia

Countries under German rule or
influence by June 1941

Neutral countries

Great Britain, the only state at war with
Germany on 21 June 1941; and the
Soviet Union, to whom Britain
immediately offered all possible help
and alliance in the fight against Nazism

0   300

Miles

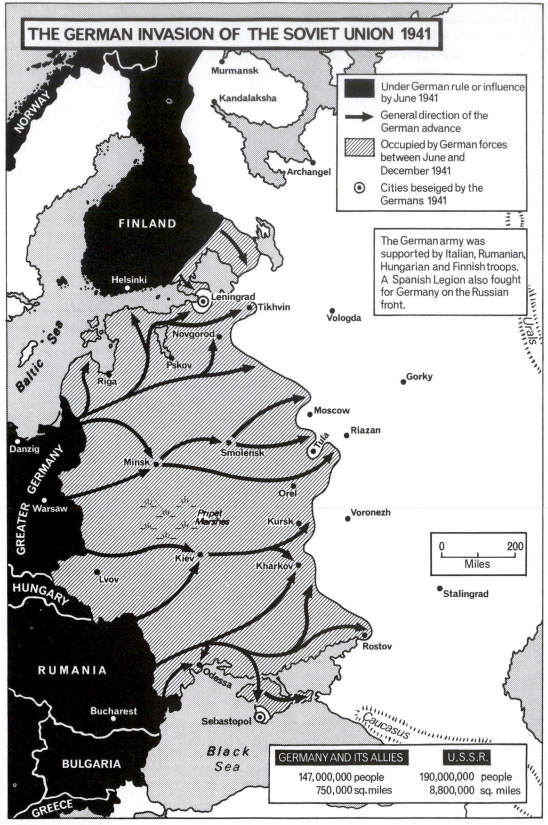

THE GERMAN INVASION OF THE SOVIET UNION 1941

Legend:

- ■ Under German rule or influence by June 1941
- → General direction of the German advance
- ▨ Occupied by German forces between June and December 1941
- ⊙ Cities beseiged by the Germans 1941

The German army was supported by Italian, Rumanian, Hungarian and Finnish troops. A Spanish Legion also fought for Germany on the Russian front.

NORWAY

Murmansk

Kandalaksha

Archangel

FINLAND

Helsinki

Leningrad

Tikhvin

Vologda

Novgorod

Pskov

Riga

Gorky

Baltic Sea

Moscow

Riazan

Danzig

Tula

Smolensk

GREATER GERMANY

Minsk

Orel

Voronezh

Warsaw

Pripet Marshes

Kursk

Urals

0 ——— 200
Miles

HUNGARY

Kiev

Kharkov

Lvov

Stalingrad

Rostov

Odessa

RUMANIA

Bucharest

Sebastopol

Caucasus

Black Sea

BULGARIA

GERMANY AND ITS ALLIES	U.S.S.R.
147,000,000 people	190,000,000 people
750,000 sq. miles	8,800,000 sq. miles

GREECE

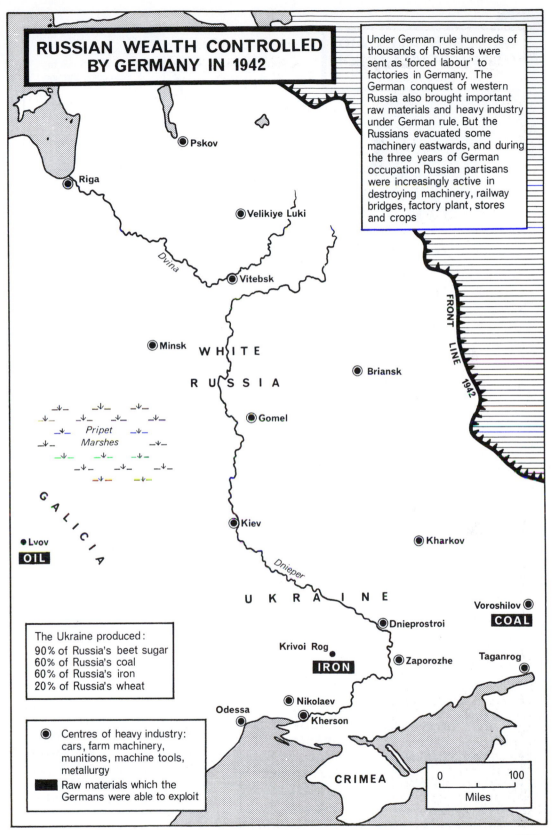

RUSSIAN WEALTH CONTROLLED BY GERMANY IN 1942

Under German rule hundreds of thousands of Russians were sent as 'forced labour' to factories in Germany. The German conquest of western Russia also brought important raw materials and heavy industry under German rule. But the Russians evacuated some machinery eastwards, and during the three years of German occupation Russian partisans were increasingly active in destroying machinery, railway bridges, factory plant, stores and crops

Pskov

Riga

Velikiye Luki

Dvina

Vitebsk

FRONT LINE 1942

Minsk

W H I T E

R U S S I A

Briansk

Gomel

Pripet Marshes

G A L I C I A

Kiev

Kharkov

Lvov

OIL

Dnieper

U K R A I N E

Voroshilov

COAL

Dnieprostroi

Krivoi Rog

IRON

Zaporozhe

Taganrog

The Ukraine produced:
90% of Russia's beet sugar
60% of Russia's coal
60% of Russia's iron
20% of Russia's wheat

Nikolaev

Odessa

Kherson

⊙ Centres of heavy industry:
cars, farm machinery,
munitions, machine tools,
metallurgy

▬ Raw materials which the
Germans were able to exploit

CRIMEA

0   100

Miles

119

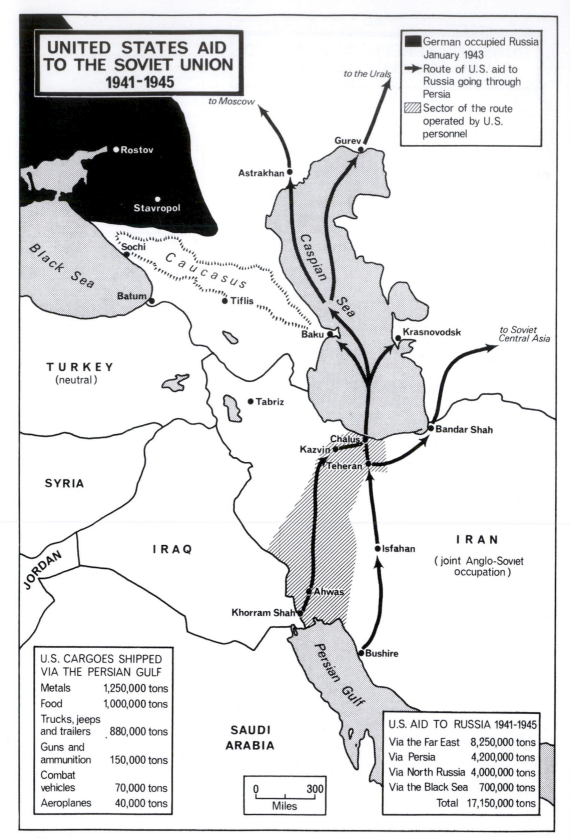

UNITED STATES AID TO THE SOVIET UNION 1941-1945

	German occupied Russia January 1943
→	Route of U.S. aid to Russia going through Persia
▨	Sector of the route operated by U.S. personnel

to the Urals

to Moscow

Rostov

Stavropol

Gurev

Astrakhan

Sochi

C a u c a s u s

Black Sea

Batum

Tiflis

Baku

Krasnovodsk

to Soviet Central Asia

Caspian Sea

TURKEY
(neutral)

Tabriz

Chalus

Kazvin

Teheran

Bandar Shah

SYRIA

I R A N
(joint Anglo-Soviet occupation)

JORDAN

I R A Q

Isfahan

Ahwas

Khorram Shah

Bushire

Persian Gulf

SAUDI
ARABIA

U.S. CARGOES SHIPPED VIA THE PERSIAN GULF

Metals	1,250,000 tons
Food	1,000,000 tons
Trucks, jeeps and trailers	880,000 tons
Guns and ammunition	150,000 tons
Combat vehicles	70,000 tons
Aeroplanes	40,000 tons

0   300
Miles

U.S. AID TO RUSSIA 1941-1945

Via the Far East	8,250,000 tons
Via Persia	4,200,000 tons
Via North Russia	4,000,000 tons
Via the Black Sea	700,000 tons
Total	17,150,000 tons

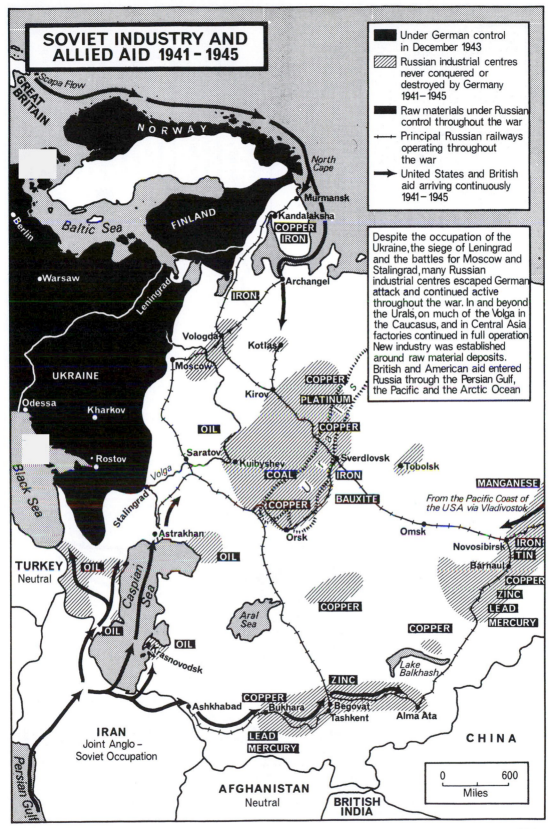

SOVIET INDUSTRY AND ALLIED AID 1941 – 1945

Under German control in December 1943

Russian industrial centres never conquered or destroyed by Germany 1941 – 1945

Raw materials under Russian control throughout the war

Principal Russian railways operating throughout the war

United States and British aid arriving continuously 1941 – 1945

Despite the occupation of the Ukraine, the siege of Leningrad and the battles for Moscow and Stalingrad, many Russian industrial centres escaped German attack and continued active throughout the war. In and beyond the Urals, on much of the Volga in the Caucasus, and in Central Asia factories continued in full operation. New industry was established around raw material deposits. British and American aid entered Russia through the Persian Gulf, the Pacific and the Arctic Ocean

GREAT BRITAIN

Scapa Flow

NORWAY

North Cape

Baltic Sea

FINLAND

Berlin

Murmansk

Kandalaksha
COPPER
IRON

Warsaw

Archangel

IRON

Leningrad

Vologda

Kotlas

Moscow

Kirov

COPPER

PLATINUM

UKRAINE

Odessa

Kharkov

OIL

COPPER

Saratov

Rostov

Volga

Kuibyshev

Sverdlovsk

Tobolsk

COAL

IRON

COPPER

BAUXITE

MANGANESE

Orsk

Omsk

From the Pacific Coast of the USA via Vladivostok

Novosibirsk

IRON
TIN

Barnaul

COPPER

ZINC

LEAD

MERCURY

Stalingrad

Astrakhan

OIL

Aral Sea

COPPER

COPPER

Black Sea

TURKEY
Neutral

OIL

Caspian Sea

OIL

Lake Balkhash

OIL

Krasnovodsk

ZINC

COPPER

Bukhara

Begovat

Tashkent

Alma Ata

Ashkhabad

CHINA

IRAN
Joint Anglo –
Soviet Occupation

LEAD
MERCURY

Persian Gulf

AFGHANISTAN
Neutral

BRITISH
INDIA

0   600
Miles

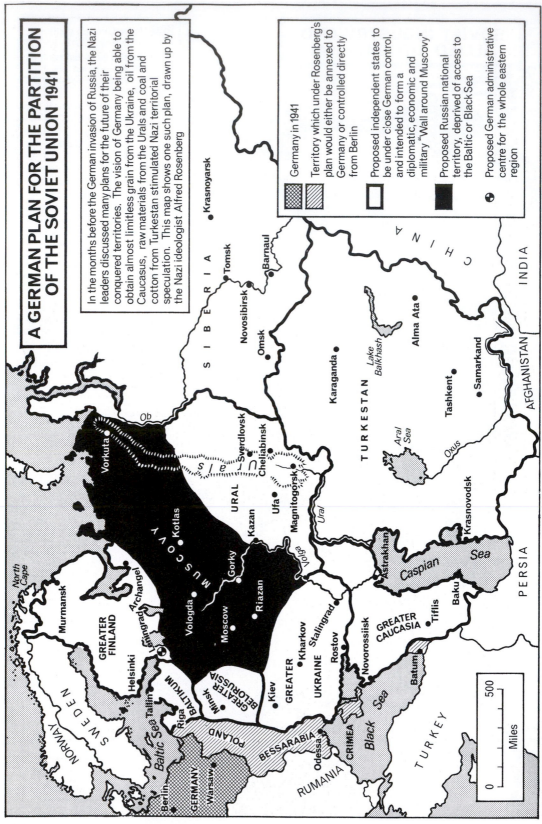

A GERMAN PLAN FOR THE PARTITION OF THE SOVIET UNION 1941

In the months before the German invasion of Russia, the Nazi leaders discussed many plans for the future of their conquered territories. The vision of Germany being able to obtain almost limitless grain from the Ukraine, oil from the Caucasus, raw materials from the Urals and coal and cotton from Turkestan stimulated Nazi territorial speculation. This map shows one such plan, drawn up by the Nazi ideologist Alfred Rosenberg.

Germany in 1941

Territory which under Rosenberg's plan would either be annexed to Germany or controlled directly from Berlin

Proposed independent states to be under close German control, and intended to form a diplomatic, economic and military "Wall around Muscovy"

Proposed Russian national territory, deprived of access to the Baltic or Black Sea

Proposed German administrative centre for the whole eastern region

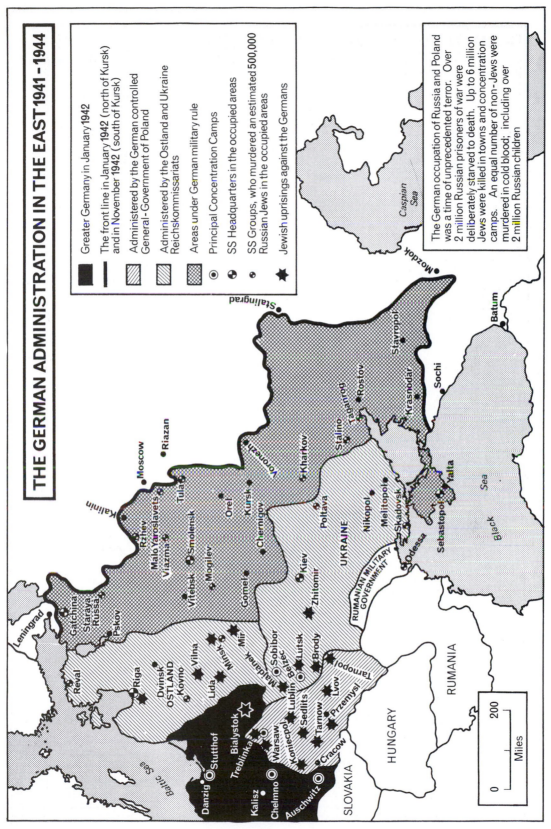

THE GERMAN ADMINISTRATION IN THE EAST 1941 – 1944

Greater Germany in January 1942

The front line in January 1942 (north of Kursk) and in November 1942 (south of Kursk)

Administered by the German controlled General - Government of Poland

Administered by the Ostland and Ukraine Reichskommissariats

Areas under German military rule

Principal Concentration Camps

SS Headquarters in the occupied areas

SS Groups, who murdered an estimated 500,000 Russian Jews in the occupied areas

Jewish uprisings against the Germans

The German occupation of Russia and Poland was a time of unprecedented terror. Over 2 million Russian prisoners of war were deliberately starved to death. Up to 6 million Jews were killed in towns and concentration camps. An equal number of non-Jews were murdered in cold blood; including over 2 million Russian children

Caspian Sea

Mozdok

Stalingrad

Batum

Sochi

Stavropol

Krasnodar

Rostov

Taganrog

Stalino

Kharkov

Voronezh

Riazan

Moscow

Kalinin

Tula

Orel

Kursk

Chernigov

Poltava

Nikopol

Melitopol

Skadovsk

Sebastopol

Yalta

Black Sea

Odessa

UKRAINE

RUMANIAN MILITARY GOVERNMENT

Kiev

Zhitomir

Gomel

Mogilev

Vitebsk

Smolensk

Viazma

Malo Yaroslavets

Rzhev

Staraya Russa

Gatchina

Pskov

Leningrad

Reval

Riga

Dvinsk

Kovno

Vilna

Lida

Minsk

Mir

OSTLAND

Sobibor

Lutsk

Brody

Tarnopol

Lvov

Przemysl

Belzec

Lublin

Majdanek

Sedlits

Tarnow

Cracow

Koniecpol

Warsaw

Bialystok

Treblinka

Stutthof

Danzig

Kalisz

Chelmno

Auschwitz

Baltic Sea

SLOVAKIA

HUNGARY

RUMANIA

0   200

Miles

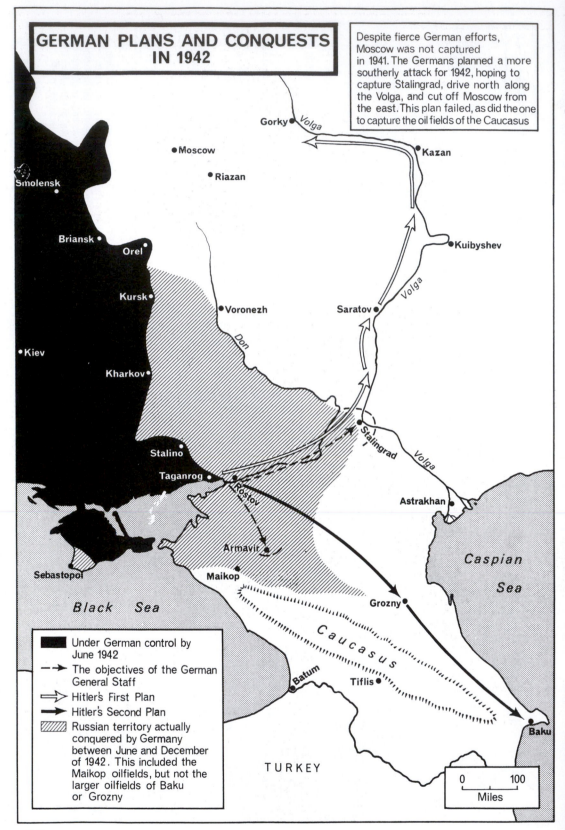

GERMAN PLANS AND CONQUESTS IN 1942

Despite fierce German efforts, Moscow was not captured in 1941. The Germans planned a more southerly attack for 1942, hoping to capture Stalingrad, drive north along the Volga, and cut off Moscow from the east. This plan failed, as did the one to capture the oil fields of the Caucasus

Gorky

Volga

Moscow

Riazan

Kazan

Smolensk

Kuibyshev

Briansk

Orel

Kursk

Voronezh

Saratov

Volga

Don

Kiev

Kharkov

Stalingrad

Volga

Stalino

Taganrog

Rostov

Astrakhan

Armavir

Caspian Sea

Sebastopol

Maikop

Grozny

Black Sea

Caucasus

Batum

Tiflis

TURKEY

Baku

Under German control by June 1942

The objectives of the German General Staff

Hitler's First Plan

Hitler's Second Plan

Russian territory actually conquered by Germany between June and December of 1942. This included the Maikop oilfields, but not the larger oilfields of Baku or Grozny

0   100
Miles

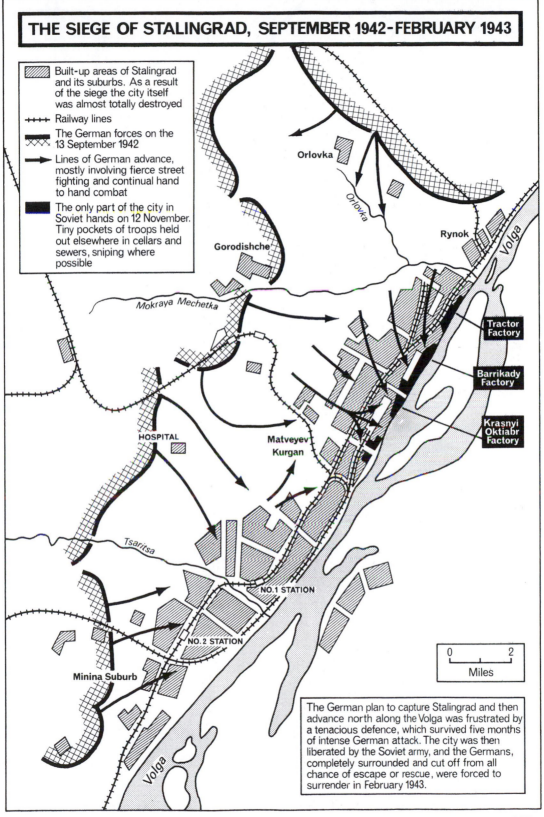

THE SIEGE OF STALINGRAD, SEPTEMBER 1942-FEBRUARY 1943

Built-up areas of Stalingrad and its suburbs. As a result of the siege the city itself was almost totally destroyed

Railway lines

The German forces on the 13 September 1942

Lines of German advance, mostly involving fierce street fighting and continual hand to hand combat

The only part of the city in Soviet hands on 12 November. Tiny pockets of troops held out elsewhere in cellars and sewers, sniping where possible

Orlovka

Orlovka

Rynok

Volga

Gorodishche

Mokraya Mechetka

Tractor Factory

Barrikady Factory

Krasnyi Oktiabr Factory

HOSPITAL

Matveyev Kurgan

Tsaritsa

NO.1 STATION

NO.2 STATION

Minina Suburb

Volga

0   2
Miles

The German plan to capture Stalingrad and then advance north along the Volga was frustrated by a tenacious defence, which survived five months of intense German attack. The city was then liberated by the Soviet army, and the Germans, completely surrounded and cut off from all chance of escape or rescue, were forced to surrender in February 1943.

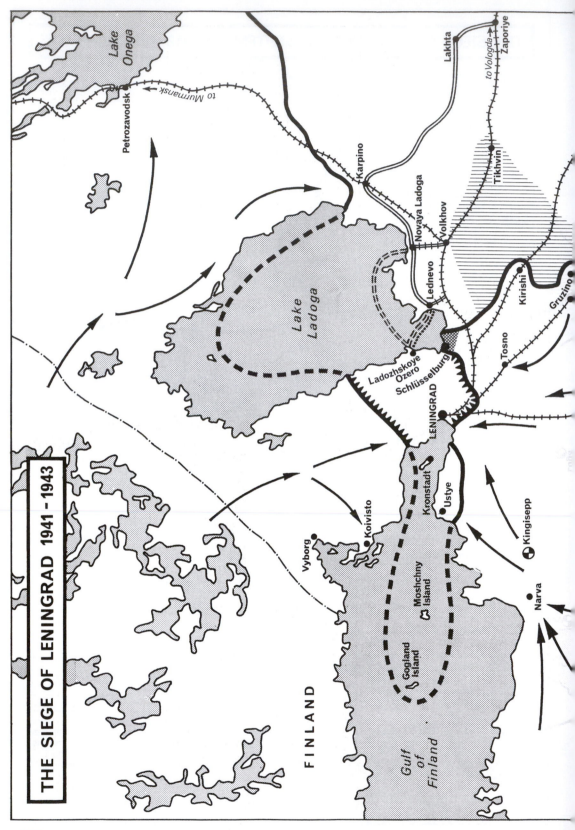

THE SIEGE OF LENINGRAD 1941 – 1943

Lake Onega

Petrozavodsk

to Murmansk →

Karpino

Lakhta

Zaporiye

to Vologda →

Tikhvin

Novaya Ladoga

Volkhov

Lednevo

Lake Ladoga

Kirishi

Gruzino

Ladozhskoye Ozero

Schlüsselburg

Tosno

LENINGRAD

FINLAND

Vyborg

Koivisto

Kronstadt

Ustye

Kingisepp

Moshchny Island

Gogland Island

Narva

Gulf of Finland

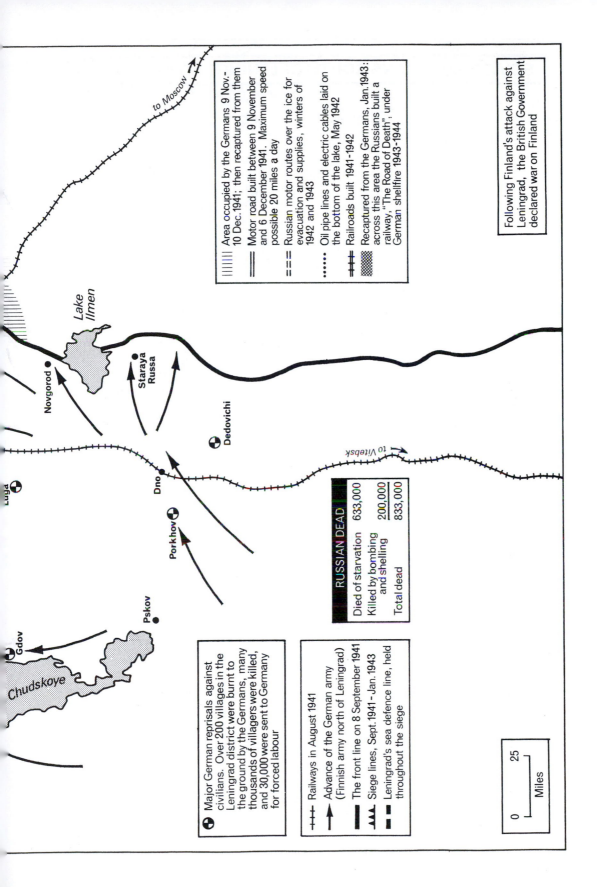

to Moscow

Lake Ilmen

Novgorod

Staraya Russa

Dedovichi

Luga

Dno

Porkhov

to Vitebsk

Pskov

Gdov

Chudskoye

RUSSIAN DEAD	
Died of starvation	633,000
Killed by bombing and shelling	200,000
Total dead	833,000

||||| Area occupied by the Germans 9 Nov.-10 Dec.1941; then recaptured from them

═══ Motor road built between 9 November and 6 December 1941. Maximum speed possible 20 miles a day

=== Russian motor routes over the ice for evacuation and supplies, winters of 1942 and 1943

•••••• Oil pipe lines and electric cables laid on the bottom of the lake, May 1942

┽┽┽ Railroads built 1941-1942

▦ Recaptured from the Germans, Jan.1943: across this area the Russians built a railway, "The Road of Death", under German shellfire 1943-1944

Following Finland's attack against Leningrad, the British Government declared war on Finland

⊕ Major German reprisals against civilians. Over 200 villages in the Leningrad district were burnt to the ground by the Germans, many thousands of villagers were killed, and 30,000 were sent to Germany for forced labour

┼┼┼ Railways in August 1941

↑ Advance of the German army (Finnish army north of Leningrad)

▬ The front line on 8 September 1941

◣◣◣ Siege lines, Sept. 1941 - Jan. 1943

▬ ▬ Leningrad's sea defence line, held throughout the siege

0   25

Miles

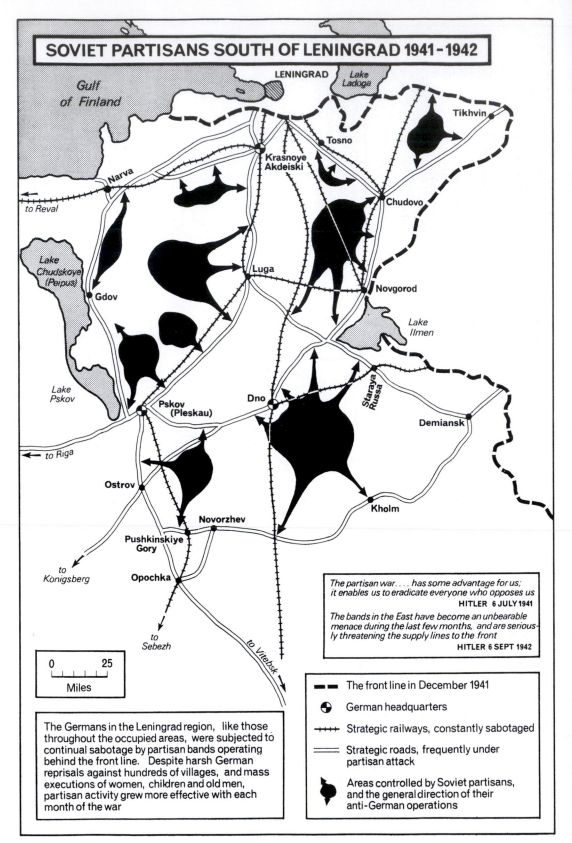

SOVIET PARTISANS SOUTH OF LENINGRAD 1941-1942

Gulf
of Finland

LENINGRAD

Lake
Ladoga

Tikhvin

Tosno

Narva

to Reval

Krasnoye
Akdeiski

Chudovo

Lake
Chudskoye
(Peipus)

Gdov

Luga

Novgorod

Lake
Ilmen

Lake
Pskov

Pskov
(Pleskau)

Dno

Starava
Russa

Demiansk

to Riga

Ostrov

Kholm

Novorzhev

Pushkinskiye
Gory

to
Konigsberg

Opochka

to
Sebezh

to Vitebsk

0   25
Miles

The partisan war.... has some advantage for us;
it enables us to eradicate everyone who opposes us
HITLER 6 JULY 1941

The bands in the East have become an unbearable
menace during the last few months, and are serious-
ly threatening the supply lines to the front
HITLER 6 SEPT 1942

- - - The front line in December 1941

⊕ German headquarters

+++ Strategic railways, constantly sabotaged

═══ Strategic roads, frequently under
      partisan attack

Areas controlled by Soviet partisans,
and the general direction of their
anti-German operations

The Germans in the Leningrad region, like those
throughout the occupied areas, were subjected to
continual sabotage by partisan bands operating
behind the front line. Despite harsh German
reprisals against hundreds of villages, and mass
executions of women, children and old men,
partisan activity grew more effective with each
month of the war

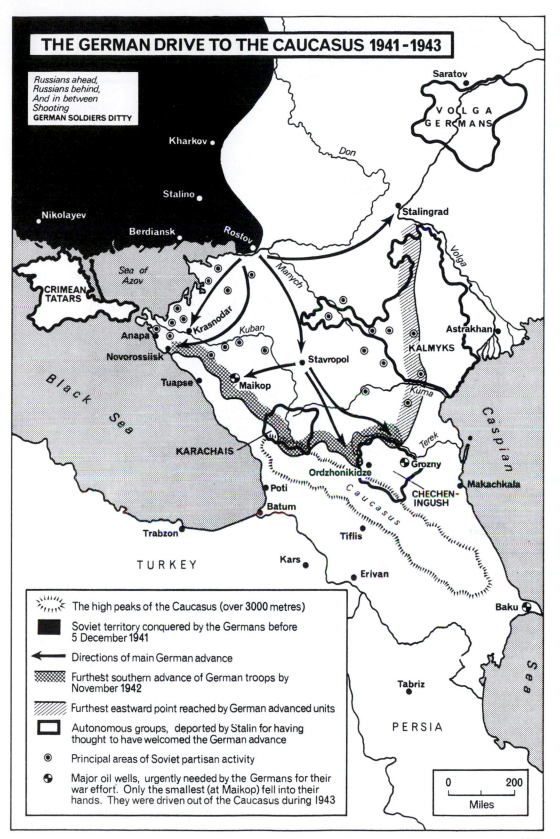

THE GERMAN DRIVE TO THE CAUCASUS 1941-1943

Russians ahead,
Russians behind,
And in between
Shooting
GERMAN SOLDIERS DITTY

Saratov

V O L G A
G E R M A N S

Kharkov

Don

Stalino

Stalingrad

Nikolayev

Berdiansk

Rostov

Volga

Sea of
Azov

Manych

CRIMEAN
TATARS

Black Sea

Krasnodar

Kuban

Astrakhan

Anapa

KALMYKS

Novorossiisk

Tuapse

Maikop

Stavropol

Kuma

KARACHAIS

Terek

Ordzhonikidze

Grozny

Caspian

Poti

CHECHEN-
INGUSH

Makachkala

Batum

C a u c a s u s

Trabzon

Tiflis

TURKEY

Kars

Erivan

Baku

Tabriz

Sea

PERSIA

The high peaks of the Caucasus (over 3000 metres)

Soviet territory conquered by the Germans before
5 December 1941

Directions of main German advance

Furthest southern advance of German troops by
November 1942

Furthest eastward point reached by German advanced units

Autonomous groups, deported by Stalin for having
thought to have welcomed the German advance

Principal areas of Soviet partisan activity

Major oil wells, urgently needed by the Germans for their
war effort. Only the smallest (at Maikop) fell into their
hands. They were driven out of the Caucasus during 1943

0   200
Miles

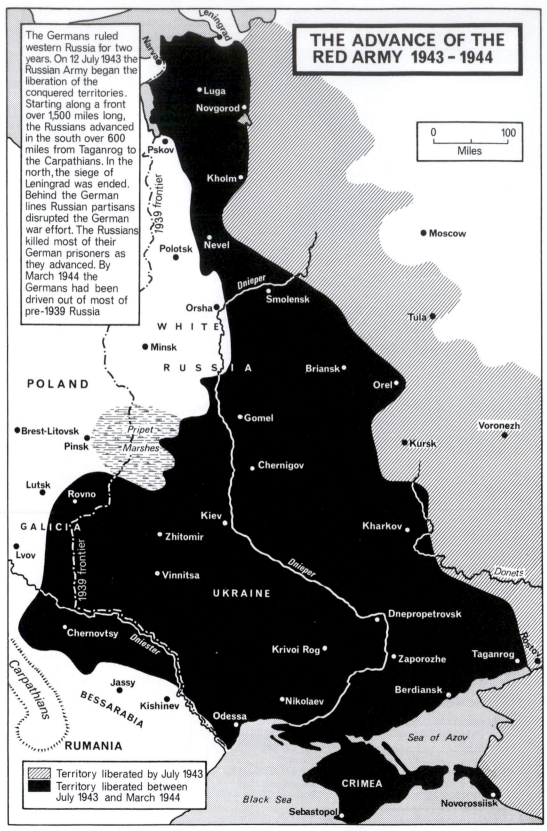

THE ADVANCE OF THE RED ARMY 1943 - 1944

The Germans ruled western Russia for two years. On 12 July 1943 the Russian Army began the liberation of the conquered territories. Starting along a front over 1,500 miles long, the Russians advanced in the south over 600 miles from Taganrog to the Carpathians. In the north, the siege of Leningrad was ended. Behind the German lines Russian partisans disrupted the German war effort. The Russians killed most of their German prisoners as they advanced. By March 1944 the Germans had been driven out of most of pre-1939 Russia

0   100
Miles

Leningrad

Narva

• Luga

Novgorod •

Pskov •

1939 frontier

Kholm •

• Moscow

Polotsk •   Nevel •

Dnieper

Orsha •   • Smolensk   Tula •

W H I T E

• Minsk   R U S S I A   Brlansk •   Orel •

P O L A N D   Pripet   • Gomel   Voronezh •

• Brest-Litovsk   Marshes   • Kursk

Pinsk   • Chernigov

Lutsk •   Rovno •

G A L I C I A   • Kiev   Kharkov •

1939 frontier   • Zhitomir

• Lvov   • Vinnitsa   Dnieper

U K R A I N E   Donets

Dnepropetrovsk •

• Chernovtsy   Dniester   Krivoi Rog •   • Zaporozhe   Taganrog •   Rostov

• Jassy   BESSARABIA   • Berdiansk

Carpathians   Kishinev •   • Nikolaev

Odessa •   Sea of Azov

RUMANIA

| Territory liberated by July 1943 |
| Territory liberated between July 1943 and March 1944 |

CRIMEA

Black Sea   Novorossiisk •

Sebastopol •

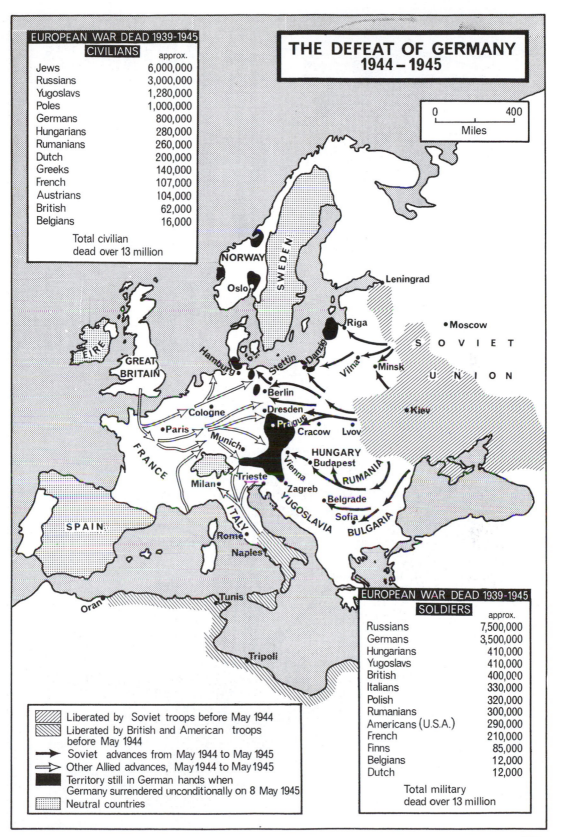

THE DEFEAT OF GERMANY 1944–1945

EUROPEAN WAR DEAD 1939-1945
CIVILIANS

	approx.
Jews	6,000,000
Russians	3,000,000
Yugoslavs	1,280,000
Poles	1,000,000
Germans	800,000
Hungarians	280,000
Rumanians	260,000
Dutch	200,000
Greeks	140,000
French	107,000
Austrians	104,000
British	62,000
Belgians	16,000

Total civilian
dead over 13 million

0 ————— 400
Miles

EUROPEAN WAR DEAD 1939-1945
SOLDIERS

	approx.
Russians	7,500,000
Germans	3,500,000
Hungarians	410,000
Yugoslavs	410,000
British	400,000
Italians	330,000
Polish	320,000
Rumanians	300,000
Americans (U.S.A.)	290,000
French	210,000
Finns	85,000
Belgians	12,000
Dutch	12,000

Total military
dead over 13 million

Liberated by Soviet troops before May 1944
Liberated by British and American troops before May 1944
Soviet advances from May 1944 to May 1945
Other Allied advances, May 1944 to May 1945
Territory still in German hands when Germany surrendered unconditionally on 8 May 1945
Neutral countries

130

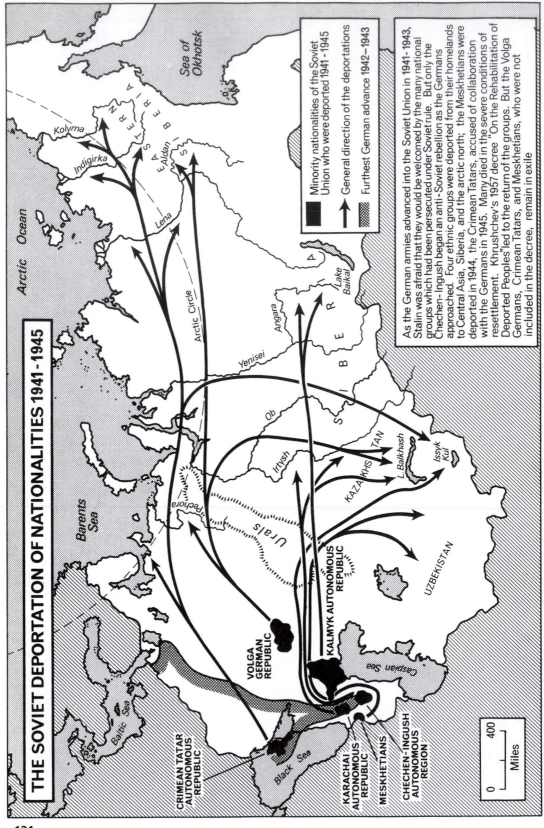

THE SOVIET DEPORTATION OF NATIONALITIES 1941-1945

Sea of Okhotsk

EASTERN

Kolyma

Indigirka

Lena

Aldan

Arctic Ocean

Arctic Circle

Yenisei

SIBERIA

Angara

Lake Baikal

Ob

Irtysh

KAZAKHSTAN

L.Balkhash

Issyk Kul

Barents Sea

Pechora

Urals

Caspian Sea

UZBEKISTAN

VOLGA GERMAN REPUBLIC

KALMYK AUTONOMOUS REPUBLIC

Black Sea

Baltic Sea

CRIMEAN TATAR AUTONOMOUS REPUBLIC

KARACHAI AUTONOMOUS REPUBLIC

MESKHETIANS

CHECHEN-INGUSH AUTONOMOUS REGION

Legend:

- Minority nationalities of the Soviet Union who were deported 1941-1945
- General direction of the deportations
- Furthest German advance 1942-1943

As the German armies advanced into the Soviet Union in 1941-1943, Stalin was afraid that they would be welcomed by the many national groups which had been persecuted under Soviet rule. But only the Chechen-Ingush began an anti-Soviet rebellion as the Germans approached. Four ethnic groups were deported from their homelands to Central Asia, Siberia, and the arctic north; the Meskhetians were deported in 1944, the Crimean Tatars, accused of collaboration with the Germans in 1945. Many died in the severe conditions of resettlement. Khrushchev's 1957 decree "On the Rehabilitation of Deported Peoples" led to the return of the groups. But the Volga Germans, Crimean Tatars, and Meskhetians, who were not included in the decree, remain in exile

0   400
Miles

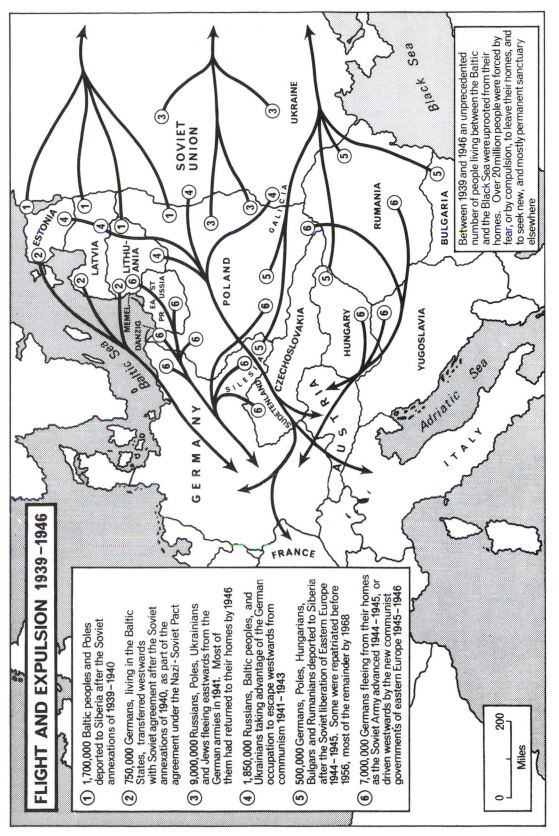

FLIGHT AND EXPULSION 1939–1946

① 1,700,000 Baltic peoples and Poles deported to Siberia after the Soviet annexations of 1939–1940

② 750,000 Germans, living in the Baltic States, transferred westwards with Soviet agreement after the Soviet annexations of 1940, as part of the agreement under the Nazi-Soviet Pact

③ 9,000,000 Russians, Poles, Ukrainians and Jews fleeing eastwards from the German armies in 1941. Most of them had returned to their homes by 1946

④ 1,850,000 Russians, Baltic peoples, and Ukrainians taking advantage of the German occupation to escape westwards from communism 1941–1943

⑤ 500,000 Germans, Poles, Hungarians, Bulgars and Rumanians deported to Siberia after the Soviet liberation of Eastern Europe 1944–1945. Some were repatriated before 1956, most of the remainder by 1968

⑥ 7,000,000 Germans fleeing from their homes as the Soviet Army advanced 1944–1945, or driven westwards by the new communist governments of eastern Europe 1945–1946

Between 1939 and 1946 an unprecedented number of people living between the Baltic and the Black Sea were uprooted from their homes. Over 20 million people were forced by fear, or by compulsion, to leave their homes, and to seek new, and mostly permanent sanctuary elsewhere

0   200
Miles

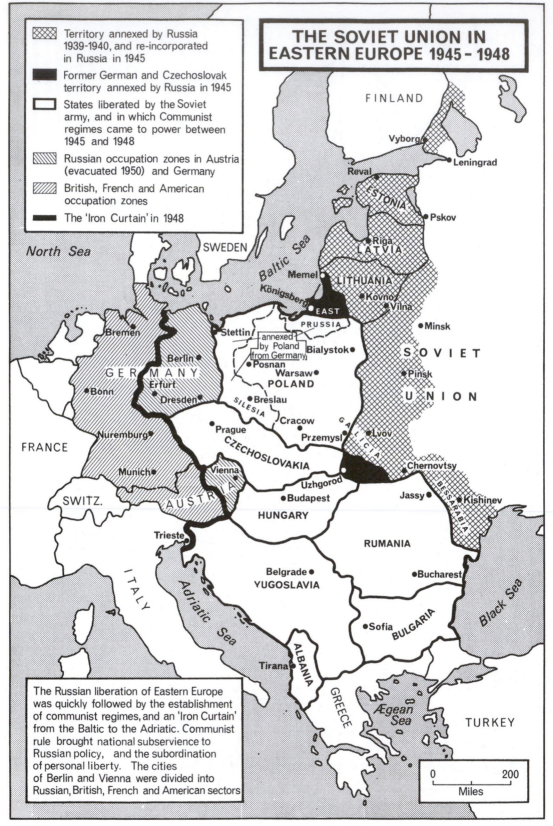

THE SOVIET UNION IN EASTERN EUROPE 1945 – 1948

Territory annexed by Russia 1939-1940, and re-incorporated in Russia in 1945

Former German and Czechoslovak territory annexed by Russia in 1945

States liberated by the Soviet army, and in which Communist regimes came to power between 1945 and 1948

Russian occupation zones in Austria (evacuated 1950) and Germany

British, French and American occupation zones

The 'Iron Curtain' in 1948

FINLAND

North Sea

SWEDEN

Baltic Sea

Vyborg

Leningrad

Reval

ESTONIA

Pskov

Riga

LATVIA

Memel

LITHUANIA

Königsberg

Kovno

Vilna

Minsk

EAST PRUSSIA

S O V I E T

Bremen

Stettin

annexed by Poland from Germany

Bialystok

Berlin

Posnan

Warsaw

Pinsk

U N I O N

Bonn

Erfurt

Dresden

POLAND

SILESIA

Breslau

Cracow

GALICIA

Lvov

GERMANY

FRANCE

Nuremburg

Prague

CZECHOSLOVAKIA

Przemysl

Chernovtsy

Munich

Vienna

Uzhgorod

Jassy

BESSARABIA

Kishinev

SWITZ.

AUSTRIA

Budapest

HUNGARY

RUMANIA

Trieste

ITALY

Adriatic Sea

Belgrade

YUGOSLAVIA

Bucharest

Black Sea

Sofia

BULGARIA

ALBANIA

Tirana

GREECE

Ægean Sea

TURKEY

The Russian liberation of Eastern Europe was quickly followed by the establishment of communist regimes, and an 'Iron Curtain' from the Baltic to the Adriatic. Communist rule brought national subservience to Russian policy, and the subordination of personal liberty. The cities of Berlin and Vienna were divided into Russian, British, French and American sectors

0   200

Miles

THE SOVIET UNION IN EASTERN EUROPE 1949-1968

0   200
Miles

FINLAND

Vyborg
Leningrad
Tallin (Reval)
Riga
Klaypeda (Memel)
Kaliningrad

SWEDEN

North Sea

Baltic Sea

SOVIET UNION

Rostock
East Berlin
EAST GERMANY
Halle
Dresden

Gdansk
Szczecin

Posnan
POLAND
Warsaw
Lodz
Wroclaw
Lublin
Cracow
Przemysl
Lvov
Kiev

WEST GERMANY

Prague
CZECHOSLOVAKIA
Brno
Bratislava
Kosice
Debrecen

FRANCE

SWITZ.
AUSTRIA
Györ
Budapest
HUNGARY
Pécs

Zagreb
Rijeka

Jassy
Cluj
RUMANIA
Arad
Odessa

Belgrade
YUGOSLAVIA
Constanza
Bucharest

ITALY

Adriatic Sea

Split
Kotor

Nish

Varna
BULGARIA
Sofia
Burgas

Black Sea

Tirana
ALBANIA
Durres
Vlone

GREECE

TURKEY

Aegean Sea

― Frontiers of communist states since 1945

Only European communist state entirely free from Soviet direction of foreign, economic and domestic policy since 1949

Only communist state within the Soviet bloc pursuing a relatively independent foreign policy since 1968

Only communist state in Europe aligned with China and refusing all contact with the Soviet Union since 1961

Only European communist state to accept Soviet guidance with equanimity

Principal areas of anti-Soviet protest and revolt 1953–1968, crushed by Soviet military intervention (East Germany, Hungary, Czechoslovakia) and by strong political pressure (Poland)

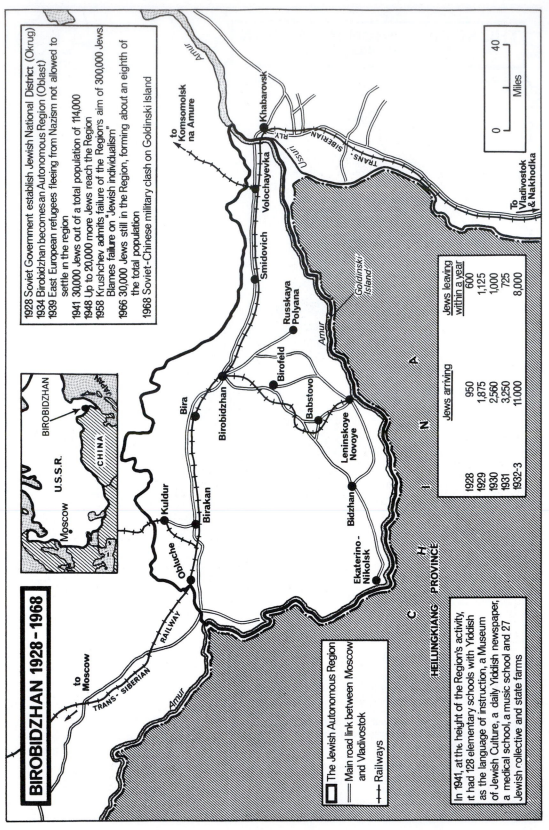

BIROBIDZHAN 1928 – 1968

1928 Soviet Government establish Jewish National District (Okrug)
1934 Birobidzhan becomes an Autonomous Region (Oblast)
1939 East European refugees fleeing from Nazism not allowed to settle in the region
1941 30,000 Jews out of a total population of 114,000
1948 Up to 20,000 more Jews reach the Region
1958 Krushchev admits failure of the Region's aim of 300,000 Jews. Blames failure on "Jewish individualism"
1966 30,000 Jews still in the Region, forming about an eighth of the total population
1968 Soviet-Chinese military clash on Goldinski Island

	Jews arriving	Jews leaving within a year
1928	950	600
1929	1,875	1,125
1930	2,560	1,000
1931	3,250	725
1932-3	11,000	8,000

In 1941, at the height of the Region's activity, it had 128 elementary schools with Yiddish as the language of instruction, a Museum of Jewish Culture, a daily Yiddish newspaper, a medical school and 27 Jewish collective and state farms

☐ The Jewish Autonomous Region
── Main road link between Moscow and Vladivostok
╫── Railways

to Moscow
TRANS - SIBERIAN RAILWAY
Amur
Obluche
Kuldur
Birakan
Bira
Birobidzhan
Bidzhan
Ekaterino - Nikolsk
Leninskoye
Novoye
Babstovo
Birofeld
Russkaya Polyana
Smidovich
Volochayevka
Khabarovsk
to Komsomolsk na Amure
Amur
Ussuri
TRANS - SIBERIAN RLY.
To Vladivostok & Nakhodka
Goldinski Island

C H I N A

HEILUNGKIANG PROVINCE

BIROBIDZHAN
U.S.S.R.
Moscow
CHINA

0   40
Miles

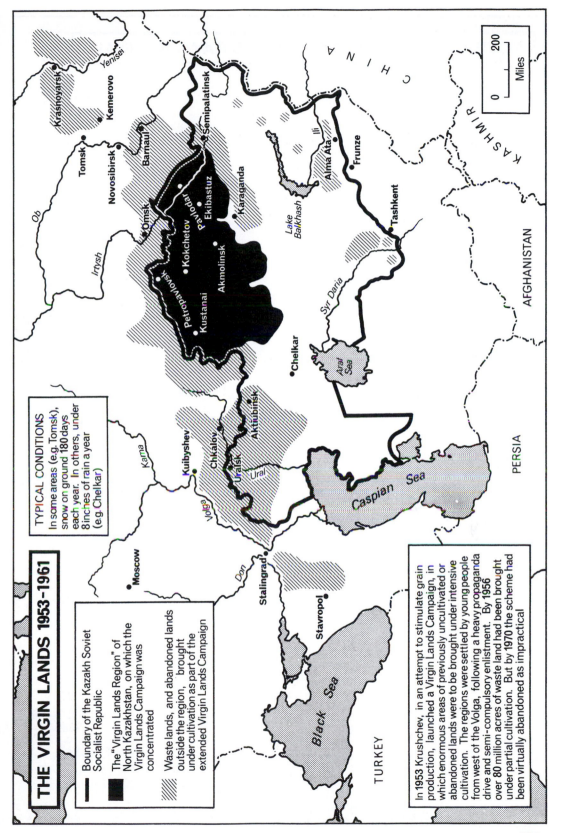

THE VIRGIN LANDS 1953–1961

Legend:

— Boundary of the Kazakh Soviet Socialist Republic

■ The "Virgin Lands Region" of North Kazakhstan, on which the Virgin Lands Campaign was concentrated

▨ Waste lands, and abandoned lands outside the region, brought under cultivation as part of the extended Virgin Lands Campaign

TYPICAL CONDITIONS

In some areas (e.g. Tomsk), snow on ground 180 days each year. In others, under 8 inches of rain a year (e.g. Chelkar)

In 1953 Krushchev, in an attempt to stimulate grain production, launched a Virgin Lands Campaign, in which enormous areas of previously uncultivated or abandoned lands were to be brought under intensive cultivation. The regions were settled by young people from west of the Volga, following a heavy propaganda drive and semi-compulsory enlistment. By 1956 over 80 million acres of waste land had been brought under partial cultivation. But by 1970 the scheme had been virtually abandoned as impractical

Map labels: Krasnoyarsk, Kemerovo, Yenisei, Tomsk, Novosibirsk, Barnaul, Semipalatinsk, Ob, Irtysh, Omsk, Pavlodar, Ekibastuz, Karaganda, Kokchetov, Akmolinsk, Petropavlovsk, Kustanai, Chelkar, CHINA, Ili, Alma Ata, Frunze, Lake Balkhash, Tashkent, Syr Daria, KASHMIR, Aral Sea, AFGHANISTAN, Kama, Kuibyshev, Chkalov, Aktiubinsk, Uralsk, Ural, Volga, Caspian Sea, PERSIA, Moscow, Stalingrad, Don, Stavropol, Black Sea, TURKEY

Scale: 0 — 200 Miles

136

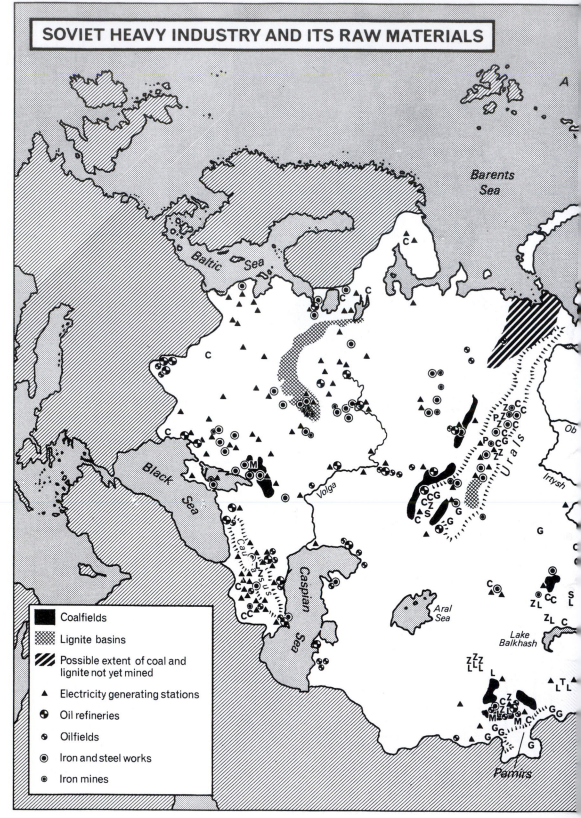

SOVIET HEAVY INDUSTRY AND ITS RAW MATERIALS

Barents Sea

Baltic Sea

Black Sea

Caucasus

Caspian Sea

Volga

Urals

Ob

Irtysh

Aral Sea

Lake Balkhash

Pamirs

Legend:

- ▬ Coalfields
- ▨ Lignite basins
- ▨ Possible extent of coal and lignite not yet mined
- ▲ Electricity generating stations
- ⊕ Oil refineries
- ⊕ Oilfields
- ◉ Iron and steel works
- ⊙ Iron mines

137

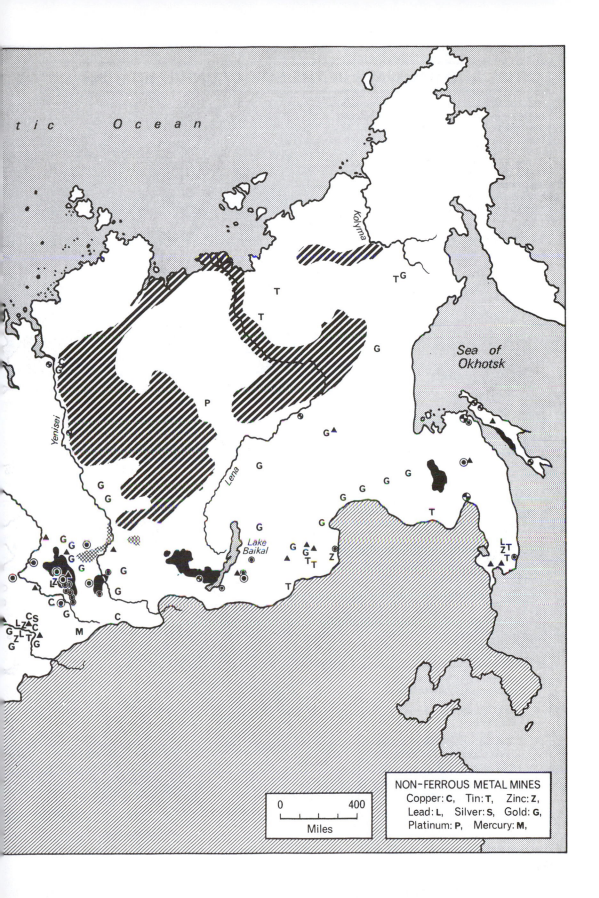

tic   O c e a n

Kolyma

T^G

T

T

G

Sea of Okhotsk

Yenisei

P

G▲

Lena

G

G

G   G   G

M

G   G

G

G   G

G

G

G   T

G   G

G   G▲   ▲

G   ▲

Lake Baikal

G   G▲   ▲

G   G   ▲

LZ   G   ▲   ▲   G   T   T   Z

C   C

C   C

CS   C

LZ   ▲   C

G   Z   L   T   ▲

G   G

L   Z   T   T

Z   T

T

0   400
Miles

NON-FERROUS METAL MINES
Copper: **C**,   Tin: **T**,   Zinc: **Z**,
Lead: **L**,   Silver: **S**,   Gold: **G**,
Platinum: **P**,   Mercury: **M**,

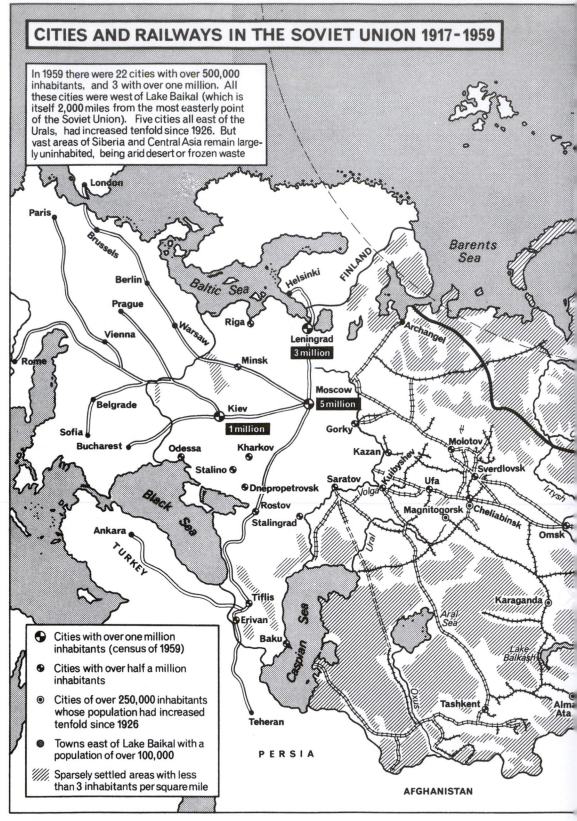

CITIES AND RAILWAYS IN THE SOVIET UNION 1917-1959

In 1959 there were 22 cities with over 500,000 inhabitants, and 3 with over one million. All these cities were west of Lake Baikal (which is itself 2,000 miles from the most easterly point of the Soviet Union). Five cities all east of the Urals, had increased tenfold since 1926. But vast areas of Siberia and Central Asia remain largely uninhabited, being arid desert or frozen waste

London
Paris
Brussels
Berlin
Prague
Vienna
Warsaw
Rome
Helsinki
Riga
Leningrad
3 million
Minsk
Belgrade
Kiev
1 million
Sofia
Bucharest
Odessa
Stalino
Kharkov
Dnepropetrovsk
Rostov
Stalingrad
Ankara
Moscow
5 million
Gorky
Kazan
Saratov
Kuibyshev
Ufa
Molotov
Sverdlovsk
Magnitogorsk
Cheliabinsk
Omsk
Tiflis
Erivan
Baku
Teheran
Tashkent
Karaganda
Alma Ata
Archangel

Barents Sea
FINLAND
Baltic Sea
Black Sea
TURKEY
Caspian Sea
Aral Sea
Volga
Ural
Oxus
Irtysh
Lake Balkash
PERSIA
AFGHANISTAN

Cities with over one million inhabitants (census of 1959)

Cities with over half a million inhabitants

Cities of over 250,000 inhabitants whose population had increased tenfold since 1926

Towns east of Lake Baikal with a population of over 100,000

Sparsely settled areas with less than 3 inhabitants per square mile

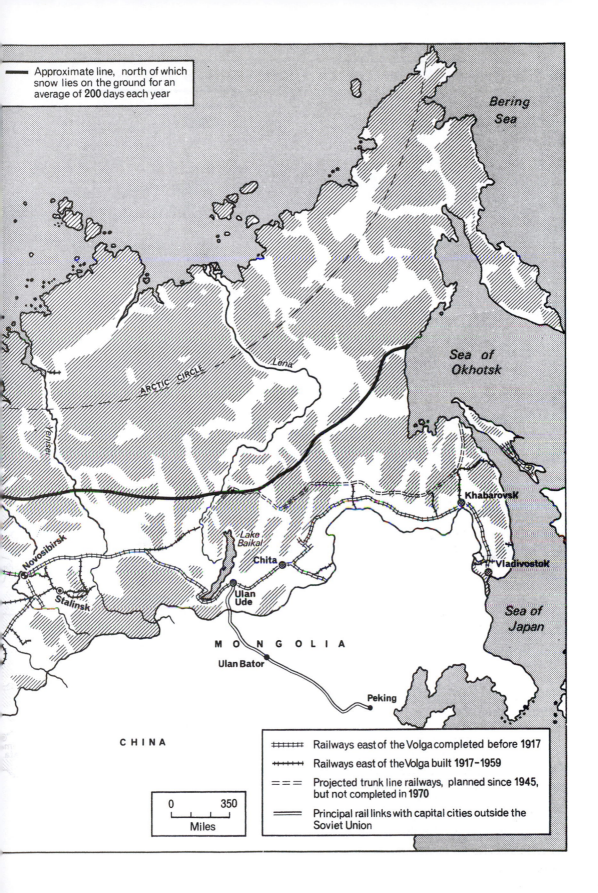

Approximate line, north of which snow lies on the ground for an average of **200** days each year

Bering Sea

Sea of Okhotsk

Lena

ARCTIC CIRCLE

Yenisei

Khabarovsk

Lake Baikal

Chita

Novosibirsk

Stalinsk

Ulan Ude

Vladivostok

Sea of Japan

M O N G O L I A

Ulan Bator

Peking

CHINA

┼┼┼┼┼┼	Railways east of the Volga completed before **1917**
┼─┼─┼─┼	Railways east of the Volga built **1917–1959**
= = =	Projected trunk line railways, planned since **1945**, but not completed in **1970**
────	Principal rail links with capital cities outside the Soviet Union

0   350

Miles

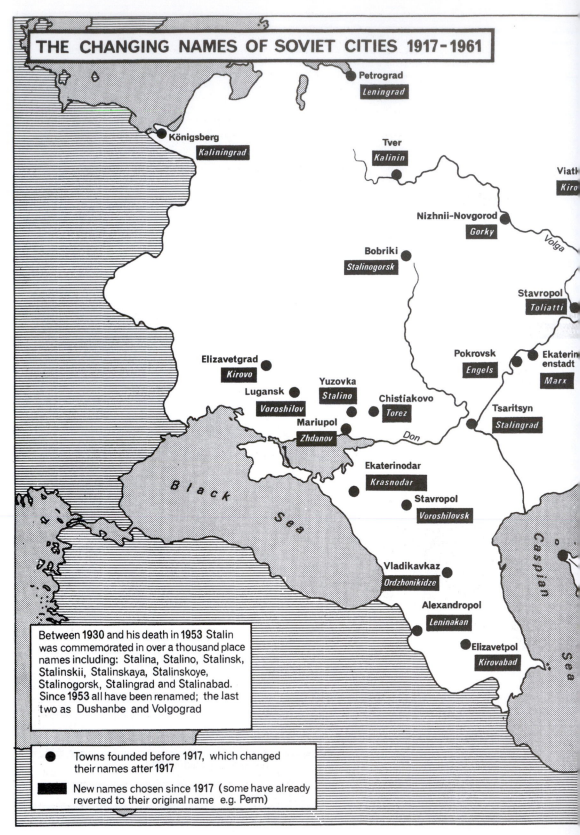

THE CHANGING NAMES OF SOVIET CITIES 1917-1961

Petrograd
Leningrad

Königsberg
Kaliningrad

Tver
Kalinin

Viatk
Kiro

Nizhnii-Novgorod
Gorky

Bobriki
Stalinogorsk

Volga

Stavropol
Toliatti

Pokrovsk
Engels

Ekaterin
enstadt
Marx

Elizavetgrad
Kirovo

Lugansk
Voroshilov

Yuzovka
Stalino

Chistiakovo
Torez

Mariupol
Zhdanov

Tsaritsyn
Stalingrad

Don

Ekaterinodar
Krasnodar

Stavropol
Voroshilovsk

Black
Sea

Caspian
Sea

Vladikavkaz
Ordzhonikidze

Alexandropol
Leninakan

Elizavetpol
Kirovabad

Between **1930** and his death in **1953** Stalin was commemorated in over a thousand place names including: Stalina, Stalino, Stalinsk, Stalinskii, Stalinskaya, Stalinskoye, Stalinogorsk, Stalingrad and Stalinabad. Since **1953** all have been renamed; the last two as Dushanbe and Volgograd

● Towns founded before 1917, which changed their names after 1917

■ New names chosen since 1917 (some have already reverted to their original name e.g. Perm)

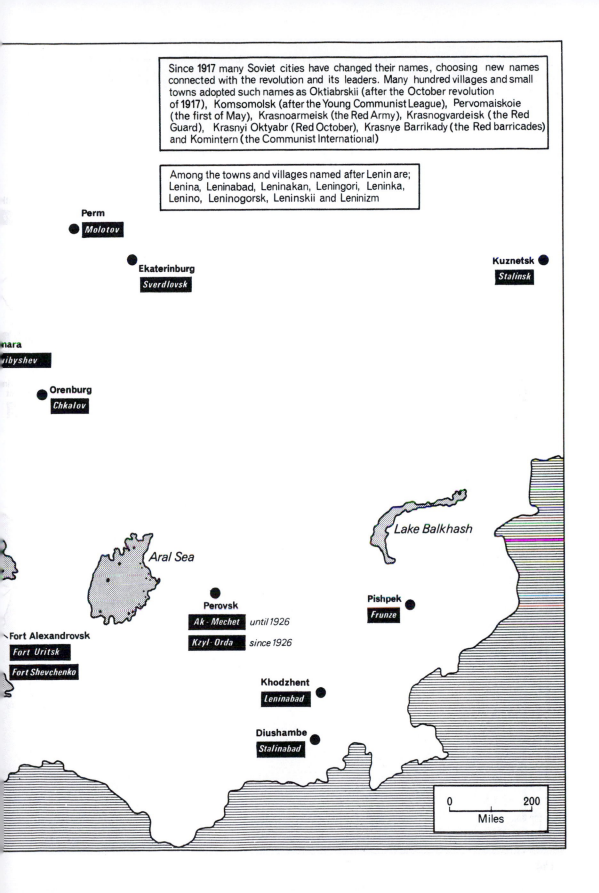

Since 1917 many Soviet cities have changed their names, choosing new names connected with the revolution and its leaders. Many hundred villages and small towns adopted such names as Oktiabrskii (after the October revolution of 1917), Komsomolsk (after the Young Communist League), Pervomaiskoie (the first of May), Krasnoarmeisk (the Red Army), Krasnogvardeisk (the Red Guard), Krasnyi Oktyabr (Red October), Krasnye Barrikady (the Red barricades) and Komintern (the Communist International)

Among the towns and villages named after Lenin are; Lenina, Leninabad, Leninakan, Leningori, Leninka, Lenino, Leninogorsk, Leninskii and Leninizm

Perm
Molotov

Ekaterinburg
Sverdlovsk

Kuznetsk
Stalinsk

nara
uibyshev

Orenburg
Chkalov

Lake Balkhash

Aral Sea

Perovsk
Ak - Mechet   until 1926
Kzyl- Orda   since 1926

Pishpek
Frunze

Fort Alexandrovsk
Fort Uritsk
Fort Shevchenko

Khodzhent
Leninabad

Diushambe
Stalinabad

0   200
Miles

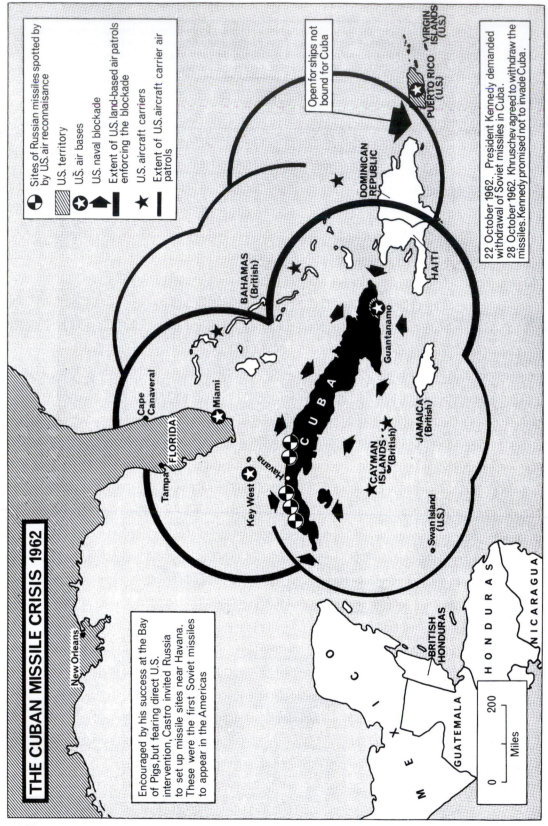

THE CUBAN MISSILE CRISIS 1962

Sites of Russian missiles spotted by U.S. air reconnaissance

U.S. territory

U.S. air bases

U.S. naval blockade

Extent of U.S. land-based air patrols enforcing the blockade

U.S. aircraft carriers

Extent of U.S. aircraft carrier air patrols

Open for ships not bound for Cuba

Encouraged by his success at the Bay of Pigs, but fearing direct U.S. intervention, Castro invited Russia to set up missile sites near Havana. These were the first Soviet missiles to appear in the Americas

22 October 1962. President Kennedy demanded withdrawal of Soviet missiles in Cuba.
28 October 1962. Khruschev agreed to withdraw the missiles. Kennedy promised not to invade Cuba.

New Orleans

FLORIDA

Cape Canaveral

Tampa

Miami

Key West

Havana

C U B A

Guantanamo

BAHAMAS (British)

CAYMAN ISLANDS (British)

JAMAICA (British)

Swan Island (U.S.)

HAITI

DOMINICAN REPUBLIC

PUERTO RICO (U.S.)

VIRGIN ISLANDS (U.S.)

M E X I C O

GUATEMALA

BRITISH HONDURAS

H O N D U R A S

NICARAGUA

0   200

Miles

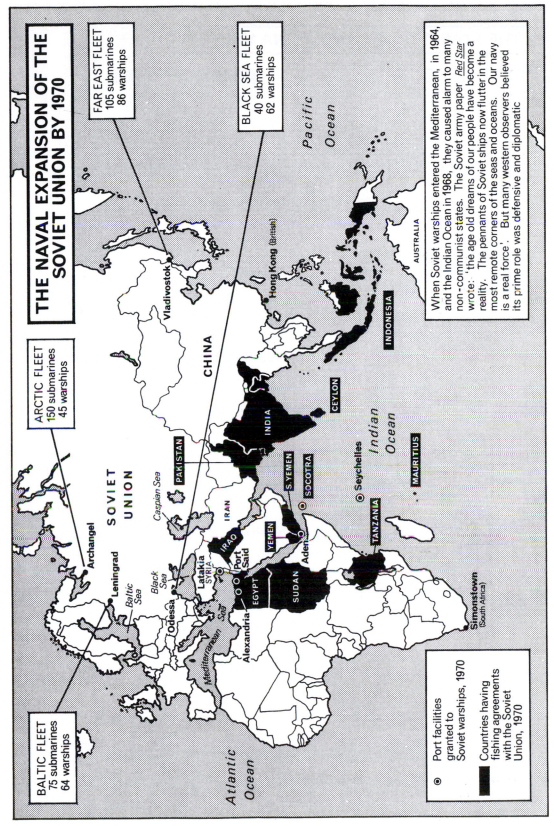

THE NAVAL EXPANSION OF THE SOVIET UNION BY 1970

FAR EAST FLEET
105 submarines
86 warships

BLACK SEA FLEET
40 submarines
62 warships

ARCTIC FLEET
150 submarines
45 warships

BALTIC FLEET
75 submarines
64 warships

Pacific Ocean

Atlantic Ocean

Indian Ocean

AUSTRALIA

INDONESIA

CHINA

SOVIET UNION

Vladivostok

Hong Kong (British)

CEYLON

INDIA

PAKISTAN

S.YEMEN

SOCOTRA

Seychelles

MAURITIUS

TANZANIA

Aden

YEMEN

IRAQ

Port Said

SUDAN

IRAN

Caspian Sea

Archangel

Leningrad

Baltic Sea

Odessa

Black Sea

Latakia
SYRIA

EGYPT

Alexandria

Mediterranean Sea

Red Sea

Simonstown
(South Africa)

When Soviet warships entered the Mediterranean, in 1964, and the Indian Ocean in 1968, they caused alarm to many non-communist states. The Soviet army paper *Red Star* wrote: 'the age old dreams of our people have become a reality. The pennants of Soviet ships now flutter in the most remote corners of the seas and oceans. Our navy is a real force'. But many western observers believed its prime role was defensive and diplomatic

◉ Port facilities granted to Soviet warships, 1970

■ Countries having fishing agreements with the Soviet Union, 1970

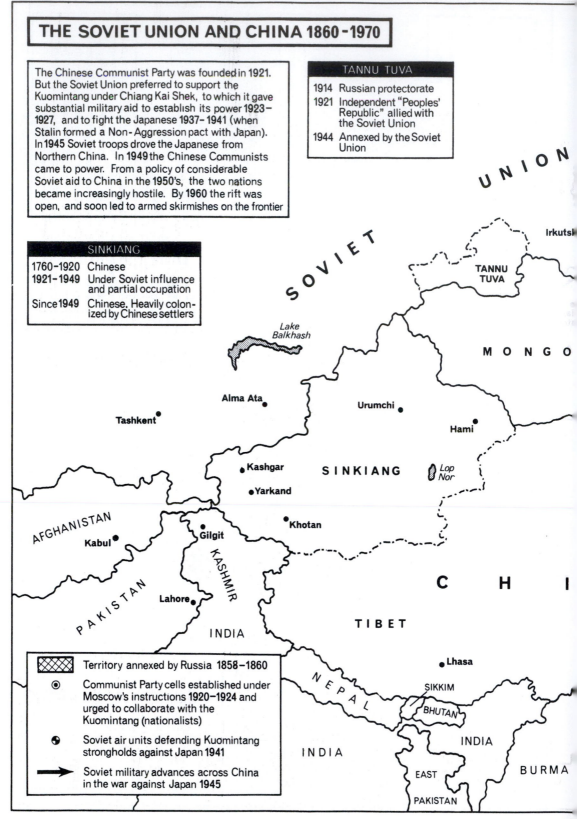

THE SOVIET UNION AND CHINA 1860-1970

The Chinese Communist Party was founded in 1921. But the Soviet Union preferred to support the Kuomintang under Chiang Kai Shek, to which it gave substantial military aid to establish its power 1923–1927, and to fight the Japanese 1937–1941 (when Stalin formed a Non-Aggression pact with Japan). In 1945 Soviet troops drove the Japanese from Northern China. In 1949 the Chinese Communists came to power. From a policy of considerable Soviet aid to China in the 1950's, the two nations became increasingly hostile. By 1960 the rift was open, and soon led to armed skirmishes on the frontier

TANNU TUVA

1914	Russian protectorate
1921	Independent "Peoples' Republic" allied with the Soviet Union
1944	Annexed by the Soviet Union

SINKIANG

1760–1920	Chinese
1921–1949	Under Soviet influence and partial occupation
Since 1949	Chinese. Heavily colonized by Chinese settlers

SOVIET UNION

Irkutsk

TANNU TUVA

MONGO

Lake Balkhash

Alma Ata

Urumchi

Hami

Tashkent

Kashgar

SINKIANG

Lop Nor

Yarkand

AFGHANISTAN

Khotan

Kabul

Gilgit

KASHMIR

C H I

PAKISTAN

Lahore

TIBET

INDIA

Lhasa

NEPAL

SIKKIM

BHUTAN

INDIA

INDIA

BURMA

EAST

PAKISTAN

Territory annexed by Russia 1858–1860

Communist Party cells established under Moscow's instructions 1920–1924 and urged to collaborate with the Kuomintang (nationalists)

Soviet air units defending Kuomintang strongholds against Japan 1941

Soviet military advances across China in the war against Japan 1945

142

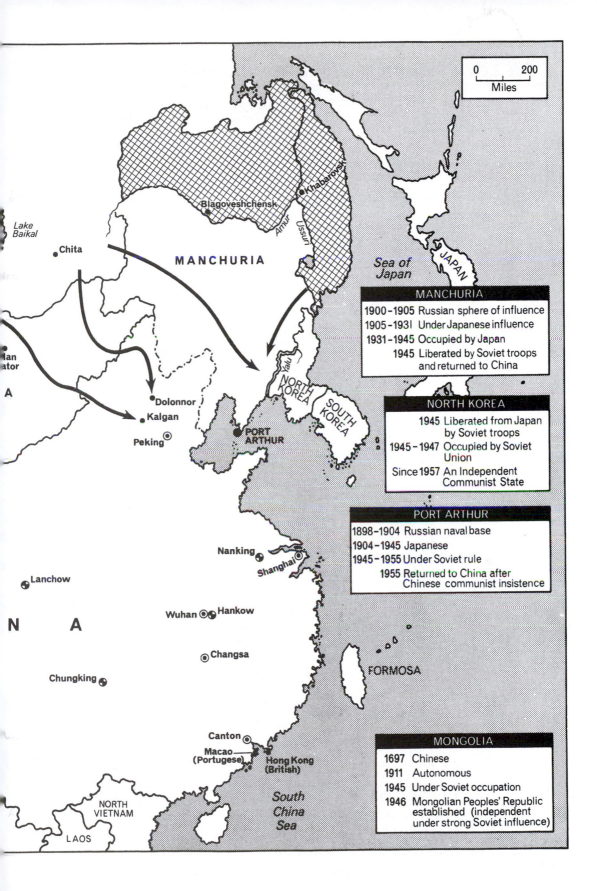

Lake
Baikal

Chita

MANCHURIA

Blagoveshchensk

Khabarovsk

Amur

Ussuri

Sea of
Japan

JAPAN

Dolonnor

Kalgan

Peking

Yalu

NORTH
KOREA

SOUTH
KOREA

PORT
ARTHUR

Nanking

Shanghai

Lanchow

N   A

Wuhan   Hankow

Changsa

FORMOSA

Chungking

Canton

Macao
(Portugese)

Hong Kong
(British)

South
China
Sea

NORTH
VIETNAM

LAOS

0   200
Miles

MANCHURIA	
1900–1905	Russian sphere of influence
1905–1931	Under Japanese influence
1931–1945	Occupied by Japan
1945	Liberated by Soviet troops and returned to China

NORTH KOREA	
1945	Liberated from Japan by Soviet troops
1945–1947	Occupied by Soviet Union
Since 1957	An Independent Communist State

PORT ARTHUR	
1898–1904	Russian naval base
1904–1945	Japanese
1945–1955	Under Soviet rule
1955	Returned to China after Chinese communist insistence

MONGOLIA	
1697	Chinese
1911	Autonomous
1945	Under Soviet occupation
1946	Mongolian Peoples' Republic established (independent under strong Soviet influence)

THE SOVIET-CHINESE BORDERLANDS 1970

Legend:
- ——— The Soviet-Chinese border
- —·—·— Other international borders
- ┼┼┼┼ Soviet, Mongolian and Chinese railways in the border area
- ▨ Land over 2000 metres (6562 feet)
- ✚ Main airfields

Caspian Sea

Aral Sea

SOVIET

to Moscow

Omsk

TRANS-SIBERIAN RAILWAY

Novosibirsk

Achinsk

Barnaul

Krasnoyarsk

Karaganda

Rubtsovsk

Biisk

Semipalatinsk

Abakan

Leninogorsk

Lake Balkash

Aktogai

Lake Zaisan

Lake Markakol

PERSIA

Tashkent

Lugovoi

Urdzhar

Zaisan

Samarkand

Panfilov

L. Alakol

Tahcheng

Diushambe

Frunze

Dzhalal

Rybachye

Alma Ata

Ebi Nor

Ulyungur Nor

Abad

Osh

Issyk Kul

Kuldja

AFGHANISTAN

Kashgar

Aksu

Urumchi

M O

PAKISTAN

KASHMIR

Lop Nor

INDIA

Lanchow

C H I N

0   250
Miles

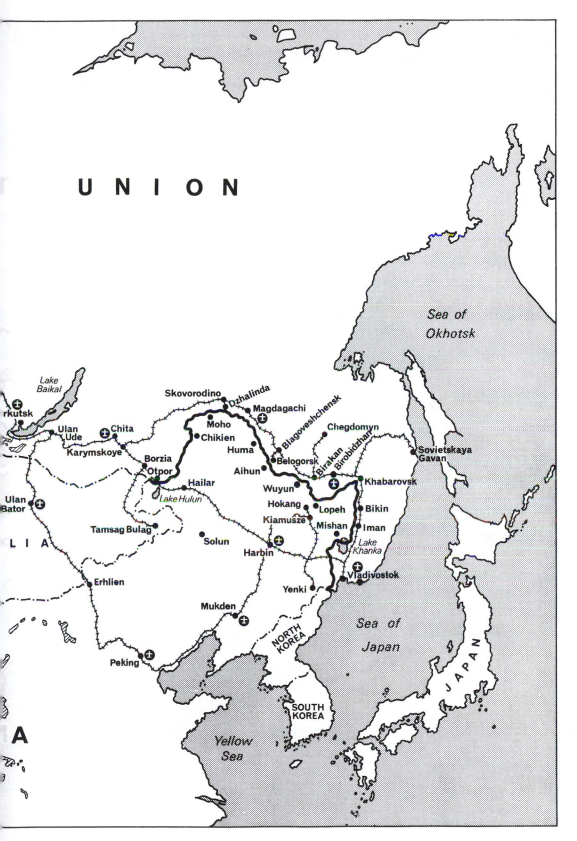

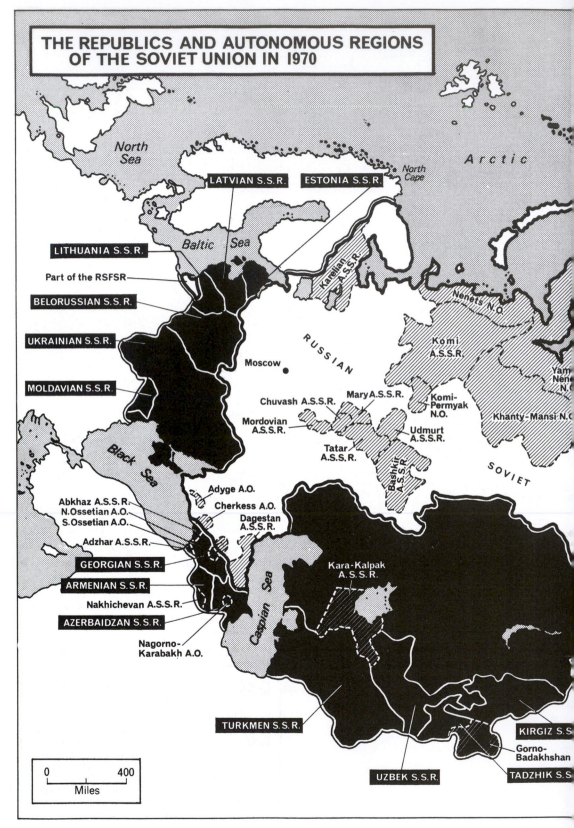

THE REPUBLICS AND AUTONOMOUS REGIONS OF THE SOVIET UNION IN 1970

North Sea

Arctic

North Cape

LATVIAN S.S.R.   ESTONIA S.S.R.

Baltic Sea

Karelian A.S.S.R.

Nenets N.O.

LITHUANIA S.S.R.

Part of the RSFSR

BELORUSSIAN S.S.R.

UKRAINIAN S.S.R.

R U S S I A N

Moscow

Komi A.S.S.R.

Yam Nene N.

MOLDAVIAN S.S.R.

Chuvash A.S.S.R.   Mary A.S.S.R.   Komi-Permyak N.O.

Mordovian A.S.S.R.

Udmurt A.S.S.R.

Khanty-Mansi N.O

Tatar A.S.S.R.

Black Sea

Bashkir A.S.S.R.

S O V I E T

Adyge A.O.

Abkhaz A.S.S.R.   Cherkess A.O.
N.Ossetian A.O.
S.Ossetian A.O.   Dagestan A.S.S.R.

Adzhar A.S.S.R.

Kara-Kalpak A.S.S.R.

GEORGIAN S.S.R.

ARMENIAN S.S.R.

Caspian Sea

Nakhichevan A.S.S.R.

AZERBAIDZAN S.S.R.

Nagorno-Karabakh A.O.

TURKMEN S.S.R.

KIRGIZ S.S

Gorno-Badakhshan

UZBEK S.S.R.   TADZHIK S.S

0   400
Miles

144

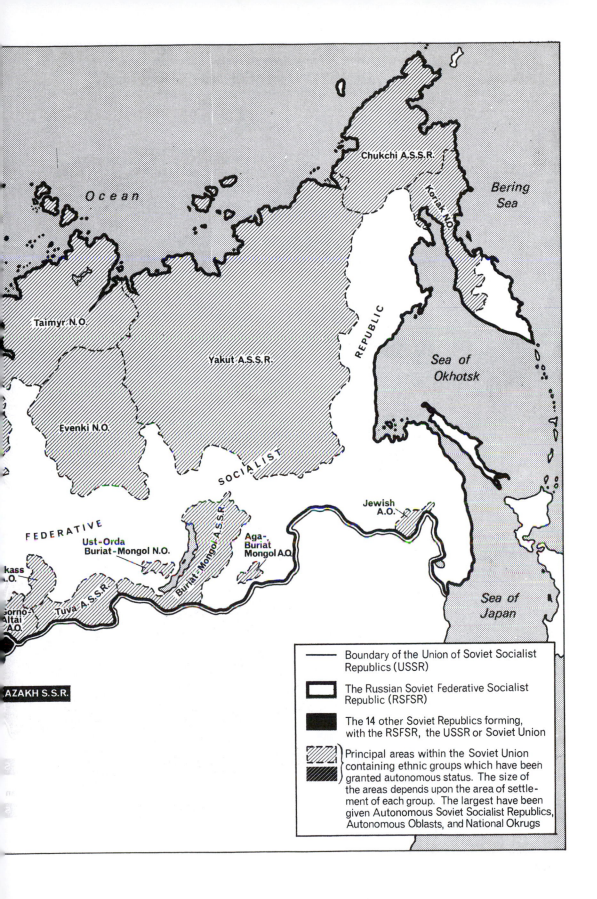

Taimyr N.O.

Chukchi A.S.S.R.

Koriak N.O.

Bering
Sea

O c e a n

REPUBLIC

Sea of
Okhotsk

Yakut A.S.S.R.

Evenki N.O.

SOCIALIST

Jewish
A.O.

FEDERATIVE

Ust-Orda
Buriat-Mongol N.O.

Buriat-Mongol A.S.S.R.

Aga-
Buriat
Mongol A.O.

kass
A.O.

Gorno-
Altai
A.O.

Tuva A.S.S.R.

Sea of
Japan

AZAKH S.S.R.

—— Boundary of the Union of Soviet Socialist
Republics (USSR)

□ The Russian Soviet Federative Socialist
Republic (RSFSR)

■ The **14** other Soviet Republics forming,
with the RSFSR, the USSR or Soviet Union

Principal areas within the Soviet Union
containing ethnic groups which have been
granted autonomous status. The size of
the areas depends upon the area of settlement of each group. The largest have been
given Autonomous Soviet Socialist Republics,
Autonomous Oblasts, and National Okrugs

RUSSIA'S WESTERN FRONTIER SINCE 1700

In 1721 Peter the Great had achieved one of Russia's main state objectives, an outlet to the ice-free waters of the Baltic. His successors continued the westward movement of Russian conquest until 1815, obtaining complete access also to the warm waters of the Black Sea. After the 1917 revolution the frontier fell back considerably, and in the north it was further eastwards than in 1721. With the victory over Germany in 1945, when Soviet troops reached Berlin, Stalin was able to advance the frontier westwards once more.

———	Russia's western frontier in 1700
	Annexed by Peter the Great in 1721
—·—·—	Russia's western frontier 1815–1914
·········	The western frontier of the Soviet Union 1921–1939
	Soviet annexations in 1945 of land never previously under Russian rule
━━━	Russia's western frontier since 1945
◉	Leased from Finland 1945–1955

Promised to Russia by Britain and France in 1915. Rejected by the Bolsheviks in 1917 on account of their "no annexations" policy. Often the aim of Russian expansionist ambition, Constantinople and the Straits have never been under Russian control.

145

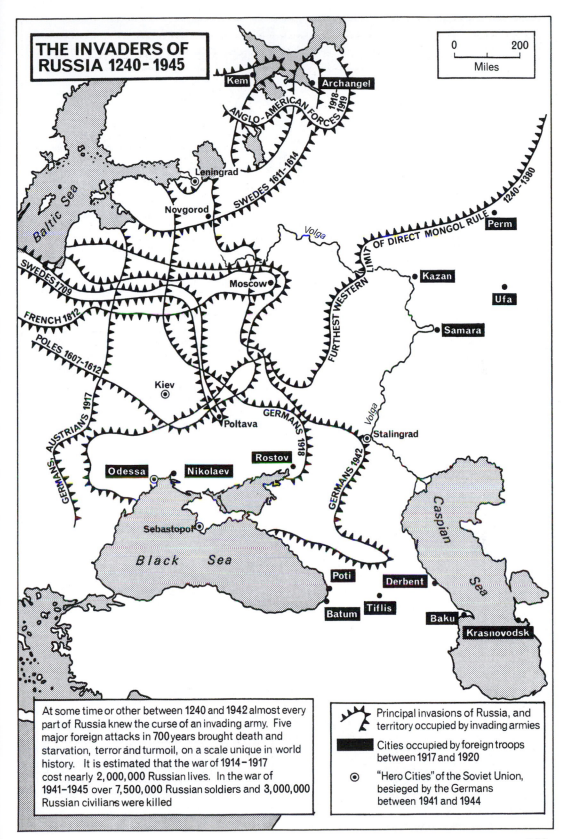

THE INVADERS OF RUSSIA 1240-1945

0   200

Miles

Kem

Archangel

ANGLO-AMERICAN FORCES

1918 1919

Leningrad

SWEDES 1611-1614

Baltic Sea

Novgorod

Volga

LIMIT OF DIRECT MONGOL RULE

1240-1380

Perm

SWEDES 1709

Moscow

Kazan

Ufa

FURTHEST WESTERN

FRENCH 1812

Samara

POLES 1607-1612

AUSTRIANS 1917

Kiev

Volga

GERMANS 1918

Poltava

Stalingrad

GERMANS, AUSTRIANS 1917

Odessa

Nikolaev

Rostov

GERMANS 1942

Caspian Sea

Sebastopol

Black Sea

Poti

Derbent

Batum

Tiflis

Baku

Krasnovodsk

At some time or other between 1240 and 1942 almost every part of Russia knew the curse of an invading army. Five major foreign attacks in 700 years brought death and starvation, terror and turmoil, on a scale unique in world history. It is estimated that the war of 1914–1917 cost nearly 2,000,000 Russian lives. In the war of 1941–1945 over 7,500,000 Russian soldiers and 3,000,000 Russian civilians were killed

Principal invasions of Russia, and territory occupied by invading armies

Cities occupied by foreign troops between 1917 and 1920

"Hero Cities" of the Soviet Union, besieged by the Germans between 1941 and 1944

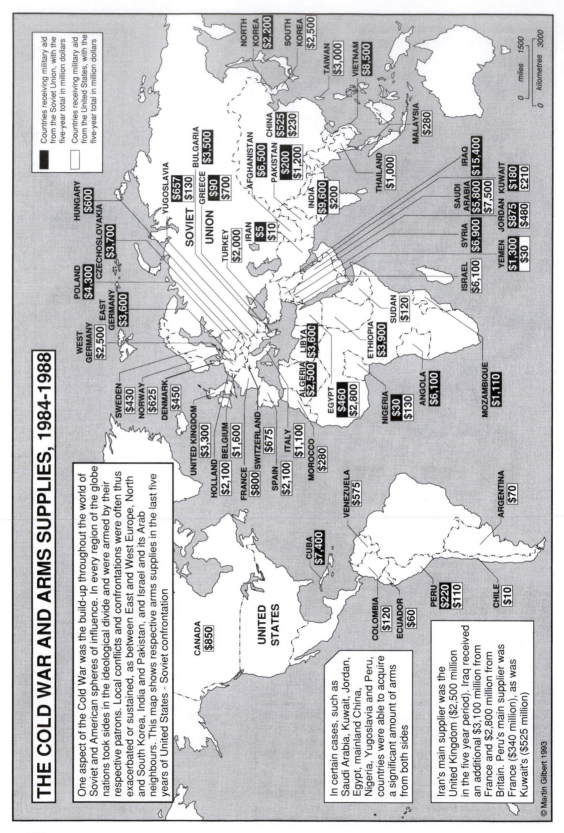

THE COLD WAR AND ARMS SUPPLIES, 1984-1988

One aspect of the Cold War was the build-up throughout the world of Soviet and American spheres of influence. In every region of the globe nations took sides in the ideological divide and were armed by their respective patrons. Local conflicts and confrontations were often thus exacerbated or sustained, as between East and West Europe, North and South Korea, India and Pakistan, and Israel and its Arab neighbours. This map shows respective arms supplies in the last five years of United States - Soviet confrontation

In certain cases, such as Saudi Arabia, Kuwait, Jordan, Egypt, mainland China, Nigeria, Yugoslavia and Peru, countries were able to acquire a significant amount of arms from both sides

Iran's main supplier was the United Kingdom ($2,500 million in the five year period). Iraq received an additional $3,100 million from France and $2,800 million from Britain. Peru's main supplier was France ($340 million), as was Kuwait's ($525 million)

Countries receiving military aid from the Soviet Union, with the five-year total in million dollars

Countries receiving military aid from the United States, with the five-year total in million dollars

0 miles 1500

0 kilometres 3000

© Martin Gilbert 1993

CANADA $850

UNITED STATES

CUBA $7,400

VENEZUELA $575

COLOMBIA $120

ECUADOR $60

PERU $220 / $110

CHILE $10

ARGENTINA $70

SWEDEN $430

NORWAY $625

DENMARK $450

UNITED KINGDOM $3,300

HOLLAND $2,100

BELGIUM $1,600

FRANCE $800

SWITZERLAND $675

SPAIN $2,100

ITALY $1,100

MOROCCO $280

WEST GERMANY $2,500

EAST GERMANY $3,600

POLAND $4,300

CZECHOSLOVAKIA $3,700

HUNGARY $600

YUGOSLAVIA $657 / $130

BULGARIA $3,500

GREECE $90 / $700

SOVIET UNION

TURKEY $2,000

IRAN $5 / $10

AFGHANISTAN $6,500

CHINA $525 / $230

PAKISTAN $200 / $1,200

INDIA $9,600 / $200

ALGERIA $2,500

LIBYA $3,600

EGYPT $460 / $2,800

NIGERIA $30 / $130

SUDAN $120

ETHIOPIA $3,900

ANGOLA $6,100

MOZAMBIQUE $1,110

ISRAEL $6,100

YEMEN $1,300 / $30

SYRIA $6,900

JORDAN $875 / $480

SAUDI ARABIA $5,800 / $7,500

IRAQ $15,400

KUWAIT $180 / $210

THAILAND $1,000

MALAYSIA $280

VIETNAM $8,500

TAIWAN $3,000

NORTH KOREA $2,200

SOUTH KOREA $2,500

147

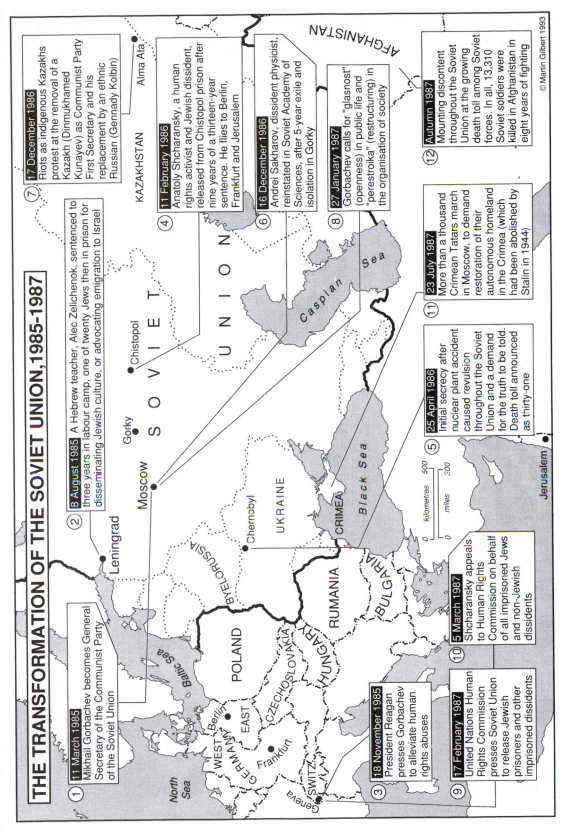

THE TRANSFORMATION OF THE SOVIET UNION, 1985-1987

① **11 March 1985** Mikhail Gorbachev becomes General Secretary of the Communist Party of the Soviet Union

② **8 August 1985** A Hebrew teacher, Alec Zelichenok, sentenced to three years in labour camp, one of twenty Jews then in prison for disseminating Jewish culture, or advocating emigration to Israel

③ **18 November 1985** President Reagan presses Gorbachev to alleviate human rights abuses

④ **11 February 1986** Anatoly Shcharansky, a human rights activist and Jewish dissident, released from Chistopol prison after nine years of a thirteen-year sentence. He flies to Berlin, Frankfurt and Jerusalem

⑤ **25 April 1986** Initial secrecy after nuclear plant accident caused revulsion throughout the Soviet Union and a demand for the truth to be told. Death toll announced as thirty-one

⑥ **16 December 1986** Andrei Sakharov, dissident physicist, reinstated in Soviet Academy of Sciences, after 5-year exile and isolation in Gorky

⑦ **17 December 1986** Riots as indigenous Kazakhs protest at the removal of a Kazakh (Dinmukhamed Kunayev) as Communist Party First Secretary and his replacement by an ethnic Russian (Gennady Kolbin)

⑧ **27 January 1987** Gorbachev calls for "glasnost" (openness) in public life and "perestroika" (restructuring) in the organisation of society

⑨ **17 February 1987** United Nations Human Rights Commission presses Soviet Union to release Jewish prisoners and other imprisoned dissidents

⑩ **5 March 1987** Shcharansky appeals to Human Rights Commission on behalf of all imprisoned Jews and non-Jewish dissidents

⑪ **23 July 1987** More than a thousand Crimean Tatars march in Moscow, to demand restoration of their autonomous homeland in the Crimea (which had been abolished by Stalin in 1944)

⑫ **Autumn 1987** Mounting discontent throughout the Soviet Union at the growing death toll among Soviet forces. In all, 13,310 Soviet soldiers were killed in Afghanistan in eight years of fighting

© Martin Gilbert 1993

148

GREAT POWER CONFRONTATION AND CONCILIATION, 1972–1979

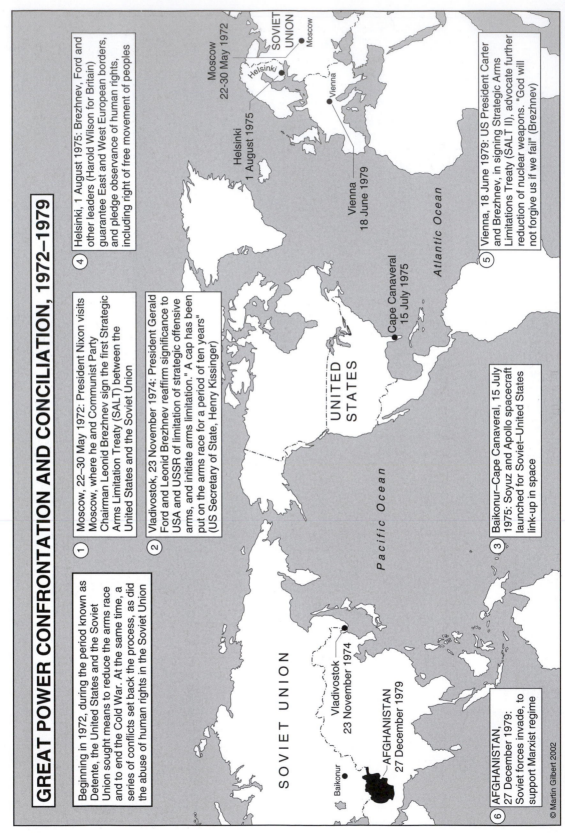

Beginning in 1972, during the period known as Detente, the United States and the Soviet Union sought means to reduce the arms race and to end the Cold War. At the same time, a series of conflicts set back the process, as did the abuse of human rights in the Soviet Union

1 Moscow, 22–30 May 1972: President Nixon visits Moscow, where he and Communist Party Chairman Leonid Brezhnev sign the first Strategic Arms Limitation Treaty (SALT) between the United States and the Soviet Union

2 Vladivostok, 23 November 1974: President Gerald Ford and Leonid Brezhnev reaffirm significance to USA and USSR of limitation of strategic offensive arms, and initiate arms limitation. "A cap has been put on the arms race for a period of ten years" (US Secretary of State, Henry Kissinger)

3 Baikonur–Cape Canaveral, 15 July 1975: Soyuz and Apollo spacecraft launched for Soviet–United States link-up in space

4 Helsinki, 1 August 1975: Brezhnev, Ford and other leaders (Harold Wilson for Britain) guarantee East and West European borders, and pledge observance of human rights, including right of free movement of peoples

5 Vienna, 18 June 1979: US President Carter and Brezhnev, in signing Strategic Arms Limitations Treaty (SALT II), advocate further reduction of nuclear weapons. "God will not forgive us if we fail" (Brezhnev)

6 AFGHANISTAN, 27 December 1979: Soviet forces invade, to support Marxist regime

SOVIET UNION

Moscow
22–30 May 1972

Helsinki
1 August 1975

Vienna
18 June 1979

Cape Canaveral
15 July 1975

Atlantic Ocean

UNITED STATES

Pacific Ocean

Vladivostok
23 November 1974

Baikonur

AFGHANISTAN
27 December 1979

Moscow

Helsinki

Vienna

SOVIET UNION

© Martin Gilbert 2002

149

GREAT POWER CONFRONTATION AND CONCILIATION, 1980–1986

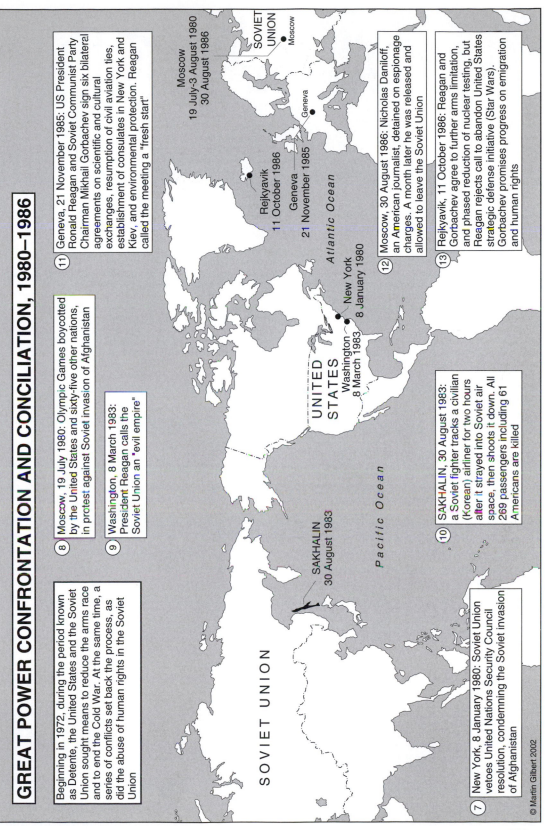

Beginning in 1972, during the period known as Detente, the United States and the Soviet Union sought means to reduce the arms race and to end the Cold War. At the same time, a series of conflicts set back the process, as did the abuse of human rights in the Soviet Union

(8) Moscow, 19 July 1980: Olympic Games boycotted by the United States and sixty-five other nations, in protest against Soviet invasion of Afghanistan

(9) Washington, 8 March 1983: President Reagan calls the Soviet Union an "evil empire"

(11) Geneva, 21 November 1985: US President Ronald Reagan and Soviet Communist Party Chairman Mikhail Gorbachev sign six bilateral agreements on scientific and cultural exchanges, resumption of civil aviation ties, establishment of consulates in New York and Kiev, and environmental protection. Reagan called the meeting a "fresh start"

(12) Moscow, 30 August 1986: Nicholas Daniloff, an American journalist, detained on espionage charges. A month later he was released and allowed to leave the Soviet Union

(13) Rejkyavik, 11 October 1986: Reagan and Gorbachev agree to further arms limitation, and phased reduction of nuclear testing, but Reagan rejects call to abandon United States strategic defense initiative (Star Wars). Gorbachev promises progress on emigration and human rights

(7) New York, 8 January 1980: Soviet Union vetoes United Nations Security Council resolution, condemning the Soviet invasion of Afghanistan

(10) SAKHALIN, 30 August 1983: a Soviet fighter tracks a civilian (Korean) airliner for two hours after it strayed into Soviet air space, then shoots it down. All 269 passengers including 61 Americans are killed

SOVIET UNION
Moscow

Moscow
19 July–3 August 1980
30 August 1986

Rejkyavik
11 October 1986

Geneva
21 November 1985

Geneva

Atlantic Ocean

New York
8 January 1980

Washington
8 March 1983

UNITED STATES

SAKHALIN
30 August 1983

Pacific Ocean

SOVIET UNION

© Martin Gilbert 2002

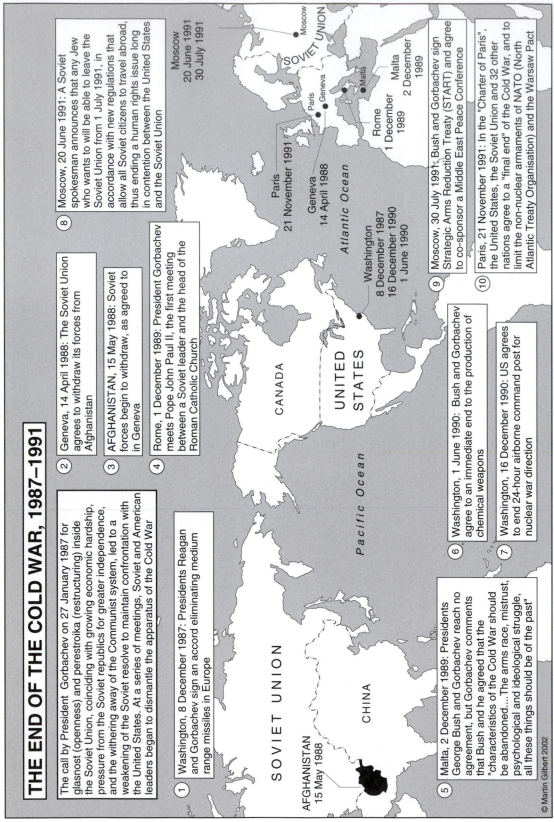

THE END OF THE COLD WAR, 1987–1991

The call by President Gorbachev on 27 January 1987 for glasnost (openness) and perestroika (restructuring) inside the Soviet Union, coinciding with growing economic hardship, pressure from the Soviet republics for greater independence, and the withering away of the Communist system, led to a weakening of the Soviet resolve to maintain confrontation with the United States. At a series of meetings, Soviet and American leaders began to dismantle the apparatus of the Cold War

(1) Washington, 8 December 1987: Presidents Reagan and Gorbachev sign an accord eliminating medium range missiles in Europe

(2) Geneva, 14 April 1988: The Soviet Union agrees to withdraw its forces from Afghanistan

(3) AFGHANISTAN, 15 May 1988: Soviet forces begin to withdraw, as agreed to in Geneva

(4) Rome, 1 December 1989: President Gorbachev meets Pope John Paul II, the first meeting between a Soviet leader and the head of the Roman Catholic Church

(5) Malta, 2 December 1989: Presidents George Bush and Gorbachev reach no agreement, but Gorbachev comments that Bush and he agreed that the "characteristics of the Cold War should be abandoned....The arms race, mistrust, psychological and ideological struggle, all these things should be of the past"

(6) Washington, 1 June 1990: Bush and Gorbachev agree to an immediate end to the production of chemical weapons

(7) Washington, 16 December 1990: US agrees to end 24-hour airborne command post for nuclear war direction

(8) Moscow, 20 June 1991: A Soviet spokesman announces that any Jew who wants to will be able to leave the Soviet Union from 1 July 1991, in accordance with new regulations that allow all Soviet citizens to travel abroad, thus ending a human rights issue long in contention between the United States and the Soviet Union

(9) Moscow, 30 July 1991: Bush and Gorbachev sign Strategic Arms Reduction Treaty (START) and agree to co-sponsor a Middle East Peace Conference

(10) Paris, 21 November 1991: In the "Charter of Paris", the United States, the Soviet Union and 32 other nations agree to a "final end" of the Cold War, and to limit the non-nuclear armaments of NATO (North Atlantic Treaty Organisation) and the Warsaw Pact

Moscow
20 June 1991
30 July 1991

Paris
21 November 1991

Geneva
14 April 1988

Rome
1 December
1989

Malta
2 December
1989

Washington
8 December 1987
16 December 1990
1 June 1990

AFGHANISTAN
15 May 1988

SOVIET UNION

CHINA

CANADA

UNITED STATES

Pacific Ocean

Atlantic Ocean

Moscow

SOVIET UNION

© Martin Gilbert 2002

THE END OF THE COLD WAR, 1992–1993

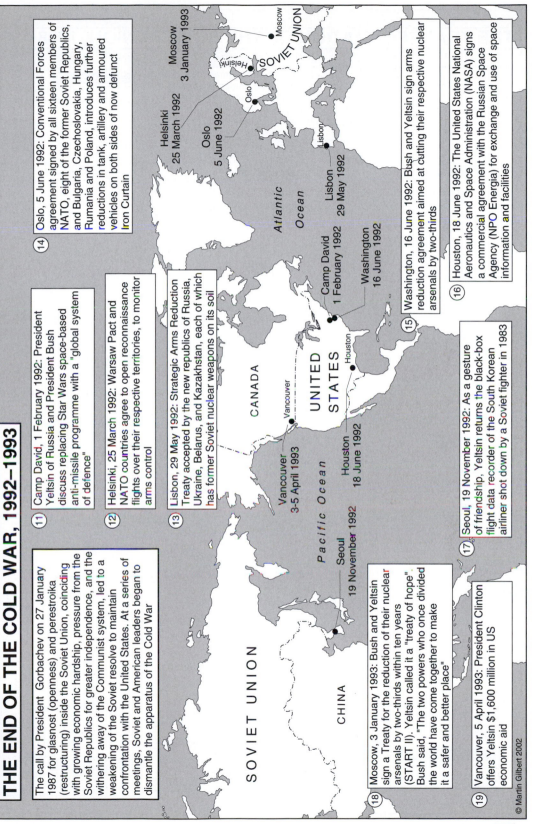

The call by President Gorbachev on 27 January 1987 for glasnost (openness) and perestroika (restructuring) inside the Soviet Union, coinciding with growing economic hardship, pressure from the Soviet Republics for greater independence, and the withering away of the Communist system, led to a weakening of the Soviet resolve to maintain confrontation with the United States. At a series of meetings, Soviet and American leaders began to dismantle the apparatus of the Cold War

11 Camp David, 1 February 1992: President Yeltsin of Russia and President Bush discuss replacing Star Wars space-based anti-missile programme with a "global system of defence"

12 Helsinki, 25 March 1992: Warsaw Pact and NATO countries agree to open reconnaissance flights over their respective territories, to monitor arms control

13 Lisbon, 29 May 1992: Strategic Arms Reduction Treaty accepted by the new republics of Russia, Ukraine, Belarus, and Kazakhstan, each of which has former Soviet nuclear weapons on its soil

14 Oslo, 5 June 1992: Conventional Forces agreement signed by all sixteen members of NATO, eight of the former Soviet Republics, and Bulgaria, Czechoslovakia, Hungary, Rumania and Poland, introduces further reductions in tank, artillery and armoured vehicles on both sides of now defunct Iron Curtain

15 Washington, 16 June 1992: Bush and Yeltsin sign arms reduction agreement aimed at cutting their respective nuclear arsenals by two-thirds

16 Houston, 18 June 1992: The United States National Aeronautics and Space Administration (NASA) signs a commercial agreement with the Russian Space Agency (NPO Energia) for exchange and use of space information and facilities

17 Seoul, 19 November 1992: As a gesture of friendship, Yeltsin returns the black-box flight data recorder of the South Korean airliner shot down by a Soviet fighter in 1983

18 Moscow, 3 January 1993: Bush and Yeltsin sign a Treaty for the reduction of their nuclear arsenals by two-thirds within ten years (START II). Yeltsin called it a "treaty of hope". Bush said, "The two powers who once divided the world have come together to make it a safer and better place"

19 Vancouver, 5 April 1993: President Clinton offers Yeltsin $1,600 million in US economic aid

Camp David
1 February 1992

Washington
16 June 1992

Houston
18 June 1992

Vancouver
3-5 April 1993

Seoul
19 November 1992

Helsinki
25 March 1992

Oslo
5 June 1992

Moscow
3 January 1993

Lisbon
29 May 1992

SOVIET UNION

CHINA

CANADA

UNITED STATES

Atlantic Ocean

Pacific Ocean

© Martin Gilbert 2002

THE TRANSFORMATION OF THE SOVIET UNION, 1988-1989

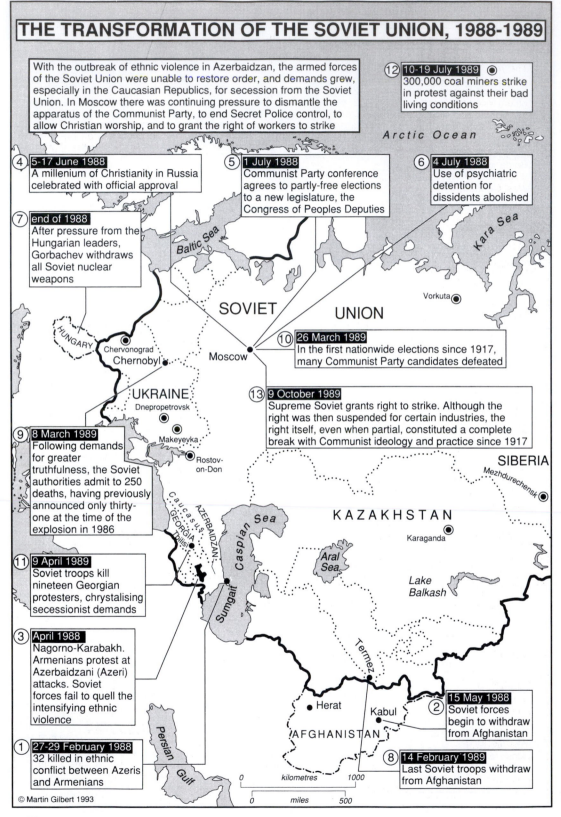

With the outbreak of ethnic violence in Azerbaidzan, the armed forces of the Soviet Union were unable to restore order, and demands grew, especially in the Caucasian Republics, for secession from the Soviet Union. In Moscow there was continuing pressure to dismantle the apparatus of the Communist Party, to end Secret Police control, to allow Christian worship, and to grant the right of workers to strike

⑫ **10-19 July 1989** ◎
300,000 coal miners strike in protest against their bad living conditions

Arctic Ocean

④ **5-17 June 1988**
A millenium of Christianity in Russia celebrated with official approval

⑤ **1 July 1988**
Communist Party conference agrees to partly-free elections to a new legislature, the Congress of Peoples Deputies

⑥ **4 July 1988**
Use of psychiatric detention for dissidents abolished

Kara Sea

⑦ **end of 1988**
After pressure from the Hungarian leaders, Gorbachev withdraws all Soviet nuclear weapons

Baltic Sea

HUNGARY

Chervonograd
Chernobyl

SOVIET   UNION

Vorkuta ◉

Moscow

⑩ **26 March 1989**
In the first nationwide elections since 1917, many Communist Party candidates defeated

UKRAINE
Dnepropetrovsk

⑬ **9 October 1989**
Supreme Soviet grants right to strike. Although the right was then suspended for certain industries, the right itself, even when partial, constituted a complete break with Communist ideology and practice since 1917

Makeyevka ◉

⑨ **8 March 1989**
Following demands for greater truthfulness, the Soviet authorities admit to 250 deaths, having previously announced only thirty-one at the time of the explosion in 1986

Rostov-on-Don

SIBERIA

Mezhdurechensk ◉

KAZAKHSTAN

Caucasus
GEORGIA
Tbilisi
AZERBAIDZAN
Caspian Sea
Karaganda ◉

⑪ **9 April 1989**
Soviet troops kill nineteen Georgian protesters, chrystalising secessionist demands

Aral Sea

Lake Balkash

Sumgait

③ **April 1988**
Nagorno-Karabakh. Armenians protest at Azerbaidzani (Azeri) attacks. Soviet forces fail to quell the intensifying ethnic violence

Termez

⑮ **15 May 1988**
Soviet forces begin to withdraw from Afghanistan

Herat
Kabul

① **27-29 February 1988**
32 killed in ethnic conflict between Azeris and Armenians

Persian Gulf

AFGHANISTAN

⑧ **14 February 1989**
Last Soviet troops withdraw from Afghanistan

0   kilometres   1000

0   miles   500

© Martin Gilbert 1993

THE COLLAPSE OF COMMUNISM IN EASTERN EUROPE, 1989

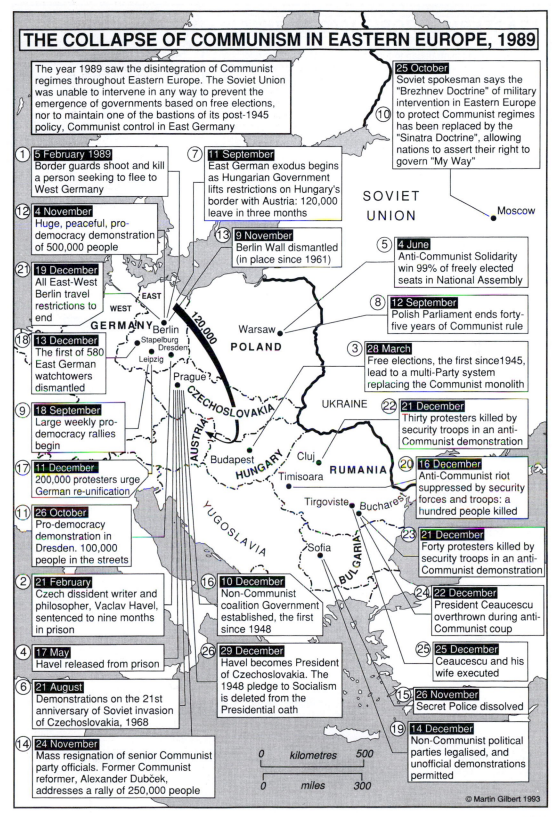

The year 1989 saw the disintegration of Communist regimes throughout Eastern Europe. The Soviet Union was unable to intervene in any way to prevent the emergence of governments based on free elections, nor to maintain one of the bastions of its post-1945 policy, Communist control in East Germany

(10) 25 October
Soviet spokesman says the "Brezhnev Doctrine" of military intervention in Eastern Europe to protect Communist regimes has been replaced by the "Sinatra Doctrine", allowing nations to assert their right to govern "My Way"

(1) 5 February 1989
Border guards shoot and kill a person seeking to flee to West Germany

(12) 4 November
Huge, peaceful, pro-democracy demonstration of 500,000 people

(21) 19 December
All East-West Berlin travel restrictions to end

(18) 13 December
The first of 580 East German watchtowers dismantled

(9) 18 September
Large weekly pro-democracy rallies begin

(17) 11 December
200,000 protesters urge German re-unification

(11) 26 October
Pro-democracy demonstration in Dresden. 100,000 people in the streets

(2) 21 February
Czech dissident writer and philosopher, Vaclav Havel, sentenced to nine months in prison

(4) 17 May
Havel released from prison

(6) 21 August
Demonstrations on the 21st anniversary of Soviet invasion of Czechoslovakia, 1968

(14) 24 November
Mass resignation of senior Communist party officials. Former Communist reformer, Alexander Dubček, addresses a rally of 250,000 people

(7) 11 September
East German exodus begins as Hungarian Government lifts restrictions on Hungary's border with Austria: 120,000 leave in three months

(13) 9 November
Berlin Wall dismantled (in place since 1961)

(5) 4 June
Anti-Communist Solidarity win 99% of freely elected seats in National Assembly

(8) 12 September
Polish Parliament ends forty-five years of Communist rule

(3) 28 March
Free elections, the first since 1945, lead to a multi-Party system replacing the Communist monolith

(22) 21 December
Thirty protesters killed by security troops in an anti-Communist demonstration

(20) 16 December
Anti-Communist riot suppressed by security forces and troops: a hundred people killed

(23) 21 December
Forty protesters killed by security troops in an anti-Communist demonstration

(16) 10 December
Non-Communist coalition Government established, the first since 1948

(26) 29 December
Havel becomes President of Czechoslovakia. The 1948 pledge to Socialism is deleted from the Presidential oath

(24) 22 December
President Ceaucescu overthrown during anti-Communist coup

(25) 25 December
Ceaucescu and his wife executed

(15) 26 November
Secret Police dissolved

(19) 14 December
Non-Communist political parties legalised, and unofficial demonstrations permitted

SOVIET UNION

Moscow

EAST
WEST
GERMANY
Berlin
Stapelburg
Dresden
Leipzig
Prague
120,000
Warsaw
POLAND
CZECHOSLOVAKIA
AUSTRIA
Budapest
HUNGARY
Timisoara
Cluj
RUMANIA
Tirgoviste
Bucharest
UKRAINE
YUGOSLAVIA
Sofia
BULGARIA

0   kilometres   500
0   miles   300

© Martin Gilbert 1993

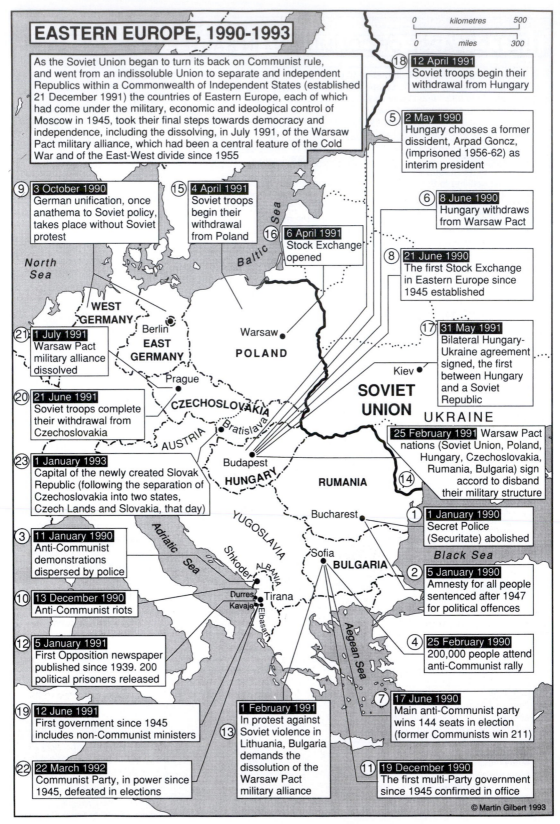

EASTERN EUROPE, 1990-1993

As the Soviet Union began to turn its back on Communist rule, and went from an indissoluble Union to separate and independent Republics within a Commonwealth of Independent States (established 21 December 1991) the countries of Eastern Europe, each of which had come under the military, economic and ideological control of Moscow in 1945, took their final steps towards democracy and independence, including the dissolving, in July 1991, of the Warsaw Pact military alliance, which had been a central feature of the Cold War and of the East-West divide since 1955

(18) 12 April 1991
Soviet troops begin their withdrawal from Hungary

(5) 2 May 1990
Hungary chooses a former dissident, Arpad Goncz, (imprisoned 1956-62) as interim president

(6) 8 June 1990
Hungary withdraws from Warsaw Pact

(8) 21 June 1990
The first Stock Exchange in Eastern Europe since 1945 established

(17) 31 May 1991
Bilateral Hungary-Ukraine agreement signed, the first between Hungary and a Soviet Republic

(9) 3 October 1990
German unification, once anathema to Soviet policy, takes place without Soviet protest

(15) 4 April 1991
Soviet troops begin their withdrawal from Poland

(16) 6 April 1991
Stock Exchange opened

(21) 1 July 1991
Warsaw Pact military alliance dissolved

(20) 21 June 1991
Soviet troops complete their withdrawal from Czechoslovakia

(23) 1 January 1993
Capital of the newly created Slovak Republic (following the separation of Czechoslovakia into two states, Czech Lands and Slovakia, that day)

25 February 1991 Warsaw Pact nations (Soviet Union, Poland, Hungary, Czechoslovakia, Rumania, Bulgaria) sign accord to disband their military structure **(14)**

(3) 11 January 1990
Anti-Communist demonstrations dispersed by police

(10) 13 December 1990
Anti-Communist riots

(12) 5 January 1991
First Opposition newspaper published since 1939. 200 political prisoners released

(19) 12 June 1991
First government since 1945 includes non-Communist ministers

(22) 22 March 1992
Communist Party, in power since 1945, defeated in elections

(13) 1 February 1991
In protest against Soviet violence in Lithuania, Bulgaria demands the dissolution of the Warsaw Pact military alliance

(1) 1 January 1990
Secret Police (Securitate) abolished

(2) 5 January 1990
Amnesty for all people sentenced after 1947 for political offences

(4) 25 February 1990
200,000 people attend anti-Communist rally

(7) 17 June 1990
Main anti-Communist party wins 144 seats in election (former Communists win 211)

(11) 19 December 1990
The first multi-Party government since 1945 confirmed in office

North Sea

Baltic Sea

WEST GERMANY
Berlin
EAST GERMANY
Prague
CZECHOSLOVAKIA
Bratislava
AUSTRIA
Budapest
HUNGARY

Warsaw
POLAND

Kiev
SOVIET UNION
UKRAINE

RUMANIA

YUGOSLAVIA
Adriatic Sea
Shkoder
ALBANIA
Durres Tirana
Kavaje Elbasan

Bucharest
Sofia
BULGARIA
Black Sea
Aegean Sea

0 kilometres 500
0 miles 300

© Martin Gilbert 1993

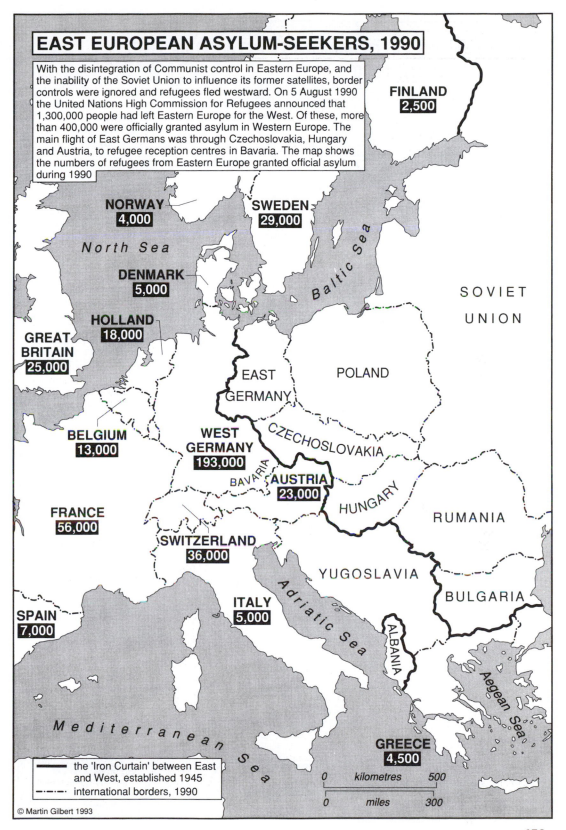

EAST EUROPEAN ASYLUM-SEEKERS, 1990

With the disintegration of Communist control in Eastern Europe, and the inability of the Soviet Union to influence its former satellites, border controls were ignored and refugees fled westward. On 5 August 1990 the United Nations High Commission for Refugees announced that 1,300,000 people had left Eastern Europe for the West. Of these, more than 400,000 were officially granted asylum in Western Europe. The main flight of East Germans was through Czechoslovakia, Hungary and Austria, to refugee reception centres in Bavaria. The map shows the numbers of refugees from Eastern Europe granted official asylum during 1990

FINLAND
2,500

NORWAY
4,000

SWEDEN
29,000

North Sea

Baltic Sea

DENMARK
5,000

SOVIET UNION

HOLLAND
18,000

GREAT BRITAIN
25,000

EAST GERMANY

POLAND

BELGIUM
13,000

WEST GERMANY
193,000

CZECHOSLOVAKIA

BAVARIA

AUSTRIA
23,000

HUNGARY

FRANCE
56,000

SWITZERLAND
36,000

RUMANIA

YUGOSLAVIA

BULGARIA

Adriatic Sea

SPAIN
7,000

ITALY
5,000

ALBANIA

Aegean Sea

Mediterranean Sea

GREECE
4,500

———— the 'Iron Curtain' between East and West, established 1945
–·–·–·– international borders, 1990

0   kilometres   500

0   miles   300

© Martin Gilbert 1993

156

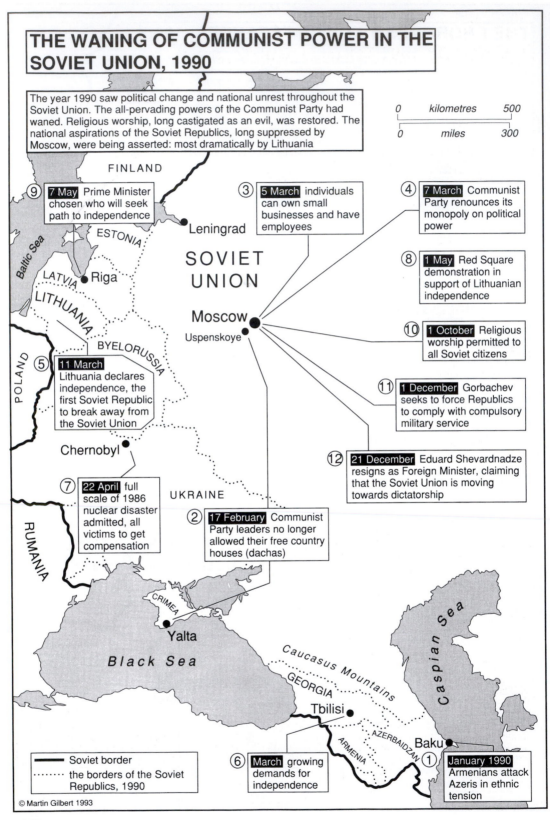

THE WANING OF COMMUNIST POWER IN THE SOVIET UNION, 1990

The year 1990 saw political change and national unrest throughout the Soviet Union. The all-pervading powers of the Communist Party had waned. Religious worship, long castigated as an evil, was restored. The national aspirations of the Soviet Republics, long suppressed by Moscow, were being asserted: most dramatically by Lithuania

0   kilometres   500

0   miles   300

FINLAND

ESTONIA

Leningrad

⑨ **7 May** Prime Minister chosen who will seek path to independence

③ **5 March** individuals can own small businesses and have employees

④ **7 March** Communist Party renounces its monopoly on political power

⑧ **1 May** Red Square demonstration in support of Lithuanian independence

SOVIET UNION

Baltic Sea

LATVIA

Riga

LITHUANIA

Moscow

Uspenskoye

⑩ **1 October** Religious worship permitted to all Soviet citizens

BYELORUSSIA

POLAND

⑤ **11 March** Lithuania declares independence, the first Soviet Republic to break away from the Soviet Union

⑪ **1 December** Gorbachev seeks to force Republics to comply with compulsory military service

Chernobyl

⑫ **21 December** Eduard Shevardnadze resigns as Foreign Minister, claiming that the Soviet Union is moving towards dictatorship

⑦ **22 April** full scale of 1986 nuclear disaster admitted, all victims to get compensation

UKRAINE

RUMANIA

② **17 February** Communist Party leaders no longer allowed their free country houses (dachas)

CRIMEA

Yalta

Black Sea

Caucasus Mountains

GEORGIA

Caspian Sea

Tbilisi

AZERBAIDZAN

Baku

ARMENIA

⑥ **March** growing demands for independence

① **January 1990** Armenians attack Azeris in ethnic tension

——— Soviet border

·········· the borders of the Soviet Republics, 1990

© Martin Gilbert 1993

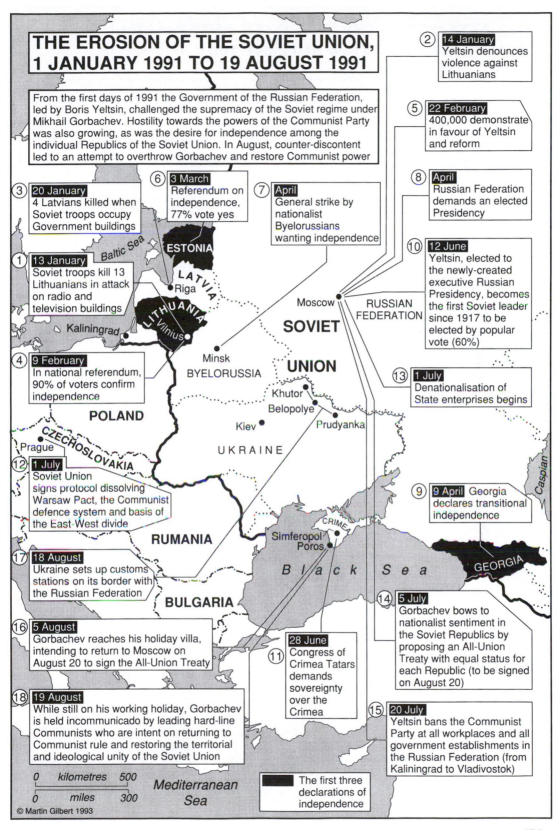

THE EROSION OF THE SOVIET UNION, 1 JANUARY 1991 TO 19 AUGUST 1991

From the first days of 1991 the Government of the Russian Federation, led by Boris Yeltsin, challenged the supremacy of the Soviet regime under Mikhail Gorbachev. Hostility towards the powers of the Communist Party was also growing, as was the desire for independence among the individual Republics of the Soviet Union. In August, counter-discontent led to an attempt to overthrow Gorbachev and restore Communist power

② **14 January** Yeltsin denounces violence against Lithuanians

⑤ **22 February** 400,000 demonstrate in favour of Yeltsin and reform

⑧ **April** Russian Federation demands an elected Presidency

⑥ **3 March** Referendum on independence, 77% vote yes

⑦ **April** General strike by nationalist Byelorussians wanting independence

③ **20 January** 4 Latvians killed when Soviet troops occupy Government buildings

⑩ **12 June** Yeltsin, elected to the newly-created executive Russian Presidency, becomes the first Soviet leader since 1917 to be elected by popular vote (60%)

① **13 January** Soviet troops kill 13 Lithuanians in attack on radio and television buildings

④ **9 February** In national referendum, 90% of voters confirm independence

⑬ **1 July** Denationalisation of State enterprises begins

⑫ **1 July** Soviet Union signs protocol dissolving Warsaw Pact, the Communist defence system and basis of the East-West divide

⑨ **9 April** Georgia declares transitional independence

⑰ **18 August** Ukraine sets up customs stations on its border with the Russian Federation

⑭ **5 July** Gorbachev bows to nationalist sentiment in the Soviet Republics by proposing an All-Union Treaty with equal status for each Republic (to be signed on August 20)

⑯ **5 August** Gorbachev reaches his holiday villa, intending to return to Moscow on August 20 to sign the All-Union Treaty

⑪ **28 June** Congress of Crimea Tatars demands sovereignty over the Crimea

⑱ **19 August** While still on his working holiday, Gorbachev is held incommunicado by leading hard-line Communists who are intent on returning to Communist rule and restoring the territorial and ideological unity of the Soviet Union

⑮ **20 July** Yeltsin bans the Communist Party at all workplaces and all government establishments in the Russian Federation (from Kaliningrad to Vladivostok)

Baltic Sea
ESTONIA
LATVIA
Riga
LITHUANIA
Kaliningrad
Vilnius
Minsk
BYELORUSSIA
Moscow
SOVIET
UNION
RUSSIAN FEDERATION
Khutor
Belopolye
Kiev
Prudyanka
UKRAINE
POLAND
CZECHOSLOVAKIA
Prague
RUMANIA
BULGARIA
CRIMEA
Simferopol
Poros
Black Sea
GEORGIA
Caspian

| 0 | kilometres | 500 |
| 0 | miles | 300 |

Mediterranean Sea

■ The first three declarations of independence

© Martin Gilbert 1993

THE ATTEMPTED COUP AND ITS AFTERMATH, 19 AUGUST 1991 TO 24 AUGUST 1991

As more Soviet Republics moved towards independence, and the powers and institutions of the Communist Party were being progressively dismantled, a group of leading Communists tried to seize power in Moscow, intent upon the restoration of Communism, and of the Soviet Union. But in Moscow itself, the head of the Russian Federation, Boris Yeltsin, rallied the forces for change, and forestalled the take-over. Within four and a half months, the Soviet Union had ceased to exist

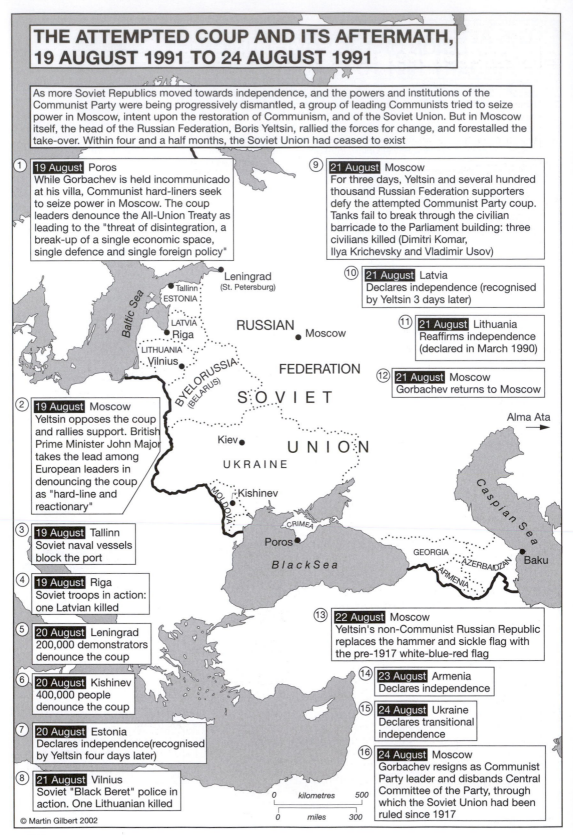

① 19 August Poros
While Gorbachev is held incommunicado at his villa, Communist hard-liners seek to seize power in Moscow. The coup leaders denounce the All-Union Treaty as leading to the "threat of disintegration, a break-up of a single economic space, single defence and single foreign policy"

② 19 August Moscow
Yeltsin opposes the coup and rallies support. British Prime Minister John Major takes the lead among European leaders in denouncing the coup as "hard-line and reactionary"

③ 19 August Tallinn
Soviet naval vessels block the port

④ 19 August Riga
Soviet troops in action: one Latvian killed

⑤ 20 August Leningrad
200,000 demonstrators denounce the coup

⑥ 20 August Kishinev
400,000 people denounce the coup

⑦ 20 August Estonia
Declares independence(recognised by Yeltsin four days later)

⑧ 21 August Vilnius
Soviet "Black Beret" police in action. One Lithuanian killed

⑨ 21 August Moscow
For three days, Yeltsin and several hundred thousand Russian Federation supporters defy the attempted Communist Party coup. Tanks fail to break through the civilian barricade to the Parliament building: three civilians killed (Dimitri Komar, Ilya Krichevsky and Vladimir Usov)

⑩ 21 August Latvia
Declares independence (recognised by Yeltsin 3 days later)

⑪ 21 August Lithuania
Reaffirms independence (declared in March 1990)

⑫ 21 August Moscow
Gorbachev returns to Moscow

⑬ 22 August Moscow
Yeltsin's non-Communist Russian Republic replaces the hammer and sickle flag with the pre-1917 white-blue-red flag

⑭ 23 August Armenia
Declares independence

⑮ 24 August Ukraine
Declares transitional independence

⑯ 24 August Moscow
Gorbachev resigns as Communist Party leader and disbands Central Committee of the Party, through which the Soviet Union had been ruled since 1917

Leningrad (St. Petersburg)
Tallinn
ESTONIA
Baltic Sea
LATVIA
Riga
LITHUANIA
Vilnius
BYELORUSSIA (BELARUS)
RUSSIAN
Moscow
FEDERATION
SOVIET
UNION
Kiev
UKRAINE
MOLDOVA
Kishinev
CRIMEA
Poros
Black Sea
GEORGIA
ARMENIA
AZERBAIDZAN
Baku
Caspian Sea
Alma Ata

0 kilometres 500
0 miles 300

© Martin Gilbert 2002

THE ATTEMPTED COUP AND ITS AFTERMATH, 25 AUGUST 1991 TO 26 DECEMBER 1991

As more Soviet Republics moved towards independence, and the powers and institutions of the Communist Party were being progressively dismantled, a group of leading Communists tried to seize power in Moscow, intent upon the restoration of Communism, and of the Soviet Union. But in Moscow itself, the head of the Russian Federation, Boris Yeltsin, rallied the forces for change, and forestalled the take-over. Within four and a half months, the Soviet Union had ceased to exist

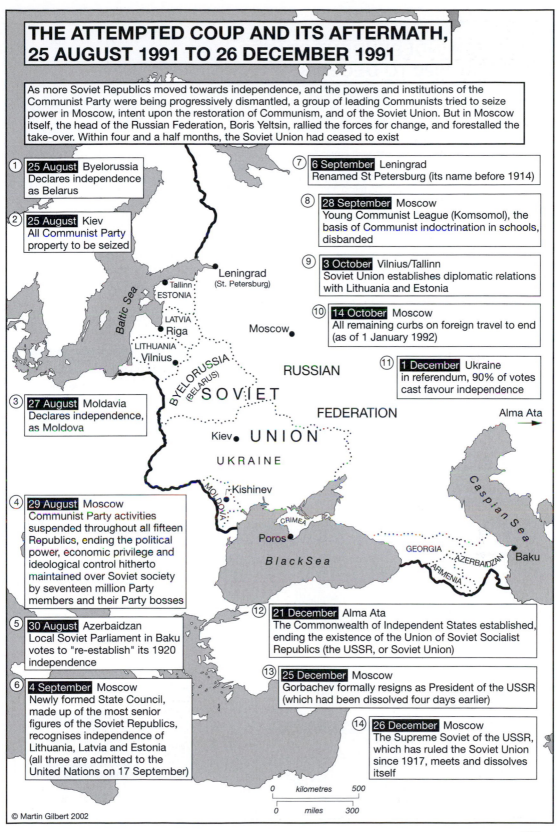

① 25 August Byelorussia
Declares independence
as Belarus

② 25 August Kiev
All Communist Party
property to be seized

③ 27 August Moldavia
Declares independence,
as Moldova

④ 29 August Moscow
Communist Party activities
suspended throughout all fifteen
Republics, ending the political
power, economic privilege and
ideological control hitherto
maintained over Soviet society
by seventeen million Party
members and their Party bosses

⑤ 30 August Azerbaidzan
Local Soviet Parliament in Baku
votes to "re-establish" its 1920
independence

⑥ 4 September Moscow
Newly formed State Council,
made up of the most senior
figures of the Soviet Republics,
recognises independence of
Lithuania, Latvia and Estonia
(all three are admitted to the
United Nations on 17 September)

⑦ 6 September Leningrad
Renamed St Petersburg (its name before 1914)

⑧ 28 September Moscow
Young Communist League (Komsomol), the
basis of Communist indoctrination in schools,
disbanded

⑨ 3 October Vilnius/Tallinn
Soviet Union establishes diplomatic relations
with Lithuania and Estonia

⑩ 14 October Moscow
All remaining curbs on foreign travel to end
(as of 1 January 1992)

⑪ 1 December Ukraine
in referendum, 90% of votes
cast favour independence

⑫ 21 December Alma Ata
The Commonwealth of Independent States established,
ending the existence of the Union of Soviet Socialist
Republics (the USSR, or Soviet Union)

⑬ 25 December Moscow
Gorbachev formally resigns as President of the USSR
(which had been dissolved four days earlier)

⑭ 26 December Moscow
The Supreme Soviet of the USSR,
which has ruled the Soviet Union
since 1917, meets and dissolves
itself

Leningrad
(St. Petersburg)

Tallinn
ESTONIA

LATVIA
Riga

Moscow

LITHUANIA
Vilnius

BYELORUSSIA
(BELARUS)

RUSSIAN

SOVIET

FEDERATION

UNION

Kiev

UKRAINE

MOLDOVA

Kishinev

CRIMEA

Poros

Black Sea

Baltic Sea

Caspian Sea

GEORGIA

AZERBAIDZAN

ARMENIA

Baku

Alma Ata

0   kilometres   500

0   miles   300

© Martin Gilbert 2002

160

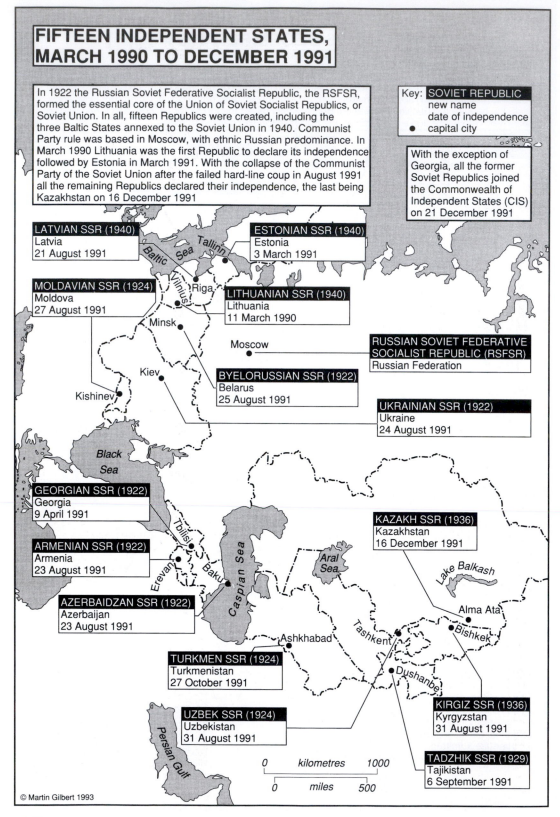

FIFTEEN INDEPENDENT STATES, MARCH 1990 TO DECEMBER 1991

In 1922 the Russian Soviet Federative Socialist Republic, the RSFSR, formed the essential core of the Union of Soviet Socialist Republics, or Soviet Union. In all, fifteen Republics were created, including the three Baltic States annexed to the Soviet Union in 1940. Communist Party rule was based in Moscow, with ethnic Russian predominance. In March 1990 Lithuania was the first Republic to declare its independence followed by Estonia in March 1991. With the collapse of the Communist Party of the Soviet Union after the failed hard-line coup in August 1991 all the remaining Republics declared their independence, the last being Kazakhstan on 16 December 1991

Key: **SOVIET REPUBLIC**
new name
date of independence
● capital city

With the exception of Georgia, all the former Soviet Republics joined the Commonwealth of Independent States (CIS) on 21 December 1991

LATVIAN SSR (1940)
Latvia
21 August 1991

ESTONIAN SSR (1940)
Estonia
3 March 1991

Tallinn

Baltic Sea

MOLDAVIAN SSR (1924)
Moldova
27 August 1991

Vilnius
Riga

LITHUANIAN SSR (1940)
Lithuania
11 March 1990

Minsk

Moscow

RUSSIAN SOVIET FEDERATIVE SOCIALIST REPUBLIC (RSFSR)
Russian Federation

Kiev

BYELORUSSIAN SSR (1922)
Belarus
25 August 1991

Kishinev

UKRAINIAN SSR (1922)
Ukraine
24 August 1991

Black Sea

GEORGIAN SSR (1922)
Georgia
9 April 1991

Tbilisi

KAZAKH SSR (1936)
Kazakhstan
16 December 1991

Aral Sea

Lake Balkash

ARMENIAN SSR (1922)
Armenia
23 August 1991

Erevan
Baku

Caspian Sea

Alma Ata

AZERBAIDZAN SSR (1922)
Azerbaijan
23 August 1991

Bishkek

Tashkent

Ashkhabad

TURKMEN SSR (1924)
Turkmenistan
27 October 1991

Dushanbe

KIRGIZ SSR (1936)
Kyrgyzstan
31 August 1991

UZBEK SSR (1924)
Uzbekistan
31 August 1991

Persian Gulf

| 0 | kilometres | 1000 |
| 0 | miles | 500 |

TADZHIK SSR (1929)
Tajikistan
6 September 1991

© Martin Gilbert 1993

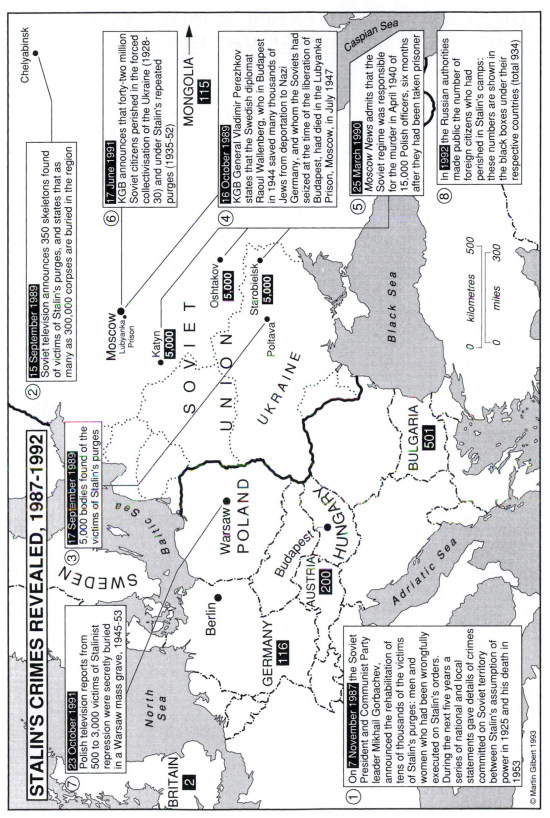

STALIN'S CRIMES REVEALED, 1987-1992

① On 7 November 1987 the Soviet President and Communist Party leader Mikhail Gorbachev, announced the rehabilitation of tens of thousands of the victims of Stalin's purges: men and women who had been wrongfully executed on Stalin's orders. During the next five years a series of national and local statements gave details of crimes committed on Soviet territory between Stalin's assumption of power in 1925 and his death in 1953

② 15 September 1989
Soviet television announces 350 skeletons found of victims of Stalin's purges, and states that as many as 300,000 corpses are buried in the region

③ 17 September 1989
5,000 bodies found of the victims of Stalin's purges

④ 16 October 1989
KGB General Vladimir Perezhkov states that the Swedish diplomat Raoul Wallenberg, who in Budapest in 1944 saved many thousands of Jews from deportation to Nazi Germany, and whom the Soviets had seized at the time of the liberation of Budapest, had died in the Lubyanka Prison, Moscow, in July 1947

⑤ 25 March 1990
Moscow News admits that the Soviet regime was responsible for the murder in April 1940 of 15,000 Polish officers, six months after they had been taken prisoner

⑥ 17 June 1991
KGB announces that forty-two million Soviet citizens perished in the forced collectivisation of the Ukraine (1928-30) and under Stalin's repeated purges (1935-52)

⑦ 23 October 1991
Polish television reports from 500 to 3,000 victims of Stalinist repression were secretly buried in a Warsaw mass grave, 1945-53

⑧ In 1992 the Russian authorities made public the number of foreign citizens who had perished in Stalin's camps: these numbers are shown in the black boxes under their respective countries (total 934)

BRITAIN **2**

GERMANY **116**

AUSTRIA **200**

BULGARIA **501**

MONGOLIA **115**

Katyn **5,000**

Oshtakov **5,000**

Starobielsk **5,000**

Chelyabinsk

Moscow
Lubyanka
Prison

Warsaw
POLAND

Berlin

Budapest
HUNGARY

Poltava

SWEDEN

SOVIET UNION

UKRAINE

North Sea

Baltic Sea

Black Sea

Adriatic Sea

Caspian Sea

kilometres
0   500

miles
0   300

© Martin Gilbert 1993

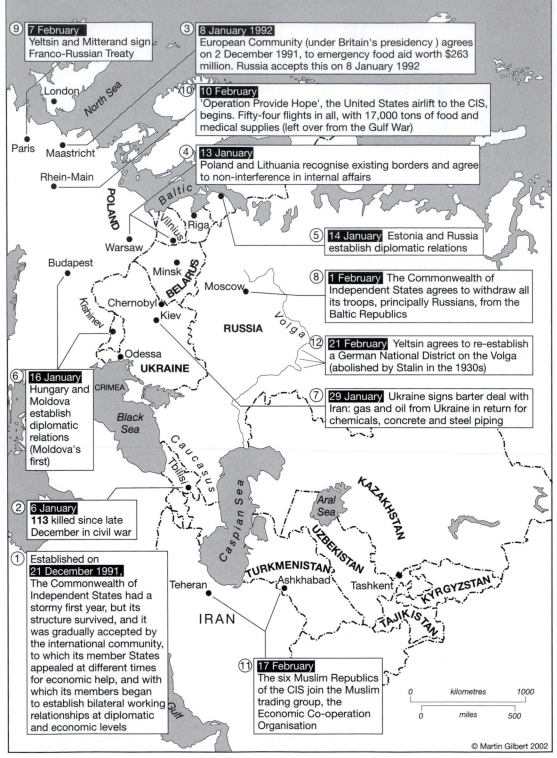

THE COMMONWEALTH OF INDEPENDENT STATES, 21 DECEMBER 1991–21 FEBRUARY 1992

⑨ 7 February
Yeltsin and Mitterand sign Franco-Russian Treaty

③ 8 January 1992
European Community (under Britain's presidency) agrees on 2 December 1991, to emergency food aid worth $263 million. Russia accepts this on 8 January 1992

⑩ 10 February
'Operation Provide Hope', the United States airlift to the CIS, begins. Fifty-four flights in all, with 17,000 tons of food and medical supplies (left over from the Gulf War)

④ 13 January
Poland and Lithuania recognise existing borders and agree to non-interference in internal affairs

⑤ 14 January Estonia and Russia establish diplomatic relations

⑧ 1 February The Commonwealth of Independent States agrees to withdraw all its troops, principally Russians, from the Baltic Republics

⑫ 21 February Yeltsin agrees to re-establish a German National District on the Volga (abolished by Stalin in the 1930s)

⑦ 29 January Ukraine signs barter deal with Iran: gas and oil from Ukraine in return for chemicals, concrete and steel piping

⑥ 16 January
Hungary and Moldova establish diplomatic relations (Moldova's first)

② 6 January
113 killed since late December in civil war

① Established on 21 December 1991,
The Commonwealth of Independent States had a stormy first year, but its structure survived, and it was gradually accepted by the international community, to which its member States appealed at different times for economic help, and with which its members began to establish bilateral working relationships at diplomatic and economic levels

⑪ 17 February
The six Muslim Republics of the CIS join the Muslim trading group, the Economic Co-operation Organisation

London
North Sea
Paris
Maastricht
Rhein-Main
POLAND
Baltic
Vilnius
Riga
Warsaw
Budapest
Minsk
BELARUS
Moscow
Kishinev
Chernobyl
Kiev
RUSSIA
Volga
Odessa
UKRAINE
CRIMEA
Black Sea
Caucasus
Tbilisi
Caspian Sea
Aral Sea
KAZAKHSTAN
UZBEKISTAN
Teheran
IRAN
TURKMENISTAN
Ashkhabad
Tashkent
KYRGYZSTAN
TAJIKISTAN
Gulf

0 — kilometres — 1000
0 — miles — 500

© Martin Gilbert 2002

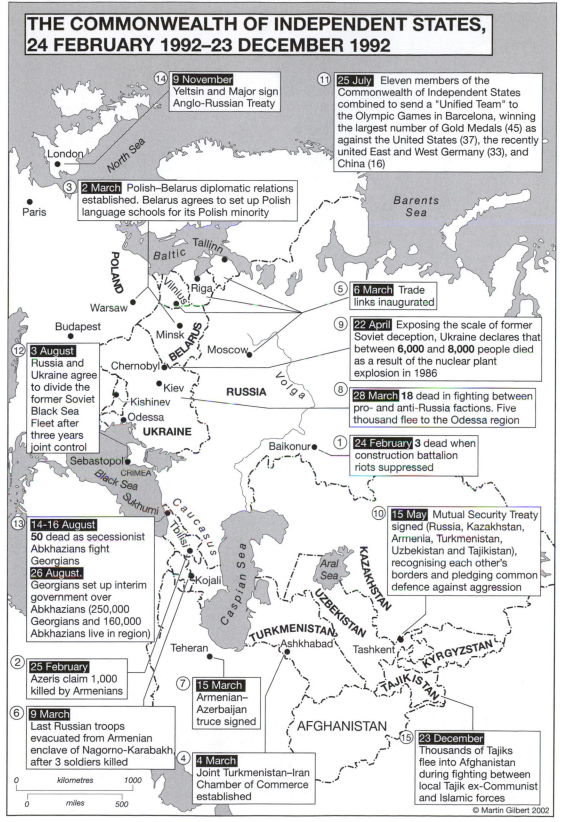

THE COMMONWEALTH OF INDEPENDENT STATES, 24 FEBRUARY 1992–23 DECEMBER 1992

⑭ **9 November**
Yeltsin and Major sign Anglo-Russian Treaty

⑪ **25 July** Eleven members of the Commonwealth of Independent States combined to send a "Unified Team" to the Olympic Games in Barcelona, winning the largest number of Gold Medals (45) as against the United States (37), the recently united East and West Germany (33), and China (16)

Barents Sea

⑬ **2 March** Polish–Belarus diplomatic relations established. Belarus agrees to set up Polish language schools for its Polish minority

Paris

London

North Sea

Tallinn

Baltic

POLAND

Vilnius

Riga

⑤ **6 March** Trade links inaugurated

Warsaw

Budapest

Minsk

BELARUS

Moscow

⑨ **22 April** Exposing the scale of former Soviet deception, Ukraine declares that between **6,000** and **8,000** people died as a result of the nuclear plant explosion in 1986

⑫ **3 August**
Russia and Ukraine agree to divide the former Soviet Black Sea Fleet after three years joint control

Chernobyl

Kiev

RUSSIA

Volga

Kishinev

Odessa

UKRAINE

Baikonur

⑧ **28 March** **18** dead in fighting between pro- and anti-Russia factions. Five thousand flee to the Odessa region

① **24 February** **3** dead when construction battalion riots suppressed

Sebastopol

CRIMEA

Black Sea

Sukhumi

Caucasus

⑬ **14–16 August**
50 dead as secessionist Abkhazians fight Georgians
26 August.
Georgians set up interim government over Abkhazians (250,000 Georgians and 160,000 Abkhazians live in region)

Tbilisi

Kojali

Caspian Sea

Aral Sea

KAZAKHSTAN

⑩ **15 May** Mutual Security Treaty signed (Russia, Kazakhstan, Armenia, Turkmenistan, Uzbekistan and Tajikistan), recognising each other's borders and pledging common defence against aggression

UZBEKISTAN

TURKMENISTAN

Teheran

Ashkhabad

Tashkent

KYRGYZSTAN

TAJIKISTAN

② **25 February**
Azeris claim 1,000 killed by Armenians

⑦ **15 March**
Armenian–Azerbaijan truce signed

⑥ **9 March**
Last Russian troops evacuated from Armenian enclave of Nagorno-Karabakh after 3 soldiers killed

AFGHANISTAN

④ **4 March**
Joint Turkmenistan–Iran Chamber of Commerce established

⑮ **23 December**
Thousands of Tajiks flee into Afghanistan during fighting between local Tajik ex-Communist and Islamic forces

0 ____ kilometres ____ 1000

0 ____ miles ____ 500

© Martin Gilbert 2002

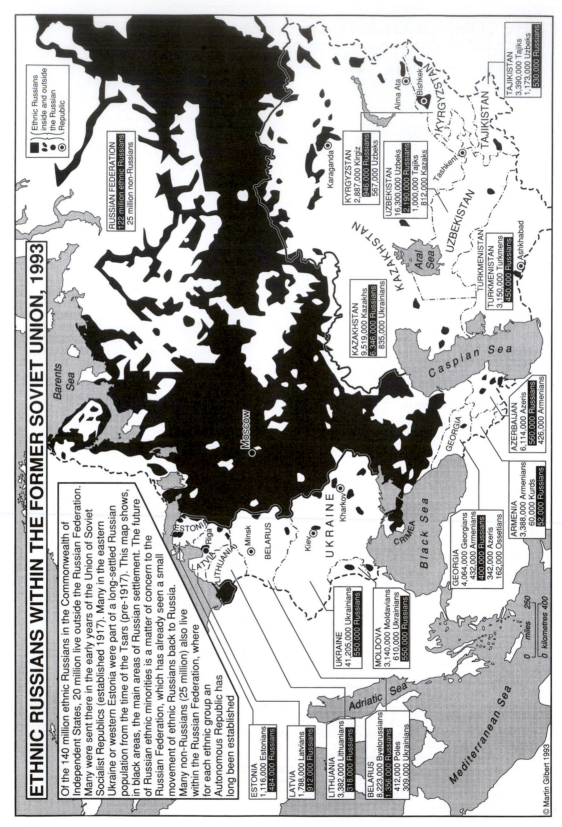

ETHNIC RUSSIANS WITHIN THE FORMER SOVIET UNION, 1993

Of the 140 million ethnic Russians in the Commonwealth of Independent States, 20 million live outside the Russian Federation. Many were sent there in the early years of the Union of Soviet Socialist Republics (established 1917). Many in the eastern Ukraine or western Estonia were part of a long-settled Russian population from the time of the Tsars (pre-1917). This map shows, in black areas, the main areas of Russian settlement. The future of Russian ethnic minorities is a matter of concern to the Russian Federation, which has already seen a small movement of ethnic Russians back to Russia. Many non-Russians (25 million) also live within the Russian Federation, where for each ethnic group an Autonomous Republic has long been established

Ethnic Russians
inside and outside
the Russian
Republic

RUSSIAN FEDERATION
122 million ethnic Russians
25 million non-Russians

KYRGYZSTAN
2,887,000 Kirgiz
946,000 Russians
567,000 Uzbeks

UZBEKISTAN
16,300,000 Uzbeks
2,190,000 Russians
1,000,000 Tajiks
812,000 Kazaks

TAJIKISTAN
3,390,000 Tajiks
1,173,000 Uzbeks
530,000 Russians

KAZAKHSTAN
9,519,000 Kazakhs
6,346,000 Russians
835,000 Ukrainians

TURKMENISTAN
3,150,000 Turkmens
450,000 Russians

AZERBAIJAN
6,114,000 Azeris
560,000 Russians
426,000 Armenians

ARMENIA
3,388,000 Armenians
60,000 Kurds
52,000 Russians

GEORGIA
4,064,000 Georgians
432,000 Armenians
400,000 Russians
342,000 Azeris
162,000 Ossetians

UKRAINE
41,205,000 Ukrainians
550,000 Russians

MOLDOVA
3,140,000 Moldavians
610,000 Ukrainians
550,000 Russians

ESTONIA
1,116,000 Estonians
484,000 Russians

LATVIA
1,788,000 Latvians
912,000 Russians

LITHUANIA
3,382,000 Lithuanians
318,000 Russians

BELARUS
8,223,000 Byelorussians
1,356,000 Russians
412,000 Poles
309,000 Ukrainians

Karaganda

Alma Ata
Bishkek
Tashkent
Ashkhabad

Moscow

Kharkov
Kiev
Minsk
Riga
ESTONIA
LATVIA
LITHUANIA
BELARUS
UKRAINE
CRIMEA

KAZAKHSTAN
KYRGYZSTAN
TAJIKISTAN
UZBEKISTAN
TURKMENISTAN
GEORGIA
AZERBAIJAN
ARMENIA

Barents Sea
Caspian Sea
Aral Sea
Black Sea
Adriatic Sea
Mediterranean Sea

0   miles   250
0 kilometres 400

© Martin Gilbert 1993

RUSSIA'S WESTERN BORDERLANDS SINCE 1991

FINLAND

St. Petersburg

Baltic Sea

ESTONIA

Pskov

LATVIA

LITHUANIA

Kaliningrad

POLAND

Western border of Soviet Union, 1945 – 1991

BELARUS

Smolensk

Moscow

RUSSIA

Bryansk

Kursk

Voronezh

Belgorod

River Don

UKRAINE

MOLDOVA

| 0 | kilometres | 300 |
| 0 | miles | 200 |

Rostov-on-Don

Yeisk

Sea of Azov

CHECHENYA

Novorossiisk

Tuapse

Sochi

Black Sea

GEORGIA

Ten years after the collapse of the Soviet Union, the new borderlands of the Russian Federation (also known as the Russian Republic, or Russia), as created in 1991, remain the borders in the first years of the twenty-first century.

Russia, with its main western border further east than at any time in its modern history, retained after 1991 the most westerly portion of the former Soviet Union: the Kaliningrad region. Formerly German East Prussia, it was annexed by the Soviet Union in 1945 (Poland annexed the southern part of East Prussia).

In August 1999 Vladimir Putin, head of Russia's Federal Security Service (the former KGB), succeeded Boris Yeltsin as President of the Russian Federation. His principal internal concern was the continuing Russian struggle against Muslim separatists in Chechenya. He also alarmed the West by the presence of the nuclear-armed Russian Baltic Sea Fleet at Kaliningrad. For his part, Putin was concerned that the extension of NATO to include both Poland and Lithuania could further isolate Kaliningrad, road and rail access to which was dependent on Lithuanian goodwill.

Kaliningrad, formerly Königsberg (a German city from 1255 to 1945), is the capital of the Kaliningrad region of a million people. It is Russia's only ice-free port and naval base on the Baltic Sea. Its population, almost entirely Russian, was brought to the region by the Soviet regime after the defeat of Germany in 1945, when the local German population either fled or was deported to Siberia. Since 1991, 10,000 ethnic Germans from other regions of the former Soviet Union – who, in the Communist years were not allowed to leave their towns – have moved freely into Kaliningrad. The region also has 40,000 Lithuanian inhabitants.

© Martin Gilbert 2002

RUSSIA AND THE SHANGHAI COOPERATION ORGANISATION (SCO)

Founded on 15 June 2001, the Shanghai Cooperation Organisation (SCO) was envisaged by the Russian President, Vladimir Putin, as a potential counterweight to the various Western groupings, among then NATO, the European Union (later expanded to included several former Soviet satellites) and the G7 leading economic nations, headed by the United States and Japan.

Outside the Persian Gulf, Kazakhstan and Russia are two of the world's leading oil producers. In 2005 the Shanghai Cooperation Organisation began consultations about energy cooperation. In December 2005, Kazakhstan inaugurated a \$3-billion pipeline to China.

On 20 September 2005 the Russian Defence Minister, Sergei Ivanov, announced that the Shanghai Cooperation Organisation would hold joint military exercises in 2006-2007 "to ensure stability in the region, and test the mobility of armed forces".

According to a poll by the All-Russian Center for the Study of Public Opinion (VTsIOM), 66% of Russians polled regret the Soviet Union's collapse. 74% linked their stance to regret over the collapse of a powerful State. 76% said that the collapse of the Soviet Union "destroyed everything people trusted and were proud of."

RUSSIA REFORM MONITOR, 5 JANUARY 2006

Member States of the Shanghai Cooperative Organisation:
CHINA
KAZAKHSTAN
KYRGYZSTAN
RUSSIA
TAJIKISTAN
UZBEKISTAN

© Sir Martin Gilbert 2006

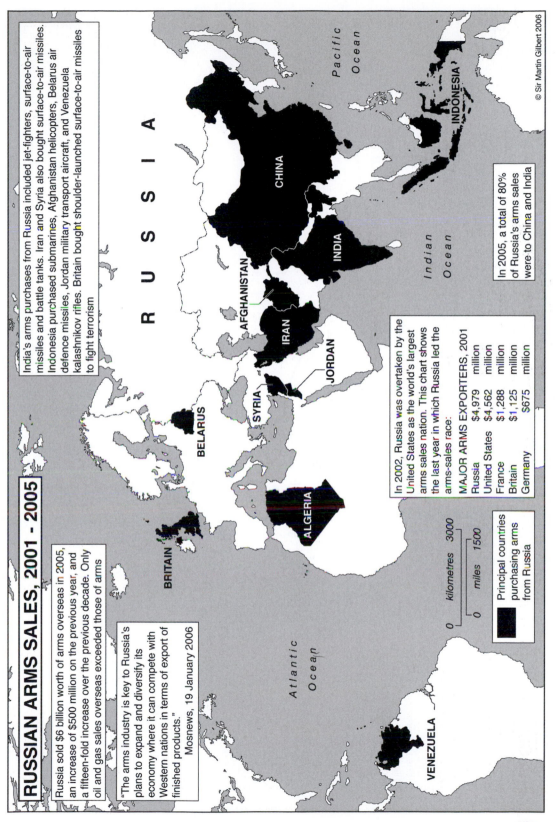

RUSSIAN ARMS SALES, 2001 - 2005

Russia sold $6 billion worth of arms overseas in 2005, an increase of $500 million on the previous year, and a fifteen-fold increase over the previous decade. Only oil and gas sales overseas exceeded those of arms

"The arms industry is key to Russia's plans to expand and diversify its economy where it can compete with Western nations in terms of export of finished products."

Mosnews, 19 January 2006

India's arms purchases from Russia included jet-fighters, surface-to-air missiles and battle tanks. Iran and Syria also bought surface-to-air missiles. Indonesia purchased submarines, Afghanistan helicopters, Belarus air defence missiles, Jordan military transport aircraft, and Venezuela kalashnikov rifles. Britain bought shoulder-launched surface-to-air missiles to fight terrorism

In 2002, Russia was overtaken by the United States as the world's largest arms sales nation. This chart shows the last year in which Russia led the arms-sales race:

MAJOR ARMS EXPORTERS, 2001

Russia	$4,979	million
United States	$4,562	million
France	$1,288	million
Britain	$1,125	million
Germany	$675	million

In 2005, a total of 80% of Russia's arms sales were to China and India

RUSSIA

CHINA

INDIA

AFGHANISTAN

IRAN

JORDAN

SYRIA

BELARUS

ALGERIA

BRITAIN

VENEZUELA

INDONESIA

Pacific Ocean

Indian Ocean

Atlantic Ocean

0 kilometres 3000

0 miles 1500

◼ Principal countries purchasing arms from Russia

© Sir Martin Gilbert 2006

168

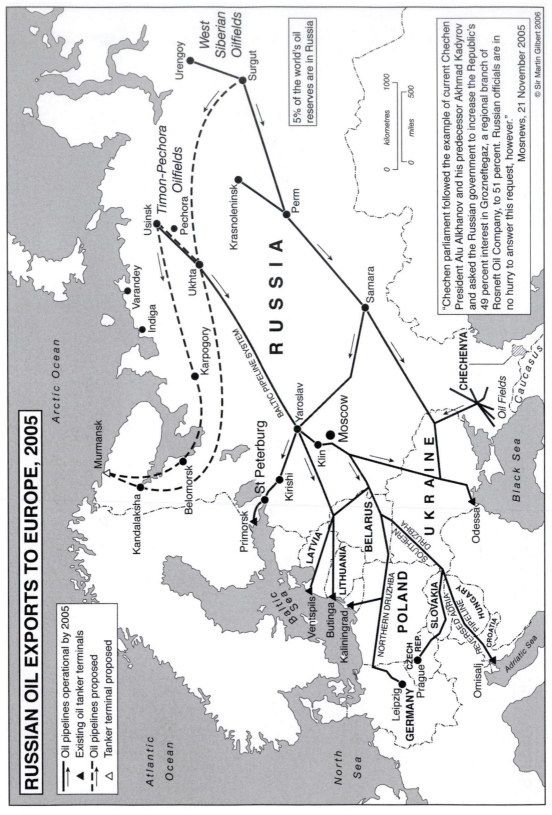

RUSSIAN OIL EXPORTS TO EUROPE, 2005

Oil pipelines operational by 2005
▲ Existing oil tanker terminals
Oil pipelines proposed
△ Tanker terminal proposed

5% of the world's oil reserves are in Russia

"Chechen parliament followed the example of current Chechen President Alu Alkhanov and his predecessor Akhmad Kadyrov and asked the Russian government to increase the Republic's 49 percent interest in Grozneftegaz, a regional branch of Rosneft Oil Company, to 51 percent. Russian officials are in no hurry to answer this request, however."
Mosnews, 21 November 2005

© Sir Martin Gilbert 2006

kilometres
miles
1000
500
0
0

West Siberian Oilfields
Urengoy
Surgut
Timon-Pechora Oilfields
Usinsk
Pechora
Krasnoleninsk
Perm
Samara

R U S S I A

Varandey
Indiga
Arctic Ocean
Murmansk
Kandalaksha
Belomorsk
Karpogory
Ukhta
BALTIC PIPELINE SYSTEM
St Peterburg
Kirishi
Primorsk
Yaroslav
Klin
Moscow

CHECHENYA
Oil Fields
Caucasus
Black Sea

U K R A I N E
Odessa

Atlantic Ocean

North Sea

Baltic Sea
LATVIA
Ventspils
Butinga
LITHUANIA
Kaliningrad
NORTHERN DRUZHBA
BELARUS
SOUTHERN DRUZHBA
POLAND
Leipzig
GERMANY
Prague
CZECH REP.
SLOVAKIA
HUNGARY
REVERSED ADRIA
ADRIA PIPELINE
CROATIA
Omisalj
Adriatic Sea

169

RUSSIAN OIL EXPORTS TO ASIA, 2005-2006

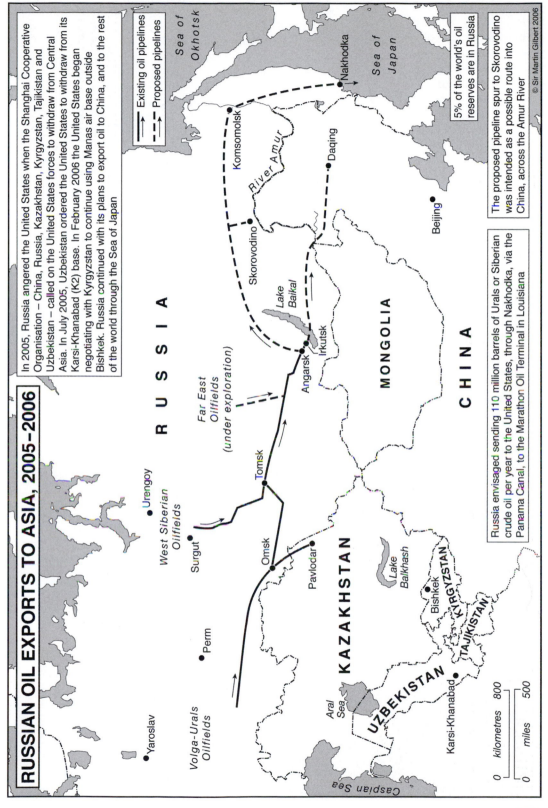

In 2005, Russia angered the United States when the Shanghai Cooperative Organisation – China, Russia, Kazakhstan, Kyrgyzstan, Tajikistan and Uzbekistan – called on the United States forces to withdraw from Central Asia. In July 2005, Uzbekistan ordered the United States to withdraw from its Karsi-Khanabad (K2) base. In February 2006 the United States began negotiating with Kyrgyzstan to continue using Manas air base outside Bishkek. Russia continued with its plans to export oil to China, and to the rest of the world through the Sea of Japan

Existing oil pipelines
Proposed pipelines

5% of the world's oil reserves are in Russia

© Sir Martin Gilbert 2006

The proposed pipeline spur to Skorovodino was intended as a possible route into China, across the Amur River

Russia envisaged sending 110 million barrels of Urals or Siberian crude oil per year to the United States, through Nakhodka, via the Panama Canal, to the Marathon Oil Terminal in Louisiana

Sea of Okhotsk

Sea of Japan

Nakhodka

Komsomolsk

River Amur

Daqing

Skorovodino

Beijing

R U S S I A

Lake Baikal

Irkutsk

Angarsk

Far East Oilfields (under exploration)

M O N G O L I A

Tomsk

C H I N A

Urengoy

West Siberian Oilfields

Surgut

Omsk

Pavlodar

Lake Balkhash

K A Z A K H S T A N

Perm

Bishkek

KYRGYZSTAN

TAJIKISTAN

Yaroslav

Volga-Urals Oilfields

Aral Sea

UZBEKISTAN

Karsi-Khanabad

Caspian Sea

0   kilometres   800

0   miles   500

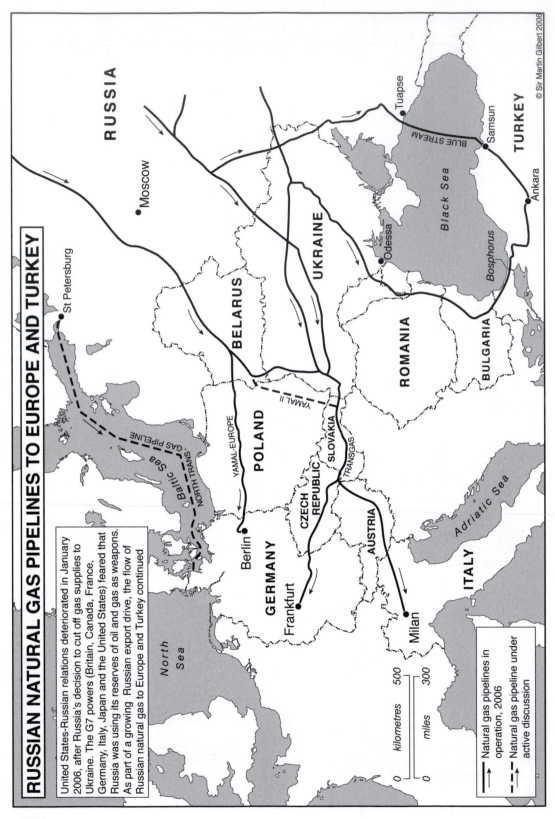

RUSSIAN NATURAL GAS PIPELINES TO EUROPE AND TURKEY

United States-Russian relations deteriorated in January 2006, after Russia's decision to cut off gas supplies to Ukraine. The G7 powers (Britain, Canada, France, Germany, Italy, Japan and the United States) feared that Russia was using its reserves of oil and gas as weapons. As part of a growing Russian export drive, the flow of Russian natural gas to Europe and Turkey continued

RUSSIA

Moscow

BELARUS

UKRAINE

St Petersburg

NORTH TRANS - GAS PIPELINE

Baltic Sea

YAMAL-EUROPE

YAMAL II

POLAND

Berlin

GERMANY

Frankfurt

CZECH REPUBLIC

SLOVAKIA

TRANSGAS

AUSTRIA

Milan

ITALY

North Sea

Adriatic Sea

ROMANIA

BULGARIA

Odessa

Black Sea

Bosphorus

BLUE STREAM

Samsun

Tuapse

Ankara

TURKEY

© Sir Martin Gilbert 2006

kilometres   500
              300
miles
0   0

— Natural gas pipelines in operation, 2006

- - - Natural gas pipeline under active discussion

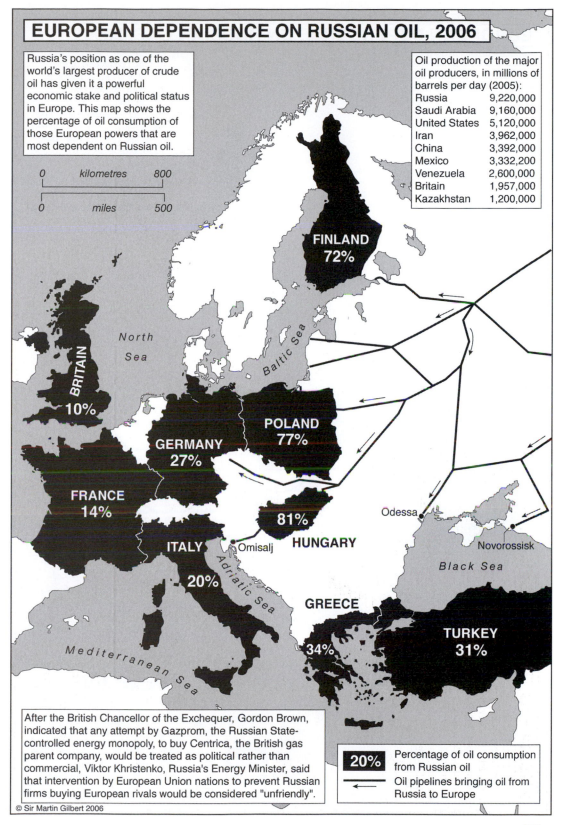

EUROPEAN DEPENDENCE ON RUSSIAN OIL, 2006

Russia's position as one of the world's largest producer of crude oil has given it a powerful economic stake and political status in Europe. This map shows the percentage of oil consumption of those European powers that are most dependent on Russian oil.

Oil production of the major oil producers, in millions of barrels per day (2005):

Russia	9,220,000
Saudi Arabia	9,160,000
United States	5,120,000
Iran	3,962,000
China	3,392,000
Mexico	3,332,200
Venezuela	2,600,000
Britain	1,957,000
Kazakhstan	1,200,000

0	kilometres	800
0	miles	500

North Sea

Baltic Sea

FINLAND
72%

BRITAIN
10%

POLAND
77%

GERMANY
27%

FRANCE
14%

81%
HUNGARY

ITALY
20%

Adriatic Sea

Omisalj

Odessa

Novorossisk

Black Sea

GREECE
34%

TURKEY
31%

Mediterranean Sea

After the British Chancellor of the Exchequer, Gordon Brown, indicated that any attempt by Gazprom, the Russian State-controlled energy monopoly, to buy Centrica, the British gas parent company, would be treated as political rather than commercial, Viktor Khristenko, Russia's Energy Minister, said that intervention by European Union nations to prevent Russian firms buying European rivals would be considered "unfriendly".

© Sir Martin Gilbert 2006

20%	Percentage of oil consumption from Russian oil
←	Oil pipelines bringing oil from Russia to Europe

172

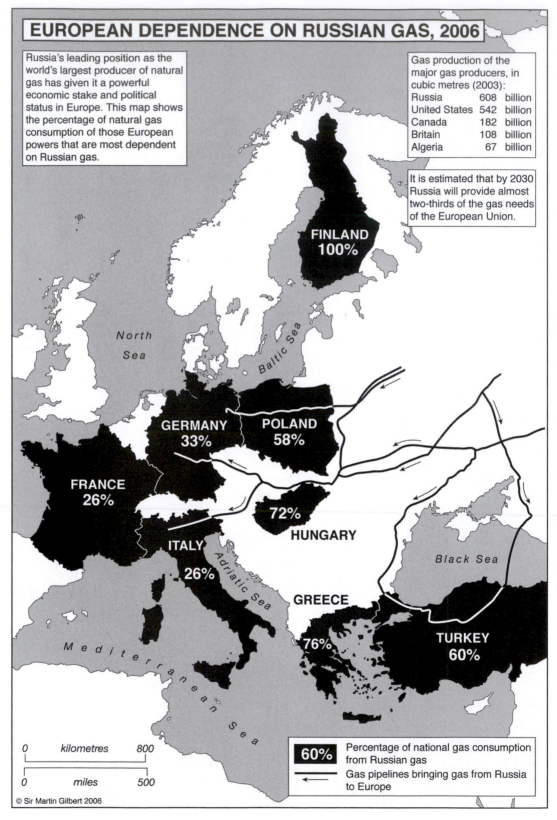

EUROPEAN DEPENDENCE ON RUSSIAN GAS, 2006

Russia's leading position as the world's largest producer of natural gas has given it a powerful economic stake and political status in Europe. This map shows the percentage of natural gas consumption of those European powers that are most dependent on Russian gas.

Gas production of the major gas producers, in cubic metres (2003):

Russia	608	billion
United States	542	billion
Canada	182	billion
Britain	108	billion
Algeria	67	billion

It is estimated that by 2030 Russia will provide almost two-thirds of the gas needs of the European Union.

FINLAND 100%

North Sea

Baltic Sea

GERMANY 33%

POLAND 58%

FRANCE 26%

72%

HUNGARY

ITALY 26%

Adriatic Sea

Black Sea

GREECE

76%

TURKEY 60%

Mediterranean Sea

| 0 | kilometres | 800 |
| 0 | miles | 500 |

60%   Percentage of national gas consumption from Russian gas

⟵   Gas pipelines bringing gas from Russia to Europe

© Sir Martin Gilbert 2006

CHALLENGING ANTI-SEMITISM AND RACISM IN RUSSIA, 2003–2006

In 2004 the number of major anti-Semitic incidents reported in Russia increased from 32 to 45. Most involved vandalism of cemeteries, monuments and property. There was also an increase in numbers of physical acts against individuals carried out by Russian extremists against Jews and other minorities, including Russian Muslims, Roma (gypsies), and foreigners. The reluctance or willingness of the the authorities to take action, within existing anti-incitement laws, was seen as a test of the Putin government's seriousness in combating anti-Semitic and racist behaviour

24 November 2004
Viktor Korchagin, a leading anti-Semite, and head of the Rusich publishing house, was placed by a district judge on two years probation for incitement of ethnic hatred. The judge then immediately revoked the punishment under the statute of limitations. on 23 December 2004 a Moscow city court cancelled the decision of the district court and transferred the case for further investigation

18 February 2004
The Russian Jewish Congress issued a statement accusing the government of covering up hate crimes and even collaborating with hate groups

5 March 2004
A bomb of about 200 kilogrammes exploded near the Institute for the Study of Judaism. The attack, which took place on the eve of the Jewish holiday of Purim, caused no injuries

9 July 2004
The Duma rejected a proposed law that would have prohibited the public display of Nazi symbols

15 December 2004
An international conference on "Antisemitism in the Former Soviet Union and the Russian Federation" was held in Moscow. It was followed by an all-Russian week against anti-Semitism and racism in more than 20 regions. Students took part in campaigns to erase anti-Semitic graffiti in many cities

December 2003
Igor Kolodezenko, a publisher of *Russkii Sibir* (affiliated to the National Sovereign Party of Russia), was given a two-year suspended sentence after being convicted of inciting ethnic hatred through anti-Semitic articles he printed in his newspaper. On 5 April 2004 a Novosibirsk court ordered the newspaper closed for promoting ethnic and religious hatred

May 2004
Nine-year-old Kursheda Sultonova, an ethnic Tadjik living with her family in St Petersburg, murdered in a racist attack. The attackers called out as they killed her: "Russia is for the Russians"

9 May 2006
As President Putin prepared to chair the G8 Summit, Amnesty International published a detailed report condemning the spread of racist violence in Russia. At least 28 racist murders were reported during 2005

November 2004
The Novgorod prosecutor's office charged a 20-year-old member of the National Sovereign Party of Russia with incitement to ethnic, racist and religious hatred. On 2 and 26 September 2003 he had planted fake explosives at the Jewish communal centre, with "Death to the Yids," and a swastika planted on them. He was sentenced to three years in prison

Racist attacks on Jews, and on asylum seekers from Africa and Asia, reported throughout 2005

October 2004
Vu Anh Tuan, a 20-year-old Vietnamese student, stabbed to death by a gang of eighteen skinheads

January 2006
Nine Jews injured in a racist stabbing in a synagogue

1 November 2004
A local human rights organization, "United Europe", informed the press that it had evidence of the distribution of neo-Nazi music and literature, and of skinhead attacks on foreigners

May 2006
A Peruvian Student killed in a racist attack

April 2006
Two Roma (gypsies) killed in an attack on a Roma camp

4 February 2004
Three Molotov cocktails thrown at the synagogue, igniting a fire in the library

Lake Onega

St Petersburg

Novgorod

Timiriazevskaya

Moscow

Orel

Voronezh

Volgograd

Cheliabinsk

Novosibirsk

Black Sea

Caspian Sea

0   500 kilometres
0   300 miles

174

A RIVAL TO RUSSIAN OIL FINDS A NEW ROUTE TO EUROPE, MAY 2006

On 28 May 2006, the first oil from oilfields in the former Soviet Republic of Azerbaijan was pumped through a newly built pipeline from Baku - through another former Soviet Republic, Georgia - to the Turkish Mediterranean port of Ceyhan. A British oil tanker moored off Ceyhan was the first ship to load that oil for shipment. The pipeline is owned by British Petroleum

The movement of Azerbaijan's oil through Turkey was a challenge to Russia's dominating position as the route for the export of oil from the countries of the former Soviet Union. But, in return for oil and gas reaching Turkey direct from Russia (see maps 171 and 172), Turkey agreed to end its medical help to wounded anti-Russian rebels from Chechenya. In return for Russian energy, Turkey sold Russia consumer goods and construction services, making Russia, by 2006, Turkey's second largest trading partner after the European Union

RUSSIA

KAZAKHSTAN

Ural River

River Don

River Volga

Aral Sea

UZBEKISTAN

UKRAINE

Caspian Sea

CHECHENYA

TURKMENISTAN

GEORGIA

Tbilisi

Black Sea

Batum

AZERBAIJAN

Baku

ARMENIA

Lake Van

Lake Urmiah

IRAN

TURKEY

Before the break-up of the Soviet Union in 1991, the Soviet Republic of Azerbaijan was the main Soviet oil producing region. Most of the oil was offshore near the port of Baku. In 1942, the prime aim of the German military thrust through the Ukraine towards Baku - a thrust that failed (see map 124) - had been aimed at securing this oil.

Ceyhan

SYRIA

After the break-up of the Soviet Union in 1991, oil from Azerbaijan had to go through Russia, through Batum, in order to reach European markets.
The new oil pipeline through independent Georgia and Turkey ended this dependence on Russia.

Mediterranean Sea

| 0 | kilometres | 500 |
| 0 | miles | 300 |

© Sir Martin Gilbert 2006

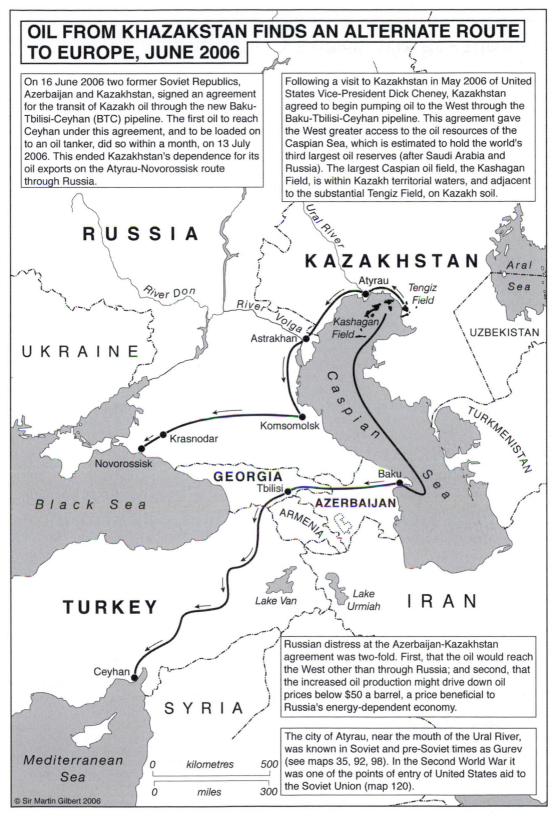

OIL FROM KHAZAKSTAN FINDS AN ALTERNATE ROUTE TO EUROPE, JUNE 2006

On 16 June 2006 two former Soviet Republics, Azerbaijan and Kazakhstan, signed an agreement for the transit of Kazakh oil through the new Baku-Tbilisi-Ceyhan (BTC) pipeline. The first oil to reach Ceyhan under this agreement, and to be loaded on to an oil tanker, did so within a month, on 13 July 2006. This ended Kazakhstan's dependence for its oil exports on the Atyrau-Novorossisk route through Russia.

Following a visit to Kazakhstan in May 2006 of United States Vice-President Dick Cheney, Kazakhstan agreed to begin pumping oil to the West through the Baku-Tbilisi-Ceyhan pipeline. This agreement gave the West greater access to the oil resources of the Caspian Sea, which is estimated to hold the world's third largest oil reserves (after Saudi Arabia and Russia). The largest Caspian oil field, the Kashagan Field, is within Kazakh territorial waters, and adjacent to the substantial Tengiz Field, on Kazakh soil.

RUSSIA

KAZAKHSTAN

Ural River

River Don

River Volga

Atyrau

Tengiz Field

Aral Sea

Astrakhan

Kashagan Field

UZBEKISTAN

Caspian Sea

Komsomolsk

Krasnodar

Novorossisk

TURKMENISTAN

GEORGIA

Baku

Tbilisi

Black Sea

AZERBAIJAN

ARMENIA

TURKEY

Lake Van

Lake Urmiah

I R A N

Ceyhan

Russian distress at the Azerbaijan-Kazakhstan agreement was two-fold. First, that the oil would reach the West other than through Russia; and second, that the increased oil production might drive down oil prices below $50 a barrel, a price beneficial to Russia's energy-dependent economy.

S Y R I A

| 0 | kilometres | 500 |

| 0 | miles | 300 |

Mediterranean Sea

© Sir Martin Gilbert 2006

The city of Atyrau, near the mouth of the Ural River, was known in Soviet and pre-Soviet times as Gurev (see maps 35, 92, 98). In the Second World War it was one of the points of entry of United States aid to the Soviet Union (map 120).

Bibliography of Works Consulted

(i) ATLASES

Baratov, R. B. (and others), *Atlas Tadzhikskoi Sovetskoi Sotsialisticheskoi Respubliki* (Dushanbe and Moscow, 1968)

Bartholomew, John (ed), *The Times Atlas of the World*, 5 vols (London, 1959)

Bazilevich, K. V., Golubtsov, I. A. and Zinoviev, M. A., *Atlas Istorii SSSR*, 3 vols (Moscow, 1949–54)

Beloglazova, O. A. (ed), *Atlas SSSR* (Moscow, 1954)

Czapliński, Wladislaw and Ladogórski, Tadeusz, *Atlas Historyczny Polski* (Warsaw, 1968)

Droysens, G., *Historischer Handatlas* (Bielefeld and Leipzig, 1886)

Durov, A. G. (General editor), *Atlas Leningradskoi Oblasti* (Moscow, 1967)

Engel, Joseph, *Grosser Historischer Weltatlas* (Munich, 1962)

Grosier, L'Abbé, *Atlas Générale de la Chine* (Paris 1785)

Hudson, G. F. and Rajchman, Marthe, *An Atlas of Far Eastern Politics* (London, 1938)

Kalesnik, S. V. (and others), *Peterburg–Leningrad* (Leningrad, 1957)

Kosev, Dimiter (and others), *Atlas Po Bulgarska Istoriya* (Sofia, 1963)

Kubijovyć, Volodymyr, *Atlas of Ukraine and Adjoining Countries* (Lvov, 1937)

Kudriashov, K. V., *Russkii Istoricheskii Atlas* (Leningrad, 1928)

Kovalevsky, Pierre, *Atlas Historique et Culturel de la Russie et du Monde Slave* (Paris, 1961)

McEvedy, Colin, *The Penguin Atlas of Medieval History* (London, 1961)

Penkala, Maria, *A Correlated History of the Far East* (The Hague and Paris, 1966)

Oxford Regional Economic Atlas: The USSR and Eastern Europe (Oxford, 1956)

Sochava, V. B. (Principal ed), *Atlas Zabaikalia* (Moscow and Irkutsk, 1967)

Taaffe, Robert N. and Kingsbury, Robert C., *An Atlas of Soviet Affairs* (London, 1965)

Terekhov, N. M. (senior editor), *Atlas Volgogradskoi Oblasti* (Moscow, 1967)

Toynbee, Arnold J. and Myers, Edward D., *Historical Atlas and Gazetteer* (London, 19.

Voznesenski (and others), *Atlas Razvitiya Khoziastva i Kultury SSSR* (Moscow, 1967)

Westermann, Georg, *Atlas zur Weltgeschichte* (Braunschweig, 1956)

Zamyslovski, Igor E., *Uchebnii Atlas po Russkoi Istorii* (St Petersburg, 1887)

(ii) MAPS

Atanasiu, A. D., *La Bessarabie* (Paris, 1919)

Bazewicz, J. M., *Polska w Trzech Zaborach* (Warsaw, n.d.)

Bazileva, Z. P., *Rossiiskaya Imperiya 1801–1861* (Moscow, 1960)

British G.H.Q., Constantinople, *Ethnographical Map of Caucasus* (Constantinople, 19.

Fedorovskaya, G. P. (publisher), *Promyshlennost Rossii 1913; Promyshlennost Soyuza SSR 1940* (Moscow, 1962)

Filonenko, W. J., *Volkstumkarte der Krim* (Vienna, 1932)

Kuchborskaya, E. P., *Rossiiskaya Imperiya 1725–1801* (Moscow, 1959)

Stanford, Edward, *Sketch of the Acquisitions of Russia* (London, 1876)

Wyld, James, *Wyld's Military Staff Map of Central Asia, Turkistan and Afghanistan* (London, 1878)

(iii) ENCYCLOPAEDIAS, REFERENCE BOOKS AND GENERAL WORKS

Baedeker, Karl, *Russland* (Leipzig, 1912)
Cole, J. P., *Geography of the USSR* (London, 1967)
Florinsky, Michael T. (ed), *Encyclopaedia of Russia and the Soviet Union* (New York, 1961)
Katzenelson, Y. L. and Gintsburg, D. G. (eds), *Evreiskaya Entsiklopediya,* 16 vols (St Petersburg, 1906–13)
Kubijović, Volodymyr (ed), *Ukraine: A Concise Encyclopaedia* (Toronto, 1963)
Pares, Bernard, *A History of Russia* (London, 1926)
Parker, W. H., *An Historical Georgraphy of Russia* (London, 1968)
Sumner, B. H., *Survey of Russian History* (London, 1944)
Utechin, S. V., *Everyman's Concise Encyclopaedia of Russia* (London, 1961)
Zhukov, E. M. (ed), *Sovetskaya Istoricheskaya Entsiklopediya,* vols 1–12 (Moscow, 1961–69)

(iv) BOOKS ON SPECIAL TOPICS

Allen, W. E. D., *The Ukraine: A History* (Cambridge, 1940)
Allen, W. E. D. and Muratov, P., *Caucasian Battlefields: A History of the Wars on the Turco-Caucasian Border 1828–1921* (London, 1953)
Allilueva, A. S., *Iz Vospominanii* (Moscow, 1946)
Armstrong, John A. (ed), *Soviet Partisans in World War II* (Madison, 1964)
Armstrong, Terence E., *The Northern Sea Route* (Cambridge, 1952)
Avalishvili, Zourab, *The Independence of Georgia in International Politics 1918–1921* (London, 1940)
Baddeley, John F., *The Russian Conquest of the Caucasus* (London, 1908)
Baddeley, John F., *Russia, Mongolia, China,* 2 vols (London, 1919)
Caroe, Olaf, *Soviet Empire: The Turks of Central Asia and Stalinism* (London, 1953)
Chamberlin, William Henry, *The Russian Revolution 1917–1921,* 2 vols (New York, 1935)
Clark, Alan, *Barbarossa: The Russo-German Conflict 1941–1945* (London, 1965)
Conquest, Robert, *The Soviet Deportation of Nationalities* (London, 1960)
Cresson, W. P., *The Cossacks, their History and Country* (New York, 1919)
Dallin, Alexander, *German Rule in Russia 1941–1945* (London, 1957)
Dallin, David J., *The Rise of Russia in Asia* (London, 1950)
Dallin, David J. and Nicolaevsky, Boris I., *Forced Labour in Soviet Russia* (London, 1948)
Dixon, C. Aubrey and Heilbrunn, Otto, *Communist Guerilla Warfare* (London, 1954)
Dubnow, S. M., *History of the Jews in Russia and Poland* (Philadelphia, 1916–20)
Eudin, X. J. and Fisher, H. H., *Soviet Russia and the West 1920–1927: A Documentary Survey* (Stanford, 1957)
Fennell, J. L. I., *Ivan the Great of Moscow* (London, 1963)
Fennell, J. L. I., *The Emergence of Moscow 1304–1359* (London, 1968)
Fischer, Louis, *The Soviets in World Affairs,* 2 vols (London, 1930)
Fischer, Louis, *The Life of Lenin* (London, 1964)
Freund, Gerald, *Unholy Alliance: Russian-German relations from the Treaty of Brest-Litovsk to the Treaty of Berlin* (London, 1957)
Futrell, Michael, *Northern Underground: Episodes of Russian Revolutionary Transport and Communications through Scandinavia and Finland 1863–1917* (London, 1963)
Greenberg, Louis, *The Jews in Russia: The Struggle For Emancipation,* 2 vols (New Haven, 1944, 1951)

Höhne, Heinz, *The Order of the Death's Head: The Story of Hitler's S.S.* (London, 1969)

Indian Officer, An (anon), *Russia's March Towards India*, 2 vols (London, 1894)

Jackson, W. A. Douglas, *Russo-Chinese Borderlands* (Princeton, 1962)

Joll, James, *The Anarchists* (London, 1964)

Kamenetsky, Ihor, *Hitler's Occupation of Ukraine 1941–1944: A study of Totalitarian imperialism* (Milwaukee, 1956)

Kazemzadeh, F., *The Struggle for Transcaucasia* (New York, 1951)

Katkov, George, *Russia 1917: The February Revolution* (London, 1967)

Kennan, George, *Siberia and the Exile System* (New York, 1891)

Kerner, Robert J., *The Urge to the Sea: The Course of Russian History* (Berkeley and Los Angeles, 1946)

Kirchner, Walther, *Commercial Relations Between Russia and Europe 1400 to 1800* (Bloomington, Indiana, 1966)

Klyuchevskii, Vasilii Osipovich, *Peter the Great* (London, 1958)

Kochan, Lionel, *Russia in Revolution 1890–1918* (London, 1966)

Kolarz, Walter, *Russia and her Colonies* (London, 1952)

Krypton, Constantine, *The Northern Sea Route* (New York, 1953)

Lang, D. M., *A Modern History of Georgia* (London, 1962)

Leslie, R. F., *Reform and Insurrection in Russian Poland* (London, 1963)

Lias, Godfrey, *Kazak Exodus* (London, 1956)

Liubavskii, M. K., *Ocherk Istorii Litovsko-Russkovo Gosudarstva* (Moscow, 1910; Russian Reprint Series, The Hague, 1966)

Lorimer, F., *The Population of the Soviet Union: History and Prospects* (Geneva, 1946)

Lyashchenko, Peter I., *History of the National Economy of Russia to the 1917 Revolution* (New York, 1949)

Maksimov, S., *Sibir i Katorga,* 3 vols (St Petersburg, 1871)

Malozemoff, A., *Russian Far-Eastern Policy 1881–1904* (Los Angeles, 1958)

Manning, Clarence A., *Twentieth-Century Ukraine* (New York, 1951)

Mazour, Anatole G., *The First Russian Revolution, 1825: the Decembrist movement* (Stanford, 1961)

Mikhailov, V., *Pamiatnaya Knizhka Sotsialista-Revoliutsionera*, 2 vols (Paris, 1911, 1914)

Miller, Margaret, *The Economic Development of Russia 1905–1914* (London, 1926)

Mora, Sylvestre and Zwierniak, Pierre, *La Justice Sovietique* (Rome, 1945)

Nasonov, A. N., *Russkaya Zemlia* (Moscow, 1951)

Nikitin, M. N. and Vagin, P. I., *The Crimes of the German Fascists in the Leningrad Region: Materials and Documents* (London, 1947)

Nosenko, A. K. (ed), *V. I. Lenin 1870–1924* (Kiev, n.d.). A collection of photographs, with 2 maps

Obolenski, Prince Eugene, *Souvenirs D'Un Exilé en Sibérie* (Leipzig, 1862)

Owen, Launcelot A., *The Russian Peasant Movement 1906–17* (London, 1937)

Park, Alexander G., *Bolshevism in Turkestan 1917–1927* (New York, 1957)

Philippi, Alfred and Heim, Ferdinand, *Der Feldzug gegen Sowjetrussland 1941–1945* (Stuttgart, 1962)

Pierce, Richard A., *Russian Central Asia 1867–1917* (Berkeley and Los Angeles, 1960)

Pipes, Richard, *The Formation of the Soviet Union: Communism and Nationalism 1917–1923* (Cambridge, Massachusetts, 1954)

Platonov, S. F., *Ocherki Po Istorii Smuti v Moskovskom Gosudarstve* (Moscow, 1937)

Pospelov, P. N., *Istoriya Kommunisticheskoi Partii Sovetskovo Soyuza,* 6 vols (Moscow, 1964–68)

Pounds, Norman J. G., *Poland Between East and West* (Princeton, 1964)

Radkey, Oliver H., *The Agrarian Foes of Bolshevism* (New York, 1958)

Rapport du Parti Socialiste Revolutionnaire de Russie au Congres Socialiste International de Stuttgart (Ghent, 1907)

Reddaway, W. R., Penson, J. H., Halecki, O. and Dyboski, R. (eds), *Cambridge History of Poland*, 2 vols (Cambridge, 1941, 1950)

Reitlinger, Gerald, *The House Built on Sand: The Conflicts of German Policy in Russia 1939–1945* (London, 1960)

Riasanovsky, Nicholas V., *A History of Russia* (New York, 1963)

Rosen, Baron A., *Russian Conspirators in Siberia* (London, 1872)

Rostovtzeff, M., *The Iranians and Greeks in South Russia* (Oxford, 1922)

Salisbury, Harrison E., *The Siege of Leningrad* (London, 1969)

Schuyler, Eugene, *Peter the Great: Emperor of Russia,* 2 vols (London, 1844)

Schwarz, Solomon M., *The Russian Revolution of 1905* (Chicago, 1967)

Serge, Victor, *Memoirs of a Revolutionary 1901–1941* (London, 1963)

Seton-Watson, Hugh, *The Russian Empire 1801–1917* (London, 1967)

Shukman, Harold, *Lenin and the Russian Revolution* (London, 1966)

Simpson, Sir John Hope, *The Refugee Problem* (London, 1939)

Skazkin, S. D. (and others), *Istoriya Vizantii*, 3 vols (Moscow, 1967)

Slusser, Robert M. and Triska Jan F., *A Calendar of Soviet Treaties 1917–1957* (Stanford, 1959)

Squire, P. S., *The Third Department: The establishment and practices of the political police in the Russia of Nicholas I* (Cambridge, 1968)

Stephan, John J., *Sakhalin* (Oxford, 1971)

Sullivant, Robert S., *Soviet Politics and the Ukraine 1917–1957* (New York, 1962)

Sumner, B. H., *Peter the Great and the Ottoman Empire* (Oxford, 1949)

Sumner, B. H., *Peter the Great and the Emergence of Russia* (London, 1950)

Suprunenko, M. I. (and others), *Istoria Ukrainskoi RSR* (Kiev, 1958)

Tikhonov, Nikolai (and others), *The Defence of Leningrad: Eye-witness Accounts of the Siege* (London, 1944)

Treadgold, Donald W., *The Great Siberian Migration* (Princeton, 1957)

Trotsky, Leon, *My Life* (London, 1930)

Vernadsky, George, *The Mongols and Russia* (London, 1953)

Wheeler, G., *The Modern History of Soviet Central Asia* (London, 1964)

Woodward, David, *The Russians at Sea* (London, 1965)

Yarmolinski, Avram, *The Road to Revolution: A Century of Russian Radicalism* (London, 1957)

Yaroslavsky, E., *History of Anarchism in Russia* (London, 1937)

Zimin, A. A., *Reformy Ivana Groznovo* (Moscow, 1960)

(v) ARTICLES

Anon, 'How the Bear Learned to Swim', *The Economist* (London, 24–30 October 1970)

Bealby, John Thomas, Kropotkin, Prince Peter Alexeivitch, Philips, Walter Alison and Wallace, Sir Donald Mackenzie, 'Russia', *The Encyclopaedia Britannica* (Eleventh edition, London and New York, 1910)

Carsten, F. L., 'The Reichswehr and the Red Army 1920–1933', *Survey* (London, 1962)

Dziewanowski, M. K., 'Pilsudski's Federal Policy 1919–21', *Journal of Central European Affairs* (London, 1950)

Footman, David, 'Nestor Makno', *St Antony's Papers No. 6: Soviet Affairs No. 2* (Oxford, 1959)

Lobanov-Rostovsky, A., 'Anglo-Russian Relations through the Centuries', *Russian Review*, vol 7 (New York, 1948)

Parkes, Harry, 'Report on the Russian Caravan Trade with China', *Journal of the Royal Geographic Society*, vol 25 (London, 1854)

Stanhope, Henry, 'Soviet Strength at Sea', *The Times* (London, 25 January 1971)

Sullivan, Joseph L., 'Decembrists in Exile', *Harvard Slavic Studies,* vol 4 (The Hague, 1954)

Wildes, Harry Emerson, 'Russia's Attempts to Open Japan', *Russian Review,* vol 5 (New York, 1945)

Yakunskiy, V. K. 'La Révolution Industrielle en Russie', *Cahiers du Monde Russe et Sovietique* (The Hague, 1961)

Index

compiled by the author